Routledge Revivals

Crime and Psychology

First published in 1943 *Crime and Psychology* reveals to the public some of the results of well-known magistrate Claud Mullin's many years of pioneering work in using the help of medical psychologists for the treatment of criminals. The book contains numerous actual cases of real scientific and social value. They show how even men who have in the past been sent to prison for serious offences can be helped, through treatment while at liberty, to lead useful lives for many years afterwards. The author also shows how psychological principles could become essential features of our system of criminal trial. This constructive and convincing book is an essential read for scholars and researchers of criminal psychology, applied psychology, criminology, and psychology in general.

T0388413

Crime and Psychology

Claud Mullins

First published in 1943
by Methuen & Co. Ltd.

This edition first published in 2021 by Routledge
2 Park Square, Milton Park, Abingdon, Oxon, OX14 4RN
and by Routledge
605 Third Avenue, New York, NY 10017

Routledge is an imprint of the Taylor & Francis Group, an informa business

© Claud Mullins 1943

Publisher's Note
The publisher has gone to great lengths to ensure the quality of this reprint but points out that some imperfections in the original copies may be apparent.

Disclaimer
The publisher has made every effort to trace copyright holders and welcomes correspondence from those they have been unable to contact.

A Library of Congress record exists under LCCN: 44006422

ISBN: 978-1-032-13254-9 (hbk)
ISBN: 978-1-003-22834-9 (ebk)
ISBN: 978-1-032-13257-0 (pbk)

Book DOI 10.4324/9781003228349

CRIME AND PSYCHOLOGY

by

CLAUD MULLINS

With an Introduction by

DR. EDWARD GLOVER

METHUEN & CO. LTD. LONDON
36 Essex Street, Strand, W.C.2

TO

THE MANY MEDICAL MEN AND WOMEN
KNOWN AND UNKNOWN TO ME
WHO HAVE FREELY GIVEN THEIR TIME AND KNOWLEDGE
IN AN EFFORT TO CURE DELINQUENTS
AND IN PARTICULAR TO
DR. ALEXANDER COSGRAVE COURT
OF WANDSWORTH, LONDON

First published in 1943

BOOK
PRODUCTION
WAR ECONOMY
STANDARD

THIS BOOK IS PRODUCED
IN COMPLETE CONFORMITY WITH
THE AUTHORIZED ECONOMY STANDARDS

PRINTED IN GREAT BRITAIN

PREFACE

Judge or no Judge, I shall be forced to write.

SIR JAMES FITZJAMES STEPHEN

He resolved to make the Bench a 'base of operations' and 'not a mere shelf'.

LESLIE STEPHEN, his biographer

Men like the late Mr. Justice McCardie and Sir William Clarke Hall are rebuked, either when alive or later when dead, for having done more than condemn their fellows to short or long terms of imprisonment. . . . What are men of this type to do ? Are they to resign office and emoluments and write pamphlets, or obtain a seat in the House of Commons ? . . . Public opinion responds more immediately to judicial criticism of the law than to any other criticism, and no humane magistrate can reasonably be expected to be for ever silent on abuses which he might otherwise be deemed to approve.

E. S. P. HAYNES [1]

THE outbreak of both wars of this century gave rise to much enthusiasm for planning better post-war worlds. Those who planned during the war of 1914 met with little success when that war was over. Their successors during the war of 1939 had even greater enthusiasm and undoubtedly better prospects, for there is greater agreement that new ideas must be tried. An unfortunate feature of the planning during the war of 1939 has been that there has been almost no planning for the post-war legal world. There has been no successor to the great, but abortive, Haldane plan for the reconstruction of our legal system. The legal world survived the war of 1914 almost untouched. Is history to repeat itself in this respect ? From a lowly legal source this book sets out to do something to prevent such repetition, to arouse interest and

[1] *More from a Lawyer's Notebook*, pp. 197-8.

v

discussion by making numerous practical suggestions for the better handling, in the post-war world, of those who may be found guilty of crime.

Books written by those on the Bench, whether high or low, are few, and there is undoubtedly a prejudice against them. Two witnesses for the defence are cited above. There is another. In 1792 Patrick Colquhoun was appointed to the office of metropolitan magistrate. In 1795 he wrote his famous *Treatise of the Police of the Metropolis*, which was a dissertation on ' the various crimes and misdemeanours and suggesting remedies for their prevention '. In his book Colquhoun pointed out the many follies in the law and procedure of his day. He set out plans for reforms. This book also tries to do both these things.

The war of 1914 provided much evidence that many cases popularly but erroneously described as ' shell shock ' could be cured or helped through attention to the unconscious emotional situation of the sufferers. From this experience came the realization that many cases of breakdown in ordinary life can be relieved by a similar approach. Then it was but a short step to the belief that some cases of delinquent conduct indicated weakness capable of relief by similar methods. Thus the psychological treatment of delinquency made great progress through discoveries during the war of 1914. But what one war encouraged another war severely checked. One result of the war of 1939 in criminal courts was that it became more difficult to obtain assistance from medical experts in psychology.

This book, therefore, is an inquest on the past, but also a programme for the future.

There are many books by psychologists which include references to the relation of modern psychology to problems of crime. Such books mostly expound psychological prin-

ciples and then turn to explain how delinquents fit into them.
It is an innovation to offer a book on crime and psychology
written by a lawyer, whose daily task is to try delinquents
and to decide what is to be done with them.   I am not
a psychologist, and such knowledge of psychology as I possess
comes mainly from experience with delinquents and from
reading.   Instead of beginning with a wide knowledge of
psychology and trying to see how delinquents are examples
of its principles, I have studied delinquents and then turned
to psychology for assistance in dealing with them.   Professional magistrates are the only men on the criminal Bench of
this country who have alone and without a jury to decide
whether those charged before them are ' Guilty ' or ' Not
Guilty '.   Therefore they have responsibilities in relation to
delinquents which others do not have.   This book is largely
the result of my experiences in court ; it deals with problems
that arise in deciding how to handle those who have been
found guilty, and also with some of the problems of criminal
trial.

In such psychological studies as I have been able to make
I have become the disciple of no particular school ; in fact,
I believe that I am inherently incapable of becoming any-
body's disciple.   It is my impression that the differences
between psychologists are more concerned with theory than
practice.   Be this as it may, I have garnered help from all
schools, content with the knowledge that psychologists treating delinquents rarely limit themselves to any particular
method.   As this book is written by a magistrate, it cannot
show blind optimism and enthusiasm, but happily a realization of the limitations and difficulties of psycho-therapy in
practice is in no way inconsistent with a genuine belief in
the merits and utility of psychology in relation to those guilty
of delinquent conduct.

In this book are many criticisms of our law and procedure, but I have written it without any desire to belittle the real merits of our system of criminal justice. The legal Adam is still sufficiently strong within me to make me prefer the English criminal system, with all its defects, to any other. I should certainly prefer to be tried in England than elsewhere if charged with a crime that I had committed, or with one of which I was innocent. Whether if guilty, I should prefer to be sentenced by an English court, I am not so certain. My attitude to English criminal law and procedure is that of Cowper to England itself : ' With all thy faults I love thee still.' In such a book as this it is not possible to avoid some discussion of weaknesses in the higher courts. As I am on the lowest rung in the judicial ladder, I would explain that an awareness of weaknesses at Assizes and Quarter Sessions is not incompatible with respect for those who administer justice there. I have just as much respect for them as those, perhaps happier, lawyers whose admiration for English criminal justice is not tempered by a belief that big reforms are necessary.

It is improbable that, if any experts in psychology read this book, they will fully approve my attempts to handle psychological theories. I shall be content if they are moved to say of this lawyer's book what Dr. Johnson said of a woman preaching : ' It is like a dog's walking on his hind legs. It is not done well. But you are surprised to find it done at all.' I must, however, meet one likely criticism. Here and there this book has too many quotations. But as I am not an expert in psychology, it seemed better, and more honest, to quote from authorities freely than to give clumsy, and probably inaccurate, summaries of what I have learned from them. I wish to thank all the authors and publishers of the books from which I have quoted.

I desire particularly to thank the following for giving permission :

Messrs. Little, Brown and Company : *Crime and Justice*, by Sheldon Glueck

Yale University Press and Oxford University Press : *New Light on Delinquency and Its Treatment*, by Dr. William Healy and Dr. Augusta F. Bronner

W. W. Norton and Company, Inc., and George Allen and Unwin, Ltd. : *A History of Medical Psychology* by Dr Gregory Zilboorg and Dr. George W. Henry

The Commonwealth Fund, New York, and Oxford University Press : *Insanity as a Defense in Criminal Law*, by Henry Weihofen

University of London Press, Ltd. : *The Young Delinquent*, by Cyril Burt

Jonathan Cape Ltd. : *Diagnosis of Man*, by Kenneth Walker

The Hogarth Press and the Institute of Psycho-Analysis : *The Unknown Murderer*, by Theodor Reik ; also *A General Selection from the Works of Sigmund Freud* by John Rickman

Kegal Paul, Trench, Trubner & Co., Ltd. : *The Psychology of C. G. Jung*, by Dr. Jolan Jacobi, and *Modern Man in Search of a Soul*, by C. G. Jung

W. W. Norton and Company, Inc., and Chapman and Hall, Ltd. : *Personality in Formation and Action*, by Dr. William Healy

George Allen and Unwin, Ltd. : *The Dilemma of Penal Reform*, by Dr. Hermann Mannheim ; *The Way to Justice*, by Heber L. Hart, and *The Criminal, the Judge and the Public*, by Franz Alexander and Hugo Staub

Williams and Norgate, Ltd. : *What we Put in Prison*, by Dr. G. W. Pailthorpe

Lindsay Drummond, Ltd. : *The Criminal in Society*, by Henry T. F. Rhodes

The Macmillan Company, New York : *Delinquents and Criminals*, by Drs. W. Healy and A. F. Bronner

Macmillan and Co., Ltd. : *Brief Life*, by Cecil Whiteley

Gratitude is also due to those invaluable institutions, the Tavistock Clinic and the Institute for the Scientific Treatment of Delinquency, both for their prolonged help in difficult cases that I have had to deal with in court and for their

permission to include in this book extracts from reports sent
by them to me in some of the cases dealt with in the following
pages.

During the first writing of this book I received much help
from my friend Dr. A. McLeod Fraser. We had many
discussions on points where his experience as a medical
psycho-therapist and mine as a magistrate came into contact.
When the book was finished, he and Dr. Rosalind Vacher
read it through most carefully, with the result that many
corrections were made. Then came a long interval during
which I continued studying. After some time I came to the
conclusion that the book must be re-cast and entirely re-
written. This was done, and in its new form it was read
by Dr. Edward Glover, who has added to my debt to him
by contributing an Introduction. My most sincere gratitude
goes out to these doctors. I could not have managed without their help, and I fully realize that they could ill spare the
time that they gave to this book. None of them is in any
way responsible for the book or for any statement in it.
In countless instances I gratefully accepted their advice,
but in some others I was headstrong, and each of these
helpful doctors will probably disagree with parts of the
book.

The many cases described in this book come from several
metropolitan courts, but mostly from South-Western court.
All the probation officers with whom I have worked have
been most helpful, both in dealing with these and countless
other cases and in co-operating in collecting the facts in the
cases here described. I thank them all, but in particular
my friend and helper Mr. Arthur Shields, senior probation
officer at South-Western court from 1934 to 1941. He was
always enthusiastic for trying to cure criminals through
psychological treatment. His patience and understanding

were unlimited, and in the early days of the preparation of this book he gave me invaluable help.

The work of magistrates is done in public, but modern methods of reporting in the newspapers that are most read are such that the public is not given any real impression of the work that magistrates do, or of the policy that they adopt. Magistrates may day by day pursue old-time methods of dealing with delinquents, make inadequate inquiries about them, send many young people to prison and talk to delinquents in technical language which they cannot possibly understand ; or magistrates may employ modern methods, seek to cure rather than to punish as many delinquents as possible, and talk to them in easy language that they will understand. In either case the public will not be told. Newspapers with large circulations seem interested only in individual cases that they can interpret as ' a story ', or whenever possible as ' a sensation '. Such reporting can provide no ground for estimating the value of the work of any magistrate. I hope that this book gives a true impression of the work that I have tried to do ; and will destroy the caricatures of this work that have from time to time been given to the newspaper-reading public.

During the long period in which this book was written I worked also on a second book, for it seemed to me that my survey of the usefulness of modern psychology in connexion with criminals would not be complete without an inquiry into the causes of crime, as seen from the psychological standpoint. By studying such causes we can the better understand the difficulties of treatment. This second book, *Why Crime ?*, will, I hope, follow the present volume after a short interval.

C. M.

LONDON,
July, 1943.

CONTENTS

		PAGE
	PREFACE	v
	INTRODUCTION BY DR. EDWARD GLOVER	xiii
1	SOME PRINCIPLES OF MODERN PSYCHOLOGY	1
2	PRACTICAL POSSIBILITIES	38
3	A FEW CASES	66
4	PUNISHMENT	99
5	FURTHER OBSTACLES	123
6	THE NEED FOR INVESTIGATION	142
7	PSYCHOLOGY AND CRIMINAL PROCEDURE	159
8	CHILDREN IN THE COURTS	181
9	THE BENCH AND THE DELINQUENT	205
	APPENDIX	226
	INDEX	229

INTRODUCTION

WHETHER he is aware of it or not, Claud Mullins has played an honourable part in a revolution which began at the close of the nineteenth century, and despite many set-backs is still gathering momentum. The discovery that man's mind, and consequently his behaviour, is activated by forces and regulated by mechanisms of which he is totally unaware was at first received with incredulous and abusive opposition : only after it had been demonstrated that by acting on these assumptions it was possible to cure or alleviate a variety of mental disorders did opposition give place to a reluctant tolerance. Even so, the ' unconscious mind ' was, and in many quarters is still regarded as a medico-psychological curiosity having little bearing on the lives of ordinary men.

Gradually the application of psycho-analytical principles (from which, directly or indirectly, most forms of modern clinical psychology derive their strength) to non-medical fields led to the conclusion that there is no variety of human behaviour, individual or social, that cannot be illuminated by understanding of man's unconscious mind. Art and literature, sociology, anthropology, philosophy and religion were in turn subjected to the unsolicited attentions of research students, confident in their belief that what governs the mind of man must of necessity be expressed also in the institutions he has created. During this period of reconnaissance the Faculty of Law stood aloof and apparently impregnable. For a time indeed it was scarcely assailed. A few articles dealing with the unconscious motivations of criminal conduct had appeared in obscure technical journals :

and of course the ' McNaghten Rules ' remained, a disconcerting legacy from a non-psychological epoch, to remind
judges that the writ of Reason does not run unchallenged
in their courts.   But until very recent times the Law, secure
in the conviction of its own sanctity, continued to carry out
undisturbed its twin functions of preserving the structure
of society from the depredations of individuals and of protecting the established rights of the individual from en-
croachment by society.   The revolutionary conception with
which the Law was about to be faced was simply that these
reciprocal functions can be more efficiently and humanely
performed if the more superstitious and retributive of legal
sanctions are replaced by unprejudiced examination and
treatment of the (conscious and unconscious) causes of law-
breaking.

   Now however little honour pioneers may gather in their
own country, they have at least the satisfaction of knowing
that they cannot justly be regarded as downright interlopers,
Greater hardihood is demanded of those who, like the
author of this courageous book, are bold enough to import
into their own professional field the more unpopular findings of an alien science.   Not only did Mr. Mullins possess
the requisite hardihood, he had sufficient patience and
conviction to apply these findings in the face of unqualified
disapproval and criticism, until, as this book shows, he
had justified beyond question his breakaway from the traditions of one of the most conservative professions.   Mr.
Mullins was not indeed the first lawyer to accept with
enthusiasm the teachings of modern psychology, but he
was the first magistrate in this country to apply them
systematically in ordinary police-court work.   This fact
deserves to be recognized, and it is right that psychologists
should be amongst the first to pay tribute to his achievements.

The present volume is itself an outstanding achievement. When the author came to record his experiences, he made the disconcerting discovery that there are no satisfactory popular books on the psychology of the unconscious, or, at least, none that would serve as a preamble to his own presentation of a new forensic psychology. With characteristic audacity he proceeded to write his own preamble. Those who are familiar with the disputes that divide the various ' schools ' of clinical psychology will best appreciate the risks the author ran by so doing.   No doubt the psychologically instructed reader will find much to criticize in his presentation ;   for Mr. Mullins hankers after eclecticism, and the psychological eclectic usually ends by alienating most of the authorities from whom he quotes.   But this should not be allowed to obscure the fact that Mr. Mullins has accepted and understood more of the basic findings of modern clinical psychology than the great majority of mental specialists in this country.   Psychologists may admire or disapprove of his effrontery, but the remedy lies in their own hands ;   they should set about writing good popular text-books.

In yet another respect the author conforms to the standards of a good revolutionary.   He is patently a good conservative, keenly aware of the fact that the aims of the law are not and never can be identical with those of medical psychology.   The Law court cannot become the exclusive preserve of the individual psychologist for the simple reason that it is itself a product of the inevitable and unending conflict between the instincts of the individual and the needs of the group.   Mr. Mullins discusses the idea of reducing this conflict by incorporating official psychological ' panels ' in the service of the courts.   So long as the law exercises punitive powers, this would not be a very desirable state of affairs.   It is important that the respective spheres of operation of the law and of medical science should be strictly delimited.   The rôle of the physician should remain that of an expert in servitude only to his own diagnostic and therapeutic ideals.   He should at all times, except with the consent of the patient or under legal duress, preserve the traditions of medical discretion.   In these days when plans for wholesale post-war ' reconstruction ' are as plentiful as blackberries, it is well that these traditions should not be forgotten.   Already the successful application of psychological ' selection tests ' to the totalitarian needs of the army threatens to influence post-war organization of civilian health services.   There is in fact more than a risk that the psychological specialist of the future may be called on by non-medical government departments to adjudicate on the normal citizen's vocational suitability.   And it would be a short step from this to compel officially appointed medical psychologists to make a daily practice of breaking their professional oaths at the behest of courts of law.   With all due respect to Mr. Mullins, I would prefer even the disadvantages of trial by jury.   Psychological diagnosis and treatment (or prevention) of social derangement, and psychological assessment of normal individuals in the interests of the State, are ' clear different things '.   The utmost vigilance is necessary to prevent psychological specialists exercising authority over the lives of normal individuals.   And as readers of Mr. Mullins's book will learn, the dividing line between the normal person and the delinquent is often a narrow one.

EDWARD GLOVER

CHAPTER I

SOME PRINCIPLES OF MODERN
PSYCHOLOGY[1]

The criminal has been regarded as sinner, moral reprobate, or anthropological monstrosity, or has been explained away as a by-product of social conditions without much individual significance. . . . Neither individual nor society is the ultimate end of the investigation. It is the relation subsisting between them at any given time which is the real subject matter. . . . A man's psychological attitude is basically determined by the relation between individual and community. . . . The value of the psychological approach cannot be overestimated. The essential point is that the reaction of individual and environment produces a psychological attitude.

HENRY T. F. RHODES [2]

MODERN PSYCHOLOGY teaches that there is a part of our mind of which we are ordinarily not aware which has a profound effect upon us in that it may influence our thoughts, our beliefs, our characters, our emotions, and our behaviour. ' Our mind is like an iceberg of which only one small part, the conscious, is above the surface.' [3]   In the larger part below the surface, that is below the level of consciousness, thoughts, feelings, wishes, and impulses may be active and have an influence upon us.

In itself this is ancient knowledge. In a book, *A History of Medical Psychology*,[4] it was stated that ' medico-psychological

[1] It is obviously not possible for a lawyer, untrained in psychology, to expound the teaching of modern psychology completely or in great detail. The object of this chapter is to refer to such psychological principles and to give such examples as will pave the way for an understanding of the utility of psychology in connection with delinquency.

[2] *The Criminal in Society*, pp. 14–15.

[3] Dr. J. R. Rees, medical director of the Tavistock Clinic, *The Health of the Mind*, p. 26.

[4] By G. Zilboorg and G. W. Henry, p. 32.

ideas are found in the literary monuments of ancient India', in the Vedas, which were composed between 1000 and 2000 years B.C. Plato wrote about the unconscious influence of experience and atmosphere on human character and conduct. Thus:

We would not have our guardians [ruling class] grow up amid images of moral deformity, as in some noxious pasture, and there browse and feed upon many a baneful herb and flower day by day, little by little, until they silently gather a festering mass of corruption in their own soul. . . . Then will our youth dwell in a land of health, amid fair sights and sounds, and receive the good in everything ; and beauty, the effluence of fair works, shall flow into the eye and ear, like a health-giving breeze from a purer region, and insensibly draw the soul from earliest years into likeness and sympathy with the beauty of reason.[1]

Even some of the distinctive ideas and methods of Sigmund Freud are suggested in some passages of Plato. ' My art ', declared Socrates, according to Plato, ' is like that of midwives, but differs from theirs, in that I attend men and not women, and I look after their souls when they are in labour, and not after their bodies.' There is definitely a psycho-analytical ring in what follows :

The triumph of my art is in thoroughly examining whether the thought which the mind of the young man brings forth is a phantom and a lie, or a fruitful and true birth. And like the midwives, I am barren, and the reproach often made against me, that I ask questions of others and have not the wit to answer them myself, is very just. The reason is, that the god compels me to be a midwife, but does not allow me to have children. So I myself am not at all wise, nor have I any invention or child of my own to show, but those who talk with me profit. . . . It is quite clear that they never learned anything from me ; all that they master and discover comes from themselves. . . . Dire are the pangs which my art is able to arouse and to allay in those who consort with me, just like the pangs of women in childbirth. . . . For I have actually known some who were ready to bite me when I deprived them of a darling folly.[2]

---

[1] *Republic*, Book 3, 401 ; Jowett's translation.
[2] ' Theaetetus,' 150 f. This extract is taken from Sir Richard Livingstone's *Plato ; Selected Passages*, pp. 19–20.

There is much here that will be familiar to those who understand the principles of psycho-analysis and the reactions that are sometimes shown by patients undergoing psycho-analysis. Indeed, the words ' all that they master and discover comes from themselves ' constitute the essence of most modern psycho-therapy. But ancient though these ideas are, it has been only in recent decades that sustained efforts have been made to study unconscious factors and by understanding them, to modify their influence where they have wrought harm.

One of the fundamental maxims of modern psychology is that what has been forgotten or repressed, or experienced only in the unconscious, is not obliterated. The belief of Freud that nothing is forgotten, in the meaning of being obliterated, has been challenged by other psychologists,[1] but there is no need for us to enter into this controversy, since for our purpose it suffices that much that has passed beyond memory, and much that has never been recorded in it, remain in the unconscious and can be powerful factors. There are, of course, various depths in the unconscious. It is a common experience of us all that what has been forgotten can often be recalled by an effort of will, or by some resumed contact or association. Such experience illustrates the working of what is termed the pre-conscious. But some impulses, ideas, and emotions, especially those which are the most important and primitive, are incapable of becoming conscious, usually because of the mentally painful conflict to which they give rise ; they are barred from consciousness by a process known as unconscious repression.

This unconscious system of the mind is in constant operation, in sleep as well as during the daily round, and it is of supreme importance to realize that what has been repressed can exercise a powerful, and often a harmful, influence on health, both physical and mental, and also on conduct. Such influence is, of course, not realized, either by the sufferer or by those around him.

[1] e.g. by Dr. Rudolf Allers in his challenging book, *The Successful Error*, p. 4.

Therefore the purpose of psycho-therapy is to restore to health those whose lives are being adversely affected by their unconscious conflicts. This is done by helping them to gain an insight into the causes of their condition. When faulty repressions giving rise to mental symptoms are corrected, the emotional tension is released. It is only as a man ' is brought to recognize the parts of his experience and the dynamics of his life with which he has lost contact that he comes to realize that his problem is within his own personality '.[1] Psycho-therapy practises the art of leading afflicted people to retrace their steps, so that by re-experiencing what has hurt and lain unconscious and by ventilating unconscious conflicts that are still active, they can secure release from the ill effects of both. Psycho-therapy seeks to trace back to its origin the symptom that has caused breakdown, to ascertain why mental pain and conflict arose and why they have persisted in such strength.

Some modern psychologists maintain that our minds are more than the repositories of experiences and that they are the repositories also of inherited instincts. They claim that just as our bodies do not really begin at conception, but are endowed with the physical characteristics of many generations of ancestors, similarly our minds are endowed with the experiences and instincts of previous generations. In this view a new-born child is in fact an elderly being, both physically and psychologically. ' The collective unconscious is the mighty spiritual inheritance of human development, reborn in every individual . . . constitution ', wrote Dr. C. G. Jung, who also maintained that our dreams are sometimes ' manifestations of the collective unconscious which, going beyond the individual conflicts ' of the dreamer, become involved in ' the primordial experience of universal human problems '.[2] This view is much disputed among modern psychologists. Thus Alfred Adler, founder of the

[1] *The New Psychology and the Teacher*, by Dr. H. Crichton Miller, p. 137.
[2] *The Psychology of C. G. Jung*, by Dr. Jolan Jacobi, pp. 33 and 69.

school of Individual Psychology, firmly denied the existence of an ' inherited unconscious '.[1] But Adler was reluctant to accept heredity in any form. What can be said without fear of dispute is that just as constitutional factors affect a man's physical development, there are constitutional factors which affect the development of the human mind. There is a psychological predisposition which constitutes, as it were, the soil in which the seed of mental conflict may later develop. Further than that we have no need to go, since the problem of inheritance has but little practical bearing on the subject of this book.[2] No psychological report that I have ever received about a delinquent has suggested atavistic causes of his behaviour. Characteristics of remote ancestors may in fact have influenced the delinquent, and I have often suspected that this must have been the case, but magistrates work in criminal courts, not in scientific laboratories.

Both our bodies and our minds develop slowly from small beginnings. Experience, like inheritance, begins before birth. During a normal pregnancy the child-to-be has every need satisfied. It is undisputed that the child's physical body can be injured or maldeveloped if the mother does not consume sufficient quantities of food containing the chemicals needed by the unborn child. Many psychologists claim that emotional experiences of the mother during the later stages of pregnancy can also affect the child in that such emotional experiences may also affect the quality of the nourishment that reaches the child in the womb. Some support for this view has come from non-psychological sources. For instance, when during the war of 1939 air raids on the civilian population of our cities began, Dame Louise McIlroy (a well-known physiologist and gynaecologist and not a psychologist by profession) pleaded for the more intensive evacuation of expectant mothers from danger areas on the following ground :

What children, born in circumstances fraught with terror for the mother, to say nothing of the physical dangers associated

---

[1] e.g. *Social Interest*, p. 148.
[2] This problem will be dealt with in my next book, *Why Crime ?*

with air raids, will be like in later life, if they do survive, it is not difficult to imagine. We still come across cases of abnormalities in individuals born during the last war. . . . Fear is one of the most deadly enemies in obstetric practice.[1]

I have had before me in court delinquents, physically normal, whose delinquent conduct was explained by medical experts, and sometimes by experienced police officers, as the indirect consequence of the fact that they were born during air raids of the war of 1914. Naturally it was impossible to test these explanations scientifically, but even allowing for an ample margin of error, it is probable that there will be many such cases during the coming years. Happily, owing to the character of most of our people, the number of children born in air raids who are adversely affected in their psychological development to any serious extent is likely to be but a small proportion ; for where no undue fear was felt, either by the parents or by those around the child, all is likely to be well with the child if its body escaped injury. But in future years our criminal courts are sure to have to deal with many who were not so fortunate. In fact, both for mothers and babies fear during air raids was an even greater danger than bombs. For present purposes air raids and bombs are merely instances of the possible effects on newly born children of experiences, physical or psychological, coming to the mother during pregnancy or confinement.

Some schools of psychological thought maintain that birth can originate unconscious experience which may have results in later life.[2] This was brought home to me when I was once discussing a man with an analytical psychologist, in general a follower of Freud's teaching. This man had a harmless form of claustrophobia in that he hated any complete enclosure of the head or any undue pressure on

---

[1] In a letter to *The Times*, 2 July 1940.
[2] In Freud's book, *Inhibitions, Symptoms and Anxiety* (pp. 103–5), and in his undelivered *New Introductory Lectures on Psycho-Analysis* (pp. 115 et seq.), Freud challenged the view of Otto Rank that birth traumas were a universal cause of neurosis.

it. He hated wearing a gas mask and would have been panic stricken had he put on a diver's helmet; he even disliked it if a child sat on his head. This, I believe, is no unusual condition. The explanation given to me was that the condition probably originated in a difficult passage of the head at birth. Such a theory sounds at first fantastic, but once it is accepted that the mind receives impressions apart from consciousness, the theory seems at least possible. Happily for the man in question, he had been brought up wisely from the psychological point of view, but had his natural aggressive instincts been unduly repressed or over-inhibited, then his form of claustrophobia could have resulted in a severe and even a crippling condition, which nothing but prolonged psycho-therapy could have relieved.

Even under the most favourable circumstances birth brings the earliest of a child's major anxieties. Apart from physical dangers, the separation from the mother involves a loss of security. With birth begin both conscious and unconscious feelings of being thwarted; what psycho-logists term frustration has begun. The child is no longer supreme. The comparative security, quiet, and content-ment of existence in the womb have given place to interfer-ence, risks, and the disappointments of human activity.

From its earliest days a child is occupied with the fulfil-ment of instinctive urges; for a time it remains supremely egocentric. But training begins almost at once and each step in this can have psychological consequences. There come a succession of new experiences, many of which are very disturbing to the child, but the love and care that it receives strengthen its sense of security and well-being. Gradually more and more adjustments have to be made, and these are far from easy for the child. Regularity in feeding, cleanliness, and so on, must involve restraints on primitive feelings. Intense anxiety, of great importance in later development, may arise if there are difficulties in breast feeding or even when feeding is not given when it is desired. Weaning is ordinarily a most anxious time for the child as well as for parents. At such times feelings of aggression are stimulated in every child.   Dr. Money-Kyrle maintained that it is the human child's helplessness, even more than the relatively long period of his dependence, that is significant in the story of mankind.   When a human child is hungry, ' he can only scream.   This is the sole mechanism for the fulfilment of his needs he is endowed with. . . .   Inevitably, therefore, he will be more subject than other young animals to fits of panic and impotent rage, which will leave a permanent impression.' [1]   This may be the reason why man is more aggressive than other animals.

If these almost innumerable crises in the life of a young child are not wisely handled, there may be at any time a stimulation of aggressive feelings which can influence either health or conduct.   Thus if a parent treats a child roughly when its rages are inconvenient, there may be dangerous consequences in the child's later life.   To endeavour to suppress childish rage, without understanding that it is perfectly normal and healthy, may make a child fearful and may create in the child a harmful feeling of guilt.   Any such undue repression of natural feelings hampers growth.   This does not mean that attempts to divert a child's rage to something more constructive are in any way to be deprecated.   On the contrary, the extreme form of modernism in education which asserts that children should always be allowed to express themselves is harmful ; every child needs to feel secure, and this necessary feeling of security is intensified by moderate and understanding attempts by adults to divert aggression and rage into useful paths.   A healthy child begins life with *L'état c'est moi* as its motto, but if a child is not brought up so as to be prepared for the time when it must realize that it is not the centre of the universe, then severe emotional stress in later life may result.   Thus both the child in an ultra old-fashioned school and a child in a self-styled progressive school can suffer from psychological strain at any time in later life.

The natural aggressiveness of a child can develop into initiative, ability to surmount obstacles, emotional independ-

---

[1] *Superstition and Society*, p. 115.

ence, and healthy self-assertion.   The child unduly sup-
pressed may suffer from a lack of initiative and self-assertion ;
it may become the tool of the evil leader.   The over-
indulged child, and particularly the child whose parents
or teachers alternate between indulgence and scolding, may
fail just because it has never learned the advantages of
obedience to the essential demands that life makes.   In
either case there will probably arise conflict between buried
impulses and the requirements of everyday life.   In either
case illness or crime may be a belated consequence.

Most people, especially the parents of young children,
believe that children are happy in their early years, but
they are unwise if they ignore the other side of the picture
of childhood.   Professor C. W. Valentine gave under the
title *The Psychology of Early Childhood* the results of his
' almost daily observations of his own five children over
a period of some twenty years ', and also of similar observations made by his former pupils and other psychologists.
His conclusion was ' that periods of contentment and
apparent enjoyment were far more frequent than displeasure,
even during the first few months, however much more
vociferously the latter might be expressed '.[1]   When I asked
a practising psycho-analyst his opinion of this conclusion,
he criticized it on the ground of ' optimism and poor
observation '.   Most grown-ups, and particularly parents
of young children, are inclined to forget all unpleasant
experiences in their own early lives.   They forget the
anxieties, terrors, and nightmares which haunted their early
childhood.   Children undoubtedly suffer terribly at times
during these years, and parents often feel powerless to
comfort them and bring them to reason.   None the less,
I feel bound to agree with the conclusion of Professor
Valentine.   I believe that it is reasonable to believe that
childhood shows a big balance of happiness, however unreal
it may be to ignore the other aspect.

But there is one prevalent idea which modern psychology
compels us to abandon ; it is mere sentimentality to believe

[1] pp. vii and 92.

that children feel undiluted love for their parents or any one else. Even towards its mother a baby feels both love and hate. There is love when needs are satisfied, but there may well be hate when satisfaction is refused. The resulting fusion of love and hate is technically described as ambivalence, which Freud characterized as 'a fundamental phenomenon of our emotional life '.[1] Another authority stated that 'love and hate are struggling together in the baby's mind; and this struggle to a certain extent persists throughout life and is liable to become a source of danger in human relationships '.[2] Unconscious conflicts of this kind can produce a sense of guilt, for guilt is likely to arise when hatred is felt towards those for whom there is also genuine love.

> And to be wroth with one we love,
> Doth work like madness in the brain.[3]

If such conflicts cannot be resolved, if children cannot from time to time express some of their real feelings, both polite and impolite, to those nearest to them, then they can become bottled-up, and this is dangerous, because in psychology, as in chemistry, undue pressure in a confined space may result in explosion. It has also to be remembered that young children suffer from a lack of means for self-expression in the interval between the yelling stage and the stage when words can be adequate. A wise upbringing enables a child to survive these strains and to become increasingly fitted to cope with life and to take his natural place in the community. But some children become solitary and inhibited because, through either suppression or indulgence, a true relationship with their parents is never developed.

[1] *Totem and Taboo*, Penguin edition, p. 208.
[2] Melanie Klein in *Love, Hate and Reparation*, p. 60.
[3] From ' Christabel ' by Coleridge ; quoted in Mrs. Melanie Klein's contribution to *Love, Hate and Reparation*. Other common sources of ambivalence are where the only child suddenly finds that there is a brother or sister, or when the grown-up son or daughter has to look after an elderly parent. In both cases love and hate are sometimes strong.

Much of the conduct of children which adults are apt to regard as deliberate naughtiness is in fact an unconscious rebellion against the standards set for them, or against the immediate circumstances in which the children are placed. When, for instance, the evacuation of children took place in the early months of the war of 1939, there was a remarkable amount of bed-wetting amongst the younger children. The journal of the National Association of Probation Officers stated at the time that ' 600 cases of bed-wetting are reported from one small county area ' ; [1] both enuresis and delinquency are linked with emotional unhappiness and a sense of insecurity.   This is an established fact.   Countless hostesses were inconvenienced, to say the least, by this development, but the children who lived with, or who could quickly be put in charge of, those who understood the reason for the bed-wetting, recovered much more quickly than children who were blamed or punished.   Children wrongly handled for bed-wetting may easily become later on problems that magistrates have to deal with. [2]

To some extent similar principles apply to adolescents and adults.   After childhood come two major events in human life when physical and psychological changes can result in conduct directed by unconscious forces.   These are adolescence and the climacteric, popularly spoken of as the change of life.   At both times the human body undergoes definite alterations and the mind experiences psychological strain.   Both when adult sexual powers emerge

[1] *Probation*, December 1939, p. 113.
[2] Dorothy Burlingham and Anna Freud, the latter a daughter of Sigmund Freud, published in *Young Children in War-Time* the valuable results of their experience with three nurseries for babies and young children affected by air raids, but not severely injured in body.   They found that ' London children were on the whole much less upset by bombing than by evacuation to the country ' (p. 41).   They stated that ' it is a common misunderstanding of the child's nature which leads people to suppose that children will be saddened by the sight of destruction and aggression. . . . Children between the age of 1 and 2 years . . . are passing through a stage of development where destruction and aggression play one of the leading parts ' (p. 29).

and when they slowly fail difficulties of character and behaviour may arise, the gravity of which is decided, not so much by the physical conditions as by the unconscious emotional state. During both adolescence and the change of life strong forces are generated in the unconscious, which may result in an absence of self-control ; the degree of self-control will depend upon the wisdom, from the psychological standpoint, of the life that has been led. Those at either stage of life sometimes behave in a manner which cannot be explained by any superficial observation. Every magistrate is brought face to face with criminal conduct by adolescents which appears inexplicable and meaningless ; also with similar conduct (both in criminal charges and in matrimonial disputes) by those of both sexes who are undergoing the change of life—that process is much less noticeable in men than in women, but men are subject to it. Unless it be realized in any such case that unconscious forces may have been at work, justice will be blind indeed.

If then, natural development can have a deep psychological influence, probably unrealized at the time, it is obvious that any unusual or catastrophic experience at any time of life may have a far deeper influence. To take a few examples at random, those who are unfortunate enough to experience a serious fire, to be subjected to some kind of sexual assault, or to have horrible experiences in war, may be influenced for life ; the feelings to which such experiences give rise may be repressed. Should this repression prove faulty, dangerous consequences in health or conduct may result at any stage of later life.

Thus from childhood onwards we and those around us seldom have any true knowledge of the reasons for our condition or our conduct. There may be no apparent reason, for instance, why one person may be made a permanent invalid, though without physical injuries, by the bursting of a bomb or shell near by, while another will remain psychologically unharmed and quickly revert to normal. In fact, those who are wounded may well be less subject to war neurosis than those who remain unwounded but who have suffered from shock. For similar reasons two men may receive similar physical wounds from shell fire, and, whereas one may become a nervous wreck through shock, the other may remain able to give a laughing account of his experiences and soon be back in the danger zone. The true difference lies in the psychological development.

So also in regard to conduct; a simple case is when a child demands something vehemently, or intolerantly insists upon the truth of some statement. Quite likely the child will care little for the object demanded or for the truth of the statement. In reality the child may well be trying out its environment, endeavouring to see whether there is near at hand any one stronger than itself. To receive the object, or to find the statement accepted, may be disconcerting to the child rather than soothing. Thus the picture of a yelling baby in a tin bath trying to get a cake of soap beyond its reach (once used as an advertisement for Pears' soap), had the caption ' He won't be happy till he gets it.' From the psychological point of view the caption was unconvincing, for the child might have yelled louder still when some one gave him the soap; he might have been thoroughly enjoying his grievance and getting much relief from his crying. Every child yearns for security, so, if some one had come along and had firmly told the yelling child that he could not have the soap, the yelling might have got louder for a few moments, but then the soothing feeling of having some one stronger near at hand might have brought about a pleasing sense of protection. Adults sometimes behave in a psychologically similar way; we cherish our grievances and find relief thereby. Again, a child will kick the object that has hurt him; he knows that the object will not mind, but the kicking gives him relief. Adults, too, do this, as every office boy knows. Similarly, a nervously exhausted parent may find relief when one of his children gives him justifiable occasion for momentary anger; he may have been trying to be self-controlled, and this opportunity for righteous anger acts as a release for pent-up discontents.

3

The more that we study modern psychology, the more we should be prepared to understand that the motives which we think dominate our actions and opinions are seldom the real ones.   In fact most of us do what we want to do, however much we may delight in feeling ourselves martyrs.   Who does not know ' the unconscious hypocrite whose passion for power takes the form of unselfishness and benevolence ' ?   Referring to such people, Professor John Macmurray wrote that ' it is so easy to feel that you are acting out of pure unselfish desire for another person's good, when you really are satisfying an unconscious passion for ordering them about '.[1]   In times of war this may be less true than normally, since totalitarian war compels men and women, either by force of law or of public opinion, to follow careers which they may dislike.   But war-time can show the truth of this psychological principle in the actions of some of those outside the armed forces ; some make themselves uncomfortable in good causes who are really seeking release from a life that they disliked.

The same principle shows itself in the motives directing the choice of partners, in either matrimony or business. A man or woman may complain that the partner lacks this or that quality, but often it was the very absence of that quality that unconsciously directed the original choice of partner ; often the quality whose lack is complained of is the very one which keeps the partnership alive.   Many women have complained in my domestic court that their husbands ' take no notice of them ', meaning that the husbands are sparing in their sexual attentions.   But sometimes both probation officer and I are convinced from the whole story that the women unconsciously chose their husbands precisely because they were not strongly sexed men.

[1] *Freedom in the Modern World*, p. 146.   Self-love can be a potent unconscious force, as magistrates see almost daily.   An example is the parent who insists on court proceedings against the man or woman who has struck the parent's child ; it is usually useless to point out that such proceedings may harm the child, for the parent is motivated by self-love, by feelings for his or her own dignity.

Many have been deterred from sympathy with the psychological point of view by reason of the emphasis which Freud and his followers have placed on sexual forces in human life. Criticism on this account is often due either to emotional prejudices about sex which are almost universal among humans, or to a lack of understanding of the meaning in which Freud used the word sex, or perhaps to both. Freud undoubtedly expanded the meaning of sexuality to include all physical and psychic forms of love. Considerable objection to this arose, even among scientists. Dr. C. G. Jung and others have put forward the criticism that human activity is too rich and too diverse to be based solely on sexual urges. It is not possible for a layman to enter into the rights and wrongs of this big controversy; I can only admit that I am more attracted to the view of Jung.[1] But whatever view is taken, all should be prepared to recognize as fact that sex, even in its conventional meaning, plays a more powerful part in promoting conduct than was ever realized by those who have not studied modern psychology.

It is undoubtedly a fact that in infancy great interest is taken in the physical body, its form, its parts and its functions. A normal and healthy child will discharge a normal and healthy volume of sexual energy by yielding to its natural desire to run about naked. It is maintained by psychologists that strong exhibitionist tendencies in a child may bear fruit in later life in such outlets as acting, public speaking and preaching. The exhibitionism of the child should mature normally, and when wisely handled a child socializes itself in time and an equally natural feeling of

[1] See the translator's preface to Jung's *Psychological Types.* I am also much drawn to the views expressed by Dr. Ian D. Suttie in his book, *The Origins of Love and Hate.* As Dr. J. A. Hadfield explained in his preface to this book, the starting-point of Suttie's conception of human life and development was the ' need for companionship ' ; Love ' is protective as well as sexual '. It follows that Suttie emphasized that ' the part played by the mother is of paramount importance in the development of the social relationships of the child '.

modesty emerges. But if parents, probably because of their own feelings of shame (the product of their own unwise education or of their own inner conflicts), are severe and critical with these natural urges, or try to suppress them as a matter of discipline, then these urges may be driven into the unconscious and a natural sexual maturity will be unlikely. If feelings of guilt in matters of sex are generated in a child, definite harm is done. A child forbidden to run about naked may later become unwilling to manifest affection ; worse still, it may grow up with its sexual energy and its love of self-display anchored to a repressed urge to show itself in the wrong way. I have found through the co-operation of psycho-therapists that some cases of indecent exposure by men of their private parts originated in such unwise suppression by their parents ; sexuality was checked—fixated, as psychologists say ; it has broken its fetters in an act which would be repugnant to any healthy man. Where exhibitionism has this origin, punishment is usually futile and the best hope lies in psycho-therapy.

That even young children are motivated by unconscious sexual forces can also be seen in many of their collective games. If a group of normal boys and girls were all dressed alike, an experienced child psychologist would probably be able to separate them into their respective sexes by watching their play. He would see through any ' tomboy ' girls ; he would find that in the main the girls were making or playing with things which they can protect, whereas the boys will be pushing things about, probably toy cars or aeroplanes. According to psychological theory, play is the natural means for expressing hidden impulses ; it can indicate the development of sexual as well as aggressive or social impulses. A psycho-analyst could probably ascertain a man's situation in regard to sexual life by studying his ordinary activities. But to believe this does not imply that all activity is prompted by sexual urges.

The principle of fixation has been mentioned. This is one of the most important principles of modern psychology.

It is best explained by means of a few illustrations. Thus the type of behaviour which a child has developed at important phases of its experience (for instance, during breast feeding, weaning, or when it is learning to be clean) may show a marked persistence in after life. Thus if a baby has unconsciously regarded weaning as a punishment for its exhibitions of aggression—a fairly normal state of affairs —it may grow up afraid of losing love and attention and thus become unduly dependent on other people. This is an illustration of a kind of fixation, frequently observed. The later dependence on other people is derived from the earlier excessive dependence on the parents.

One type of fixation in particular is of special importance in work among delinquents, namely the fixation of the natural homo-sexual tendencies which, I am told, develop their first form and strength about the age of 3 or 3½. Between the ages of 10 to 15 both sexes pass through a normal homo-sexual stage, as well as manifesting adolescent forms of interest in the opposite sex. The boy, for example, may have predominantly male friendships ; he has ' chums ' or ' pals ' and may love being in a ' gang ' ; a girl may have an ardent affection for a school-mistress or for an older girl. With the normal development of interest in the other sex homo-sexual inclinations should fade. But sometimes the homo-sexual phase persists, resulting in reluctance to enjoy association with those of the opposite sex. Any lack of understanding in parents or teachers of these natural phases may seriously interfere with mental growth. Unwise suppression of early homo-sexuality, or the imposition of an attitude of secrecy towards such matters, may result in a pathological condition where the homo-sexual phase persists until it develops into perversion. Fixated homo-sexuality can result later in conduct which is criminal ; many kinds of crime not apparently linked with homo-sexual tendencies may be thus caused. So great is sometimes the fear of this natural instinct, if it has assumed false proportions, that suicide can be the result. But homo-sexual instincts that are healthily sublimated can intensify the value of friendship with the same sex ; the popular member of a club, regiment, trade union, and so on, may be the product.

What are called mother (or father) fixations are also of mportance. Then, the impression made by the mother, natural and valuable in itself, has remained so strong that she has become unconsciously the pattern for all women. The result may well be either an unhappy marriage, where a wife has been selected because of her apparent likeness to the mother, or no marriage at all, when no such woman has turned up. Marriage cases in domestic courts often reveal the consequences of the former. In such cases trouble has arisen because of the unconscious desire to have all arranged as mother used to arrange things. As a result of this trouble there is an unhealthy eagerness to return to mother, and mother usually receives back her child, quite regardless of the immense damage that she is causing to the marriage ; misquoting the old saying, ' My son is my son to the end of my life, my daughter's my daughter for all her life.' Magistrates also see the mother-fixated son who has never married. His natural development has been frustrated, and if his abnormalities have been directed towards sexual activity, he is a very difficult person to handle. Some primitive races have special ceremonies to mark the emancipation from the guardianship of the mother.[1] Such ceremonies here would, if they were practicable, prevent much misery and failure. Far too many men have never married because of mother-fixations, and, while many lead blameless lives from the standpoint of the criminal law, some are driven to criminal conduct, sexual or otherwise. Women's lives can also be unconsciously directed by a repressed fear of, or fixation to, father, especially when father has been excessively dominating or over-indulgent. Both types of father may be the cause of an unhappy marriage, of an unhappy spinsterhood, or of abnormal conduct.

Where fixations of any kind have resulted in serious con-

[1] *The Psychology of C. G. Jung*, by Dr. Jolan Jacobi, p. 106.

sequences, including criminal conduct, cure by mere punishment is unlikely. Relief will come best through psychotherapy, which will bring into consciousness the conflict arising from the fixation and thus put an end to the trouble.

Enough has been written to show that it is poetry, not science, to say with Henley :

> I am the master of my fate,
> I am the captain of my soul.

It may be humiliating for man to realize that his personality is influenced, sometimes dominated, by unconscious forces within him. But many of the discoveries of modern science have been humiliating to man's pride. Both this world and man are not so central in the scheme of things as our ancestors believed. But man is slowly learning that many of his physical ills are not the will of God, but are within his own power to overcome. Similarly man has to learn that the psychological forces that influence him can be brought within the control of science. To realize that human character and conduct may be the consequence of unconscious forces, and be warped as the result of repressed experiences and fixations, is the ' open sesame ' to advance, to such preventive measures as a wiser and more scientific education and also to remedial measures such as re-education and psycho-therapy.

There are many who cannot face this realization. They feel that psychology, with its exploration of the unconscious mind, involves too great an invasion of their personalities, too great a disturbance in their lives. They are apt to resent any inquiry into their unconscious activities. So they belittle the teachings of modern psychology and without inquiry deny the validity of its discoveries. But in fact man is strengthened, not weakened nor robbed of his independence, when he realizes and understands the unconscious forces that drive him on. Past repressions, unconscious reactions to past experiences, fixations, or any conflicts of which he has never been conscious, may be holding him back and limiting his usefulness. Psychological disorders can gravely affect physical as well as mental health.   Restoration to health generally can be achieved by psycho-therapy.   Those who are not strong enough to face realities may have to be left with their weaknesses, phantasies and limitations ; many such are seen in our criminal courts, and they will be dealt with in the course of this book.   But the further psychological knowledge advances and the better that methods of therapy become, the fewer there will be of those whom psychology cannot reach.

Without accepting the extreme view that man is wholly directed by unconscious forces, we should at least recognize, what is now an undoubted scientific fact, that some conduct of sane people can be so directed.   What is of special importance for the purposes of this book is that some of the conduct which society for its self-protection terms criminal, and which accordingly results in an appearance in a criminal court, is in reality not a consequence of deliberate choice.   This is a scientific fact which the criminal law has so far only admitted to the extent that special laws and special treatment exist for those who are insane or mentally deficient ; those, in other words, who in most of their activities cannot be regarded as reasonable beings. But it is fundamental in all schools of psychology that many, able to live apparently normal lives, cannot in particular spheres of action be regarded as responsible.   This is a factor which the criminal law has not yet accepted.[1]   In-deed, the results in criminal law and procedure must be revolutionary when it becomes accepted that the personality of apparently normal human beings may be such that particular lines of conduct are influenced, or determined, by unconscious forces ; that, for example, a ' respectable ' person, leading a useful and otherwise blameless life, may be driven to some criminal act because he or she suffers from some psychological disorder which is not entirely disabling.   It is inevitable that modern psychology, in

[1] The Criminal Justice Bill of 1938–9 proposed to provide machinery for dealing with psychological disorders in those who remain at liberty.   See Chapter 4 of this book.

proportion as it becomes generally accepted, must affect deeply existing conceptions of the criminal law about self-responsibility. At present the law demands that delinquents are either generally responsible or generally irresponsible, and those coming within the latter category are not permitted to continue to live in freedom. But psychology teaches that there are innumerable half-way houses ; that people can be safe for living in the community who are irresponsible in one line of conduct.

Our traditional and existing criminal law is based upon the assumption that man from childhood onwards has in all activities a free choice between good and evil, except those who can be certified insane or mentally deficient. To-day this assumption is being assailed, and for some decades the attack upon it has been growing in intensity. The question of self-responsibility, it was said so long ago as 1882, ' has excited a controversy between the medical and the legal professions '.[1] But not only are doctors and lawyers involved. Ever since the conversion of St. Augustine of Hippo to the conventional Christian faith in 386, ecclesiastical opinion has accepted the freedom of the will and thus justified the doctrine of sin, the free choice of wrong against right. From the Christian Church the law inherited this belief. Crime, like sin, was the free choice of wrong-doing in preference to right conduct. The belief that such wrong-doing deserved punishment thus became deeply embedded in the law. It was once carried to what we now regard as extreme lengths. Even dumb animals were convicted and punished, a system that survived in some countries until modern times. In English civil law the same principle was at work ; chattels which had been the immediate cause of the death of a human being could be forfeited to the king, to be used ' in works of charity for the appeasement of God's wrath '.[2] Even so late as

[1] Sir James Fitzjames Stephen, *History of the Criminal Law*, vol. 2, p. 124.
[2] Sir Edward Coke (1552–1634), a Chief Justice, in his *Institutes*, vol. 3, ch. ix.

1842 the Court of Exchequer was occupied in deciding whether a railway engine could be made ' deodand ' (as objects so forfeited were called) four times over because it had killed four people.[1] This case led to the abolition of deodands by Parliament in 1846. But some modern schools of psychological thought would claim that the execution of animals for crime, or the condemnation of a railway engine, is not more extravagant than is sometimes the criminal law to-day.

Primitive law was unable to make any distinction between criminal acts committed by those who were responsible and such acts when committed by the irresponsible. Thus ' the primitive Germanic law has often been criticized on the ground that it paid attention only to the external injury and took no notice of the accompanying intention '.[2]   Such a distinction is only possible when judicial power is strong. ' It is always easy to say that a man is guilty of manslaughter, larceny, bigamy, but it is often most difficult to pronounce what extent of moral guilt he has incurred and consequently what measure of punishment he has deserved.'[3]

English criminal law still takes up a jealous attitude about responsibility. Responsibility is presumed ; every one but children accused of crime is presumed sane unless it is affirmatively proved on his behalf that he is insane. This doctrine has been repudiated by the laws of many of the states in the United States of America, where the presumption has been reversed ; ' since a sound mind is essential to criminal responsibility, the prosecution must prove beyond a reasonable doubt that the accused was mentally capable of the criminal intent required to constitute the crime charged '.[4]   But in this country there has been no vocal demand that such a drastic change should be made.   The attitude of English criminal law appears to be based on

[1] *The Queen* v. *Eastern Counties Railway*, 10 M. & W., p. 58.
[2] *A History of Continental Criminal Law*, by C. L. von Bar, p. 68.
[3] Sir Henry Maine in *Ancient Law*, 1930 edition, p. 400.
[4] *Insanity as a Defence in Criminal Law*, by Henry Weihofen, p. 158.

the conception that crime has whenever possible to be condemned; as it would be improper to condemn as criminals those who are definitely irresponsible, their number must be restricted as much as possible, lest the guilty should escape their deserts. There is much to be said for this point of view, and a belief in the teaching of modern psychology is not wholly inconsistent with it.

Conflicts concerning criminal responsibility date back many centuries. The *History of Medical Psychology*, by Drs. Gregory Zilboorg and George W. Henry, gave a detailed account of the conflict in the sixteenth century between the opinions of the doctor Johann Weyer (1515–88) and the lawyer Jean Bodin (1530–96):

In the personality of Bodin the law defied medicine with a strict and uncompromising ' No Trespassing '. The problem of the relationship between medicine and law is a very old one, of course, but it was Weyer who was the first in the history of medicine to present a systematic criticism of that branch of the law governing the punishment of the mentally sick, and it was Bodin's questionable honor to be the first to respond negatively to this legitimate demand of medicine.

Summarizing the opinions of Bodin, the authors wrote that ' a physician who waves his medical flag a bit too threateningly against the judicial branch of the government is an even more dangerous defender of Satan, for the human art of medicine might serve as too attractive a screen for concealing the ill will of the true collaborators of the devil '.[1] Such fears have persisted and exist to-day.

As an illustration of the jealous attitude of English law on this question of responsibility it is worth mentioning that under modern legislation it is possible for trials to take place, and for punishment to be inflicted, when the main point to be established by the prosecution is that the defendant was in fact irresponsible at the time that the alleged criminal act was committed. It sounds Gilbertian, and so it is; but it is fact as well. Under the Infanticide Act, 1938 (which extended and re-enacted an Act of 1922),

[1] p. 239.

a mother can be prosecuted, and sent to imprisonment for life, if she has caused 'the death of her child under twelve months' and if 'at the time of the act or omission' the 'balance of her mind was disturbed by reason of her not having fully recovered from the effect of giving birth to the child or by reason of the effect of lactation'. This strange Act of Parliament had for its purpose to spare such miserable women from a verdict of murder and its consequent sentence to death. There was, therefore, humanity in these Acts. Was there psychology? That question needs to be asked and answered. There is no psychological or logical justification for prosecutions for infanticide. If the legal tradition had been less strong that crimes demand punishments, the reform of 1922 and 1938 would have taken a very different shape. Where the police are satisfied that the death of a child was caused by the mother under circumstances coming within the words just quoted from the Act of 1938, there should be no trial at all. The woman might be brought before a magistrates' court [1] under a procedure similar to that of juvenile courts for children 'in need of care or protection', so that there might be some supervision by a woman probation officer. But the whole machinery of charge, trial, and possible punishment is an anachronism in these days of psychological teaching.

The first time that I had to hear evidence in a prosecution for infanticide I could not resist the thought that any psychologist would be indignant at the whole proceedings. Medical evidence was called by the prosecution to prove the abnormality of the woman's mind at the time of the

---

[1] Throughout this book I have used the name magistrates' courts instead of courts of summary jurisdiction, petty sessional courts, or police courts. This is the name adopted by the Magistrates' Association and in my opinion is the most suitable. The word 'summary' gives an impression of superficiality and undue haste. Police courts would appear to be run by the police, whereas, as nobody knows better than the police, they are not so run. These courts are run by magistrates, and the fact should be recognized in their name. Harm has been done by the names that have in fact been used.

killing. The woman, who for months before the trial had lain in hospital, was in such a bad condition that a nurse had to sit next to her the whole time. When evidence of the child's death was being given, I shamelessly told the nurse to engage the woman in conversation, so that she should not hear the evidence—a definite illegality on my part. The woman tugged nervously at her handkerchief during the proceedings and periodically burst into tears. I felt ashamed of the English system of criminal law. I had to commit the woman for trial. After the trial before judge and jury and a verdict of guilty, the judge said : ' I cannot find it in my heart to send you to prison for what you have done,' and bound her over. I can only describe such proceedings as a useless and unnecessary form of torture. Just because the mind of the prosecution and defence are concentrated on the question of responsibility, the real questions in such a case are completely neglected. Had I been more than a conduit pipe in the case, I should have directed investigations about why this miserable woman killed her child, why for this illegitimate, unwelcome child there was no order for maintenance by the father, and so on. But such vital points were irrelevant in the legal proceedings.

Between legal and psychological conceptions of responsibility for criminal acts a great gulf exists, but one that varies in width. A superficial student of English criminal law would get the impression that all is clear, but in fact the law is less finite than seems to be the case.

The basis of the criminal law on responsibility is still, strange though it may appear, certain general rules laid down in 1843, before the sciences of psychiatry and modern psychology were established. The story is this : one Daniel McNaghten shot a Mr. Edward Drummond on 20 January 1843, in the belief that Drummond, who was Sir Robert Peel's secretary, was Peel himself. McNaghten cherished a bitter, but unjustified, grievance against Peel. He was tried for murder at the Central Criminal Court by Lord Chief Justice Tindal, sitting with two other judges and a jury. Medical evidence was called for the defence to the effect that McNaghten was of unsound mind at the time of the shooting by reason of morbid delusions. The jury acquitted on this ground. A public outcry followed, the extent of which was well illustrated when in March 1943 *The Times* printed several extracts ' From *The Times* of 1843 '. These came from a heated discussion in the House of Lords and from letters to the editor, both indignant and cynical. The House of Lords decided to make use of an old custom whereby the judges of the High Court can be required to advise the House on general legal principles. As this custom infringes the traditional (and in my opinion harmful) principle of English legal procedure that judges only declare the law in particular cases argued before them,[1] Mr. Justice Maule separated himself from his brother judges and rather peevishly gave his own hurried answers to the questions put. Through Lord Chief Justice Tindal the other judges, also somewhat reluctantly, gave their considered answers.[2] The essence of these answers lay in the following statement :

The jurors ought to be told in all cases that every man is presumed to be sane, and to possess a sufficient degree of reason to be responsible for his crime, until the contrary be proved to their satisfaction ; and that to establish a defence on the ground of insanity, it must be clearly proved that, at the time of the committing of the act, the party accused was labouring under such a defect of reason, from disease of the mind, as not to know the nature and quality of the act he was doing, or if he did know it, that he did not know he was doing what was wrong.[3]

It is important to realize that the judges were answering certain questions, not endeavouring to define insanity in

---

[1] This procedure was used again in 1898, in the case of *Allen* v. *Flood*, [1898] A.C. 1. The judges gave individual opinions, and disagreed substantially among themselves.

[2] Questions and answers are set out in Clark and Finelly's reports, vol. 10, pp. 200 onwards.

[3] In these answers the judges used verbose language, many ambiguous words and expressions and even tacitly accepted some false scientific theories of the time. For details, see *Insanity as a Defense in Criminal Law*, by Henry Weihofen.

legal terms. They emphasized that 'the facts of each particular case must of necessity present themselves with endless variety and with every shade of difference in each case'. From the beginning these McNaghten Rules have given rise to interminable controversies. Writing in a book that was first published in 1883, Sir James Fitzjames Stephen, a judge of the High Court and a great authority on the criminal law, stated that he could not

help feeling, and I know that some of the most distinguished judges on the Bench have been of the same opinion, that the authority of the answers is questionable, and it appears to me that when carefully considered they leave untouched the most difficult questions connected with the subject, and lay down propositions liable to be misunderstood.[1]

The most difficult aspect of the problem of legal responsibility was not touched on by the judges who laid down the McNaghten Rules for the simple reason that they were not asked to pronounce upon it. What is to be done when it is claimed by the defence that at the time of the act complained of the will-power of the accused was defective although he knew the 'nature and quality of the act he was doing'? The accused may even have known that what he was doing was wrong and yet have been driven to commit the act by an irresistible impulse. This great problem was left out in the questions put to the judges, but it was an old one. In the sixteenth century Johann Weyer had pleaded for the acceptance of a defence of irresistible impulse.[2] In a famous case of 1800 this issue had been raised ; one James Hadfield was tried for shooting at George III in Drury Lane theatre, and at his trial his counsel, the famous Erskine, submitted that he should not be held responsible because of delusions at the time. 'Reason,' he urged, 'is not driven from her seat, but distraction sits down upon it along with her.' Erskine's powerful advocacy persuaded the trial judge, Lord Kenyon,

[1] *History of the Criminal Law of England*, vol. 2, p. 154.
[2] *A History of Medical Psychology*, by G. Zilboorg and G. W. Henry, p. 243.

to stop the case.[1]   A similar case was that of Oxford, tried
in 1840 for shooting at Queen Victoria.   Lord Denman,
Lord Chief Justice, told the jury that ' if some controlling
disease was in truth the acting power within him which he
could not resist, then he will not be responsible '.   The
jury gave a verdict of ' Not Guilty, he being insane at the
time.' [2]   With these cases in the law reports, it seems
strange that the judges in the McNaghten case were not
asked to pronounce upon their legal validity.

Despite this defect of the Rules and of much criticism
at the time and since, the authority of the McNaghten Rules
has actually increased in modern times.   The influence of
Lord Hewart, Lord Chief Justice from 1922 to 1941,
worked consistently to prevent any widening of the law
concerning irresponsibility.   None the less, as two modern
writers have put it, ' though the doctrines laid down after
McNaghten's trial remain theoretically unaltered, the practical administration of them affords a wider immunity than
their language would at first sight seem to recognize '.[3]

Some years after the McNaghten Rules, in 1859, a remarkable statement to a jury was made by that famous judge
Baron Bramwell.   ' If an influence,' he said, ' be so powerful as to be termed irresistible, so much the more reason
is there why we should not withdraw any of the safeguards
tending to counteract it.' [4]   Here Baron Bramwell revealed
much ignorance of the dynamics of human behaviour, since
if an influence is irresistible, the threat of punishment would
not be likely to counteract it.   But despite this statement,
judicial pronouncements tending to authorize a defence of
irresistible impulse continued.[5]

In modern times the belief that ' controlling disease ' can
be accepted as a valid defence continued to be raised.   In

[1] 27 How. State Trials, 1282.
[2] 9 C. and P., p. 546.
[3] *Mentality and the Criminal Law*, by O. C. M. Davis and
F. A. Wilshire, p. 109.
[4] *R.* v. *Haynes*, 1 F. and F., p. 667.
[5] *Mentality and the Criminal Law*, pp. 110 et seq.

the notorious case of Ronald True, tried for murder in 1922, Mr. Justice McCardie instructed the jury as follows : ' Even if the prisoner knew the physical nature of the act and that it was morally wrong and punishable by law, yet was he through mental disease deprived of the power of controlling his actions at the same time ? ' [1] The judge added that if the jury answered that question in the affirmative, they should bring in a verdict of ' Guilty but Insane '. This statement went considerably further than the McNaghten Rules. But Lord Hewart would not let it stand. The jury convicted True (in the face of strong medical evidence) and an appeal was made. In the Court of Criminal Appeal Lord Hewart complained that the judge ' had allowed on the question of insanity a latitude going beyond the rule in McNaghten's case ' and expressly over-ruled the statement of Mr. Justice McCardie quoted above.[2]

Ronald True was not hanged, for after the appeal the Home Secretary set in motion a procedure established by an Act of Parliament of 1884 [3] ; he deputed three eminent experts to examine True and they unanimously certified him to be insane.[4] As a result of this case the Lord Chancellor of the day (Lord Birkenhead) appointed a strong committee ' to consider and report upon what changes, if any, are desirable in the existing law, practice, and procedure relating to criminal trials in which the plea of insanity as a defence is raised . . .' Of this committee Lord (then Lord Justice) Atkin was chairman. In 1924 the committee reported. They approved generally of the existing law and stated that ' the present rules of law for determining criminal responsibility, as formulated in the

[1] *The Times*, 6 May 1922.
[2] 127 Law Times, p. 563.
[3] This action was much criticized at the time, mainly on the ground that no similar action was taken in another murder case in which a young hotel servant had murdered Lady White. There was no substance in this unfortunate comparison. In view of the facts in the True case, the Home Secretary was bound to act under the Criminal Lunatics Act, 1884.
[4] True was confined in the Broadmoor Criminal Lunatic Asylum.

4

rules in McNaghten's case, are in substance sound '. They stated : ' in our opinion the existing rule of law is sound that a person may be of unsound mind and yet be criminally responsible '. But by 1922 modern psychology had developed. Psychological evidence was laid before the committee and in consequence the committee recommended the following important addition to the McNaghten Rules :

> It should be recognised that a person charged criminally with an offence is irresponsible for his act when the act is committed under an impulse which the prisoner was by mental disease deprived of any power to resist.

This was the view expressed by Mr. Justice McCardie in the True case, the view which the Court of Criminal Appeal criticized. It was in effect the view advanced over forty years previously by Sir James Fitzjames Stephen.[1] This report was referred to twelve High Court judges, of whom, it is believed, ten advised against the adoption of this recommendation.[2] The suggested change in the law has never been made. In an appeal in the year following the publication of this report Lord Hewart again expressed his strong objections : ' It is the fantastic theory of uncontrollable impulse which, if it were to become part of our criminal law, would be merely subversive. It is not yet part of the criminal law and it is to be hoped that the time is far distant when it will be made so.'[3] Whether judicial opinion will change cannot be prophesied, but interesting speculations arise from the fact that Lord Caldecote, who succeeded Lord Hewart as Lord Chief Justice in 1941, was a member of the Atkin Committee and signed the report without reservation.

[1] ' If it is not, it ought to be the law of England that no act is a crime if the person who does it is at the time when it is done prevented either by defective mental power or by any disease affecting his mind from controlling his own conduct, unless the absence of the power of control has been produced by his own default.' *History of the Criminal Law in England*, vol. 2, p. 168.
[2] Taylor's, *Medical Jurisprudence*, vol. 1, p. 806.
[3] *R. v. Kopsch*, 19 Crim. App. Rep., p. 51.

Most psychologists and psychiatrists firmly believe that there are many men and women of unsound mind who knew perfectly well, when they committed an act that was criminal, both what they were doing and that authority would consider their act wrong. Here is, therefore, a substantial conflict between science and law.

It would be more difficult now than in 1924 to secure the recommended extension of the McNaghten Rules by agreement between psychiatrists and lawyers, because in many quarters there has been a considerable hardening of psychological opinion. Any present-day inquiry into the subject would find that the evidence given to the Atkin Committee on behalf of the Medico-Psychological Association would be regarded as anaemic by many psychologists and psychiatrists. The legal and judicial world would be more alarmed than ever, and it would be found that scientific opinion is more divided than it was in 1922. For the teaching of Freud was quite definite that there is no freewill, as freewill is generally understood : ' There is within you a deeply rooted belief in psychic freedom and choice ', he wrote, but ' this belief is quite unscientific ' ; such a belief ' must give ground before the claims of a determinism which governs even mental life '.[1] In another work Freud accepted the view that ' the conduct through life of what we call our ego is essentially passive ' and that ' we are " lived " by unknown and uncontrollable forces '.[2] Such a dogma means in effect that whether a man does an act which the law terms criminal, as also whether a man goes for a walk or stays at home, passes a shop or goes in, and whether he pays for his goods or steals, all is governed by internal forces independent of the will.

There are many who would deny that problems of freewill lie within the sole jurisdiction of the scientist ; there are even scientists who would agree with them in this.

[1] *Introductory Lectures on Psycho-Analysis*, pp. 87–8.
[2] This quotation from Freud's *The Ego and the Id* is taken from Dr. John Rickman's book, *A General Selection from the Works of Sigmund Freud*, p. 250.

Thus an eminent surgeon, Mr. Kenneth Walker, maintained that, before the whole universe can be accepted as
a gigantic machine, with man as part of its mechanism,
'two assumptions have been made by the scientist : the
first the assumption that effects can always be calculated
from causes, and the second that an object is analysable
without remainder into its parts and is capable of classification in terms of these '. Mr. Walker disputed these
assumptions, and in his view ' the nature of man can never
be discovered by ruling out all methods of investigation
that do not conform to scientific standards '.[1]   There are
experienced psychologists who recognize the contribution
of religion and philosophy to discussions about free will.
Thus Professor William McDougall, who accepted much
of Freud's teaching, criticized Freud's ' quite gratuitous
insistence on rigid determinism '.[2]   The followers of Jung
are not determinists, and most of them would agree that the
problem is at least as much one of religion and philosophy
as of science.

It seems obvious that in the present stage of human
development the criminal law cannot accept determinist
dogmas ; if it did, all reform of criminal law and procedure would be totally irrelevant.   With determinism,
criminal law and procedure must abdicate.   There would
be no necessity for Bench or lawyers in criminal courts to
study the elements of modern psychology, as I should like
to see them doing ; they would have to find other occupa-
tions, for criminals would henceforth be solely the concern
of the medical profession.   There would be no reform of
the McNaghten Rules, since they would lose all validity ;
nobody would be responsible for his actions.   Erewhon
would come to life.

But the question of extending these Rules is in fact of
less importance than appears at first sight.   It would be
useful to have an inquiry into the experience of the many

---

[1] *Diagnosis of Man*, pp. 93–5.   Freud in his book *The Future
of an Illusion* would not accept this.
[2] *Psycho-Analysis and Social Psychology*, p. 112.

States in the United States of America which have incorporated into their laws an exemption from responsibility
for criminal acts by those who acted under irresistible
impulse. But it is my opinion that no good can come
from any attempt to reconcile substantive law, so far as
tests for criminal responsibility are concerned, with the
psychiatric opinion of to-day. I doubt whether it would
be worth while even to press for the adoption of the recommendation of the Atkin Committee. There are other ways
in which progress can be made without bringing about
a serious conflict between legal and judicial opinion on the
one hand [1] and some schools of psychiatric opinion on the
other.

The truth is that the issue concerning determinism has
no practical bearing on present-day criminological or penological problems. In practice it matters nothing whether
the determinist view is right or wrong. The university
chair is the place where metaphysicians, philosophers, etc.
should expound theories about the absence of free will.
Dr. Johnson said, according to Boswell, that ' all theory is
against the freedom of the will : all experience for it '.[2]
Be the theory what it may, it is with experience that criminal
law is mainly concerned. Both those who formulate our
criminal law and those who apply it to accused and convicted people have the duty, so it seems to me, to realize
that modern psychology teaches that the freedom of the
will is not so universal as has hitherto been assumed. But
the true line of progress lies, I would suggest, not in
acquitting large numbers on the ground of irresponsibility,

[1] Lord Birkenhead propounded the dangerous doctrine that
Governments cannot introduce ' schemes for legal reform ' unless
they ' act with the concurrence of great judicial personages and
with the general assent of the instructed minds of the professions '—
Points of View, vol. 2, p. 29. This is an ancient doctrine, and
I would agree with the great Romilly in denouncing it as ' a most
unconstitutional doctrine '—*Three Criminal Law Reformers*, by
Coleman Phillipson, p. 255. Unfortunately this doctrine is in
practice observed, except on rare occasions.

[2] Under date Wednesday, 15 July 1778.

but in adequate investigations after conviction. In technical language, it is adjective law, not substantive law, that needs to be reformed, namely, procedure at and after trial.

In the report of Drs. East and Hubert, to be dealt with at length in the next chapter, there is this wise sentence : ' The psychological treatment of crime has incurred a measure of distrust because its exponents have sometimes failed to draw a distinction between irresponsibility and culpability.' [1] This distinction points to a practical solution of most difficulties about free will. There would not be likely to be any grave conflict between lawyers and psychologists if progress was made in the direction, not of widening the law of irresponsibility, but of providing greatly improved methods for investigating the real culpability of delinquents when the facts have been proved or admitted. To struggle about whether verdicts should be ' Guilty ' or ' Guilty but Insane ' [2] would, I suggest, be to side-track progress. Even if the determinists got their way, only fresh problems would be created.

The point of vital importance is that there are two ways of doing justice to those who have been driven to criminal acts by internal forces not under their control ; either they can be found ' Guilty but Insane ' and be dealt with under the laws of lunacy and mental defect, or they can be held technically guilty and dealt with by the court, after adequate inquiry by experts, from the point of view of cure (which does not necessarily exclude punishment). [3] A man whose unconscious impulses lead him to murder must for some time yet be dealt with on the first method. Far more numerous are those who are apparently normal but who in one line of conduct of no great enormity are motivated

[1] Paragraph 43.
[2] The words ' Guilty but Insane ' are, of course anomalous. It is said that we owe them to Queen Victoria, who objected to a man being found not guilty on account of insanity who had attempted her life. In most States of the United States the form used is ' Not Guilty by reason of insanity '—see Weihofen's book, p. 264.
[3] Chapter 4 deals with this question.

by unconscious impulses; such people should be dealt with on the second method. Subsequent chapters will develop these ideas in greater length.

The bias of English law is likely to remain in favour of self-responsibility. In the future that can be foreseen it is likely to remain difficult for those who have committed acts in breach of the criminal law to escape the label ' guilty '. This seems to me as it should be. In the life of every human being there are times of exceptional emotional strain, just as ordinarily there are periods of physical illness. From birth onwards every man and woman is in both physical and psychological danger. But health consists not in the absence of crises, but in the ability to overcome them, in the power to absorb the abnormal and to place it in proper perspective. Both body and mind have to digest much that is inimical to ideal development, and we have every reason to be thankful that this is so, since we do not live in an ideal world. There is no such thing as a normal life, whether physically or psychologically, and happily all but a small minority are capable of resisting the ' slings and arrows of outrageous fortune '. In most people expert psycho-therapists could, if they wished, and if they received sufficient co-operation, find traces of the abnormal. Only harm is done when the importance of ordinary abnormalities is exaggerated. This is so even where no unpleasant consequences follow from the conduct of the patient. But when it is a question of responsibility or irresponsibility for criminal conduct, exaggeration becomes dangerous both for the patient and for the whole community. The criminal law contains so much that needs altering; energies devoted to attempts to secure the adoption of the determinist view are not only futile, but distracting.

Before we leave the question of irresponsibility one further point must be mentioned, namely, the fitness of a jury to decide about these questions. I do not share the enthusiasm for juries that British lawyers usually show. Both from practice before juries at the Bar and from watching the fate of accused persons whom as magistrate I commit for trial by jury, I long ago formed the opinion that the whole system of trial by jury has outlived its usefulness. It was invaluable in the days of judges who were not impartial. It is an anachronism in the democratic days of the free Bench, a free Parliament, and a free Press. I agree entirely with Mr. Henry Weihofen in the following criticism :

Is there anyone who seriously thinks that the jurymen in even an appreciable minority of cases decide the question of sanity or insanity by a dispassionate and judicial application of the test given them by the judge ? Whether a jury will return a verdict of ' Guilty ' or ' Not guilty by reason of insanity ' depends primarily upon the dramatic quality of the offense charged . . . ; upon the personality and appearance of the defendant, his lawyer and the prosecutor ; . . . upon a thousand and one legally irrelevant facts appealing to the jury's ' common sense '.[1]

I believe that opinion is growing, both in this country and in the United States, that trial by jury should be slowly abolished ; already many steps in this direction have been taken. Magistrates now try over eighty per cent of indictable (the more serious) charges ; this process is likely to go further. The time may come when cases that magistrates cannot try will pass into the hands of three judges, who will try the facts without a jury.[2] But be juries superfluous or essential in ordinary cases, there can surely be no wisdom in submitting to them intricate issues about responsibility. If the encephalogram establishes itself in judicial favour in trials where responsibility is in issue, the presence of a jury in such cases must become superfluous. This complicated device records the electrical currents in the brain and, it is claimed, can show the distinction between the normal functioning of the brain and the abnormal. In March 1943 a High Court judge admitted evidence

[1] *Insanity as a Defense in Criminal Law*, p. 9.
[2] In his book *The Way to Justice*, this suggestion was made by Mr. Heber L. Hart. As will be shown in later chapters, Cecil Whiteley also suggested a reform on these lines for three kinds of criminal offence.

of its recordings in a trial for murder at the Central Criminal Court.[1] The jury had no alternative to accepting these findings and brought in a verdict of ' Guilty but Insane '. But if juries have no alternative to accepting the findings of a machine, these findings might just as well be accepted without the jury. In the words of Dr. Bernard Hollander : ' That the question of insanity in a case of murder should be left for decision to the wisdom of a jury seems to me outrageous.' [2] There are on record cases of grave insanity where the jury refused to accept convincing scientific evidence ; the case of Ronald True was one. There are also cases where juries have brought in verdicts of ' Guilty but Insane ' from purely sentimental motives, usually because they did not desire the accused to be sentenced to death. I have never heard from any psychiatrist any approval of the present system. Many of the difficulties arising from questions of responsibility arise from the fact that juries are the deciding tribunals.

[1] *R. v. Lees Smith.*
[2] *The Psychology of Misconduct*, p. 214.

CHAPTER 2

PRACTICAL POSSIBILITIES

The question to be considered in the future will not be how
to balance the past wrong by a supposed equivalent of inflicted
pain, but how to remove the mischief that is working.

GEORGE IVES [1]

IN assessing the practical possibilities of applying psychological principles to the treatment of crime it has always to be
remembered that a diagnosis, the simpler task of a psycho-
therapist, is of little value in itself to a court, or to those in
charge of a delinquent.   Indeed, a mere diagnosis usually
embarrasses.   Psychology in connexion with crime must
stand or fall according to its ability by treatment to deflect
delinquents from further criminal acts.

The use of psycho-therapy in the treatment of delinquents
was a slow development of the twenty-five years preceding
the war of 1939.   By the outbreak of that war considerable
results had been achieved.   I hope that in a small way the
cases set out in the next chapter, some of those that have
fallen to me to handle, will be accepted as confirming that by
1939 the psycho-therapeutic method of dealing with
delinquents was a practical and established method.   In
March 1934, an official investigation, restricted in its scope,
was begun in Wormwood Scrubs prison, London, ' to
ascertain the value of psychological treatment in the prevention and cure of crime '.   The treatment was given by
Dr. W. H. de B. Hubert to cases selected by Dr. W. Norwood
East [2] in conjunction with the medical officers of the prison
service.   The detailed report [3] of this experimental treatment

[1] *A History of Penal Methods*, p. 340.
[2] At the time the medical member of the Prison Commission.
[3] *The Psychological Treatment of Crime*, published by H.M.
Stationery Office.

38

was published in March 1939, and attracted much attention in the circles interested in penology. But unfortunately the outbreak of war six months later prevented the report from penetrating far beyond those circles. It would be lamentable if the report, despite its limitations, shared the fate of so many official publications.

The method adopted by Drs. Norwood East and Hubert was that 'medical officers of prisons should submit the case of any prisoner who was thought to be suitable for psychological investigation and treatment'. The reports of the medical officers were then considered by Dr. Hubert and 'correlated with any further information that might be available from the official files relating to the prisoner'.[1] The whole investigation was restricted to male prisoners over 17. The selected men, considered suitable for treatment, were transferred to Wormwood Scrubs prison, London, there to be investigated by Dr. H. T. P. Young, the senior medical officer of Wormwood Scrubs prison, and later with Dr. Norwood East in consultation. Treatment, if finally found desirable, was carried out by Dr. Hubert in the prison. No attempt was made 'to apply the tenets of any particular school' of psychological thought.[2] '406 cases were seen in all and were investigated to determine their suitability for treatment'; and 'of these 214 were approved for treatment'.[3] The report made abundantly clear that the two doctors were never guilty of wishful thinking; they took extreme care not to claim for psycho-therapy more than could by justified by proved experience.

One criticism can reasonably be made against the whole scheme of work. A great opportunity was missed when the experimental work described in the report was restricted to delinquents over 17 years of age. The most hopeful

[1] Paragraph 34.
[2] Paragraph 61. Professor R. S. Woodworth in his book, *Contemporary Schools of Psychology*, stated that 'only a minority of psychologists have become adherents of any of the schools' (p. 15). He wrote of American conditions.
[3] Paragraph 69.

delinquents for the psycho-therapist are children and young adolescents. They are nearer in time to the repressions and fixations that have resulted in, or contributed to, their misconduct. They are less sceptical about new methods for receiving help ; adult patients are often either consciously or unconsciously in resistance to the treatment which they are about to undergo and probably they meet with some scepticism from those about them. In the psycho-analysis of adults many hours are often necessary to overcome these resistances. But the methods that have been worked out for children are attractive and can sometimes conquer resistance quickly. Even the hard-boiled adolescent of modern times usually has an easier approach to psycho-therapy than has the adult. Therefore it would have been of great value if, alongside the practical work of Dr. Hubert, similar work had been done among delinquent children and adolescents by doctors experienced in child guidance and work among adolescents. It would have been easy to select cases on similar lines in Approved Schools. Had this been done, and a combined report been issued, there would assuredly have been less ground for that tone of pessimism which characterizes the report. During the early months of 1939 an inquiry into certain psychological aspects of juvenile crime was planned by the Home Office and by Mr. A. M. Carr-Saunders, Dr. Hermann Mannheim, and Dr. E. C. Rhodes ; such inquiry was to be parallel to the inquiry into juvenile crime generally, which the Home Office had in 1938 delegated to these three experts.[1] Unfortunately the outbreak of war made the psychological project impossible. All the more the pity, therefore, that parallel to the East-Hubert researches psychological inquiries into both juvenile and adolescent delinquency were not made.

The East-Hubert report must not be regarded as a treatise on the general possibilities of treating delinquents by psycho-therapy, for the cases studied and treated belonged to a special group of delinquents. The report stated that ' the

[1] Published in 1942 under the title *Young Offenders*. See pp. ix, 54, and 156.

great majority of the cases seen were early recidivists. Of the cases approved for treatment, 72 had, between them, 215 previous convictions.'[1] No wonder that these cases were termed ' a difficult recidivist class ', for with this type of delinquent psycho-therapy, while it has its triumphs, labours under a severe handicap. The gloomy statistical results of the East-Hubert investigation are partly due to this fact. In addition, it has to be remembered that all the prisoners had been sentenced without any regard to treatment, that they were serving ordinary sentences of imprisonment, and that the psychological treatment took place within prison walls. These are points which will come up for discussion later. The statistical results were as follows [2] :

Class of Offender	Approved for Treatment	Treatment Concluded	At Liberty	Re-Convicted [3]	Still Serving Sentence
Borstal Group . .	29	18	6	15	8
Adolescent Group [4]	34	30	29	13	2
Adult Group . .	27	19	14	8	5
Sexual Offenders .	124	102	92	20	12

Such statistics are a poor advertisement of the efficacy of psychological treatment among delinquents, but the severe limitations of the investigation are the real explanation. The general conclusion of Drs. East and Hubert was that ' psycho-therapy is, and is likely to remain, a specialized method of treatment usefully applied to but a comparatively small number of disorders '.[5] When this report was

[1] Paragraph 96.   [2] Paragraphs 99 and 154.
[3] Paragraph 158 stated that ' at the most any treated case in our series can only have been out of prison four years at the present time, while the majority have been at liberty for much shorter periods '. Probably later statistics would present an even more gloomy picture here.
[4] As in the ordinary way no one could be sent to prison at that time under 16, no adolescents under that age could be included in the investigation.
[5] Paragraph 160.

published, I discussed it with several experienced psycho-therapists and gathered the impression that the report would be appreciated among medical psychologists for its case histories and not for the value of its conclusions. Many medical men and women took strong objection to the report on account of its bias in favour of treatment during incarceration.

There are cases in the East-Hubert report itself which support the belief that psycho-therapy for delinquents can-not be judged fairly by the results of the work done by Drs. East and Hubert. Their work often came too late in the lives of the delinquents. In some cases included in the report the success achieved was avowedly restricted by this fact. Thus Case LXIV ends with these words : ' It is doubtful if enough was achieved to prevent further offences in the future. If treated a little earlier in his career, success could have been confidently anticipated.' That prisoner of 33, we are told in the report, ' came from a very respectable family. He frequently played truant at school.' Truancy from school often shows the need for psychological investiga-tion. But the story of this case goes further : ' He . . . obtained employment as a clerk, but resigned in eighteen months as he became depressed and suffered from nocturnal enuresis and a feeling of inferiority.' This should have been recognized as another red light. Enuresis (bed-wetting) may be, as we saw in the previous chapter, a clear indication of emotional abnormality, and emotional abnormality, if not psychologically treated, can result later in criminal acts. This prisoner ' was eventually arrested, and since the age of 17 had been convicted seven times for shopbreaking, theft and forgery. He had been detained in a Borstal Institution. He had served a sentence of four years' penal servitude, as well as shorter terms of imprisonment.' At the time of his treatment this man was serving a sentence of twenty-two months' imprisonment for warehouse-breaking. The account of the case in the report—and that is the limit of my knowledge of it—does not state that at any time between his being found guilty and his sentence there had been a thorough medical and psychological examination of him. But the account gives much more evidence that at all times there was an acute need for such an examination :

He had before this [the series of offences which had led up to his last conviction] borrowed his sister's underclothing, stolen that belonging to other women, and had also bought similar articles and dressed himself up in them to stimulate phantasy. He also obtained satisfaction by self-flagellation accompanied by phantasies of complicated masochistic relationships. The enuresis did not persist, but he was always sexually inferior.

These conditions had probably existed in lesser degree in that man's childhood, and if he had then had the benefit of treatment, or even mere advice, from a trained psychologist, his future might then have been quite different. Perhaps if his parents had been less ' very respectable ', he might have had the advantage of being charged before a juvenile court for some minor delinquency ; he doubtless committed, like plenty of healthy children, acts contrary to the criminal law. Perhaps also his juvenile court would have seen his need for psychological examination and sent him to a Child Guidance Clinic. But it is useless to ponder over the might-have-beens. Let us see how this miserable man when young tried to help himself. The report of the case continues :

He was concerned about his condition and studied psycho-analytic literature in order to gain some insight into his condition. He read some of Freud's works and studied Krafft-Ebing's writings on sadism and masochism. The only effect, however, was to make him feel physically nauseated.

Dr. Hubert was able to diagnose the complaint of this case and ' treatment was carried out over a considerable period '. But it is no tribute to our system of criminal justice that this occurred first after all these sentences to Borstal and prison.

It is highly probable that at all times there are in our prisons some men and women who might be leading useful, or at least harmless, lives if their conduct had been examined from the psychological point of view when they first came within the criminal law. Had this been done, it might have been possible for any necessary treatment to have been given without imprisonment.

The tragedy of the undiscovered psychopath was investigated by Dr. Hermann Mannheim, a judge of the Court of Appeal in Berlin and professor of Laws in the Berlin University before the coming of Nazi rule. He was given facilities to make a special investigation into the problem of recidivism in England and for that purpose he examined the calendars of the Central Criminal Court and of the London Quarter Sessions. In his book, *Social Aspects of Crime in England between the Wars*, Dr. Mannheim summarized his results.[1] Many of the gloomy lists of past records, he showed, indicate that in the early days of the criminals' breaches of the law there were indications calling for psychological inquiry. Had psycho-therapy been available when these recidivists were young, perhaps they could have had their energies turned into useful paths. The argument is, of course, hypothetical, but I believe that many recidivists could have been saved if they had undergone psycho-therapy at the right age. I agree that there are others who could not have been other than they are.

One more criticism of the East-Hubert report needs to be mentioned. It seems to be unnecessary that in the report so much space was given to the cases that were wholly unsuitable for psycho-therapy. The authors declared that ' psycho-therapy as an adjunct to an ordinary prison sentence appears to be effective in preventing, or in reducing the chance of, future anti-social behaviour, provided the cases to which treatment is applied are carefully chosen '.[2] This will be generally accepted. But it is difficult to see the justification for including in the report cases for whom psycho-therapy was found not to be suitable at all. Thus the account of Case X ends with the words : ' It is doubtful whether such a case would receive benefit from any sort of training or discipline.' Similar judgments occur frequently and prompt the question why such cases were included in the report. If some physician wished to convince professional

[1] Chapter 12.   [2] Paragraph 158.

and public opinion that a new method existed for curing cancer, he would scarcely dilate on details of cases where the disease was too far advanced for the new treatment to be attempted. The hopeless cases set out in the report merely prove that at the time some medical officers in the prison service had little knowledge of what psycho-therapy can and cannot achieve. Surely the failures that were relevant in such a report were those where psycho-therapy was tried for a considerable time and proved inadequate, not those where it was impracticable for psycho-therapy to be tried at all.[1] The drawback of including cases where treatment had no chance is that they may reduce the prospects of the report being accepted as evidence of the utility of psycho-therapy for delinquents. Having regard to the wide gulf between the law and modern psychology, it is most desirable that gradually a mutual understanding between them shall arise. But this will not be encouraged by accounts in an official publication of hopeless cases where psycho-therapy could not even be begun.

Criticism of the East-Hubert report is less valuable than the question, raised in the report, of the pros and cons of giving psycho-therapy during a sentence of imprisonment and giving it while delinquents are at liberty, having been placed by their trial court on probation under the supervision of a probation officer.[2] I have an invincible dislike of most dichotomies and believe that both forms of treatment will continue to be necessary. But as in a considerable

[1] In Case XIX, a lad of eighteen, the preliminary observation ' gave the general impression of considerable organic cerebral deterioration '. He was found ' unsuitable for psycho-therapy '. As no psychological disorder was discovered, it is difficult to see why the case was mentioned in the report. Other such cases could be cited.

[2] All our criminal courts have power to place on probation all delinquents, except murderers (and a few others who are extremely rare). This means that the question of penalty is held over and is never raised if the delinquents behave themselves. Such delinquents are placed under the supervision of probation officers who are usually trained social workers. Probation usually lasts a year, but can last three years.

5

number of cases the choice between these methods is difficult, it is worth while entering in some detail into the merits and demerits of each. The bias of Drs. East and Hubert led them to say that ' the use of psycho-therapy on probation . . . should be confined largely to first offenders, to cases in which the offence is a comparatively minor one and where experience has shown psycho-therapy on probation is likely to be more effective than the use of probation alone '.[1] This is the worst sentence in the report. There is, as we shall see, a mass of evidence to show that psycho-therapy, while the delinquent is at liberty, but under supervision, can be successful both with those with several previous convictions, even prison sentences, and with those who have committed serious offences. Even my own cases in the next chapter afford some indication of this. The authors also stated that ' only a psychiatrist of wide experience can exercise a wise discrimination in any particular case as to whether psychological treatment can be recommended with a reasonable chance of success if unaided by imprisonment '.[2] The last words make a startling assumption. There are very real drawbacks to treatment in prison. It is significant that the medical officer of Wormwood Scrubs prison, where the experimental treatment was given, wrote in his appendix to the report that ' the atmosphere of distrust which penetrates prisons from without is one of the principal obstacles to the recovery of the sense of citizenship in the offender '. He also admitted that ' imprisonment remains an expression in concrete form of the loss of public confidence in the ability of those who have committed crime to discharge their social obligations '. Many will say that the essence of psychological treatment is the stimulation of self-confidence and that its forcible stamping out, which life in prison involves, must militate against the success of treatment. Not only is there an ' atmosphere of distrust ' and a repression of self-confidence in prison ; there is also shame and discouragement, monotony and lack of free comradeship. These are factors that must work against the success of psychological

[1] Paragraph 168.   [2] Paragraph 49.

treatment.   Even the fact that meals are served regularly and in no way depend on effort is a handicap, one that is to some extent mitigated nowadays by the earnings scheme and facilities for purchasing comforts.   It is well known that men and women can become almost model prisoners, causing no trouble, and yet be unfitted for free life.   When Dr. Grace Pailthorpe made her investigations into women held in custody, she found that there was in prison an atmosphere that intensified the difficulties of her work.   The ' inevitable reaction ', she wrote, of the women to the unnatural conditions in which they were living was ' to make them suspicious of any further interference from outside sources '.[1] Her considered opinion was that ' the application of psycho-analysis is impossible as long as the subject is in prison, since the conditions are unsuitable for carrying out that technique '.[2]   But Dr. Pailthorpe had no opportunity to try treatment in prison, so ' impossible ' is probably too strong a word.   To some extent a skilled therapist would be able to create his own atmosphere and thereby to undo some of the effects of prison life.   His ' rapport ' should not be dependent on the circumstances under which his patient lives, but in fact it probably would be in many cases.

There are, we must admit, some advantages in treatment in custody.   Thus in some psychological states the beneficial effects of treatment cannot be experienced until its conclusion ; at any stage there may be a return to criminal conduct ; in the early weeks of treatment it is possible that a repetition of criminal acts may even be prompted by the treatment.   When an offender who has been placed on probation is brought before a court on account of an early repetition of the offence, it would require an unusual psychological insight on the part of the Bench not to put an end to both liberty and treatment ; the Bench would be more likely to take up the position that the delinquent had had his chance

[1] *What We Put in Prison*, p. 41.   Dr. Pailthorpe's *Studies in the Psychology of Delinquency*, a report made to the Medical Research Council of the Privy Council, is in my opinion a more valuable work.   [2] Ibid., p. 129.

and, as he had failed to take advantage of it, he must go to prison. This should not happen. When there is such repetition of offences, a report ought to be obtained from the psycho-therapist in charge of the case before any drastic step is taken by the court.

An important recommendation in the report was the establishment of ' a penal institution of a special kind ' for dealing with ' abnormal and unusual types '.[1] There is much to be said for the establishment of such an institution, but it is difficult to see how in it many of the drawbacks inherent in treatment during imprisonment could be avoided. If the abnormality of the cases were not of a dangerous type, the institutions might be created on the lines of the newer Borstal Institutions and the camp for adult prisoners, none of which has any enclosing walls. If possible, I should like to see such an institution containing others besides psycho-pathic cases, for the association of those undergoing psycho-therapy with prisoners not needing treatment would probably assist the treatment without doing harm to the ordinary prisoners.

The Criminal Justice Bill of 1938–9 proposed to enlarge the powers of our courts for dealing with those needing psycho-therapy without the necessity of ordering their imprisonment. This was a most welcome recognition of the weakness of the criminal law that was mentioned in my first chapter. The new proposals recognized that plenty of psychopathic delinquents can be made safe by treatment without imprisonment. For such cases it was proposed to empower courts ' to include in the probation order a pro-vision requiring the probationer to submit (for such period not extending beyond twelve months from the date of the order as may be specified therein [2]) to treatment by or under

[1] Paragraph 172.
[2] There was at the time a strong feeling among those interested in the psychological treatment of delinquents that this limitation to treatment for one year was unscientific. But it has always to be remembered that there are many cases where treatment for a number of years would be just as ineffective as treatment for one year.

the direction of a duly qualified medical practitioner with a view to the improvement of the probationer's mental condition '.[1] Treatment, which was to be directed only with the delinquent's consent, could be residential or non-resident. If non-resident, it could be given at an institution or by an individual psycho-therapist. In fact, many of the powers proposed to be given to courts by this Bill could have been exercised under the existing law. Probation orders can legally include terms about ' any other matters as the court may, having regard to the particular circumstances of the case, consider necessary for preventing a repetition of the same offence or the commission of other offences '.[2] In the numerous cases that I have handled I have inserted in the probation orders, pursuant to these general powers, a term that the delinquents shall submit to medical treatment as directed ; this, of course, only when consent has been given. The main benefit that would follow the enactment of such a scheme as was included in the Criminal Justice Bill would be, not the power to order treatment, but the power to pay for it. Hitherto, courts endeavouring to obtain the psychological treatment of their delinquents have been dependent on the charity of the medical profession or of psychological clinics. A State scheme would provide for payment for treatment out of public funds, the delinquents presumably contributing as much as their means make possible.

Most psychologists will agree that no institution can really take the place of family life. I once heard a distinguished psycho-therapist say that any home, with a small ' h ', is always better than any Home, with a capital. This was an exaggeration, but the truth in the remark needs to be emphasized, especially as there is in official circles an excessive belief in the virtues of institutional life. So far as children are concerned it has been well said that ' the fact

---

[1] ' Mental treatment ' was defined as including ' any treatment designed to cure or alleviate his mental condition '. In some cases, therefore, physical or surgical treatment could be included.
[2] Criminal Justice Act, 1914, section 8.

of managing children in large numbers is bound to tend towards a blurring of personality '. The result is ' a child coming out of an institution with the individuality of a registered number rather than the personality of a human being '.[1] The natural method is for children to be cared for by two parents, not by a number of well-meaning people. In the report of the Prison Commissioners for 1937 the following statement was printed from the Governor of the Borstal Institution for girls at Aylesbury :

A remarkable feature of the receptions during the year has been the greatly increased number (32 as against 13) from the Home Office Approved Schools. These girls present a very serious problem in the life of the institution. In the first place, many of them are already institutionalised, and a long experience of Homes and schools has taught them how to get through their time with the minimum effort and without the slightest feeling of personal responsibility.

. . . These constitute the small and obviously inadequate attempts to minimise the dangers of discharging, even though under supervision, a girl who has probably known nothing but institutional life for years and is now required to live the life of a free adult without ever having been a free child.

There is much bitter truth in this, and it applies to both sexes. Institutionalised youths and girls know next to nothing about such things as the necessity to look after clothes, what they cost, what it costs to re-sole a pair of shoes, and so on. Young people have to learn that holes in shoes are uncomfortable and that if shoe-money is spent on sweets or cigarettes, discomfort follows. If in fact the evil effects of institutional life are influencing the patients, the

[1] *The Needs of Youth*, a report made to the King George Jubilee Trust Fund by A. E. Morgan, M.A., LL.D., pp. 135–6. Another drawback of Approved Schools is that ' there are immense difficulties inherent in running a school where the good boys are sent away as soon as they are fit to become prefects, for a selection of the unfittest elder boys remains to set a bad example '.—*A Note Book for the Children's Court*, by Margery Fry and Champion B. Russell (Howard League), p. 18. This also applies to all semi-penal institutions.

efficacy of psycho-therapy must be hampered. This applies to all types and ages.

A factor which weighs heavily in favour of psycho-therapy while a delinquent is on probation is that then the delinquent will presumably be making an effort to be self-supporting ; that he should lead an industrious life is one of the terms that appear in all probation orders. This effort is helpful in the treatment. An extra effort is usually involved in the necessary travelling to the psycho-therapist ; this also can have curative value. A London psycho-therapist once told me that whenever possible he advised his provincial clients to live at home, rather than live in a London nursing home or hotel ; he regarded the effort that his patients would have to make in travelling to and from London as a valuable assistance in the treatment. Of course there is another aspect of this ; sometimes the effort to reach the psycho-therapist after a day's work will so tire the patient that the treatment is handicapped. This has been a problem even in London. I have found it sometimes difficult to persuade delinquents to go regularly to the West End for treatment when their homes are in Hackney, Battersea, or Wandsworth ; people in London are local-minded, and to many Londoners a journey to the West End, or to Denmark Hill (the Maudesley Hospital), involves a distinct effort. These problems of distance are a far greater obstacle in rural areas and can only be solved when more medical men and women up and down the country are trained in psycho-therapy.

But the greatest advantage of treatment while delinquents are at liberty is the fact that the court is trusting them. From the outset of the treatment they are beginning to live down their offence and to get back their self-respect. They have a staunch new friend in the probation officer, who is not the agent of a punitive machine if delinquents are making an effort to conform to the terms of their probation orders. With adults particularly, it is difficult to be creative in penal institutions. The probation system should be creative from the beginning. On probation delinquents should be conscious that the world is friendly ; ' He restoreth my soul ' should be their inmost feeling.

When a delinquent is being dealt with under the probation system, it is important that courts should realize that to undergo psycho-therapy involves a considerable invasion of personal privacy and liberty, and also considerable effort. One of the witnesses before the Feversham Committee on Voluntary Mental Services (another Committee whose report was inundated by the outbreak of war in 1939) stated that ' physical illness is still " respectable " as compared with " nerves " or " mental disorder ", and it is certainly pleasanter to swallow a bromide mixture than to lay bare one's soul, though possibly sometimes less effective '.[1]   This is well put. It is insufficiently realized how great is the effort required for successful psychological treatment. Where there has been reluctance to recognize psycho-therapy as a suitable means for dealing with delinquents, the reason may well be that it has been assumed that psycho-therapy is an easy way out for the delinquent. This is far from the truth. When a court persuades a delinquent to submit to psychological treatment, it is wise to give a warning that hard work is involved, and that the doctor is not going to do that work.

Where a court decides in favour of treatment while on probation, it is of importance that the court itself should follow up the case ; it is not sound policy to leave all questions about treatment to probation officers, excellent though they often are. It is becoming more frequent for defending lawyers to plead on behalf of their clients that psychological treatment should be directed, so it is essential that courts see that the directions that they give in their probation orders are carried out. I once tried a professional man for driving a car when under the influence of drink to such an extent as to be incapable of having proper control of it. I convicted and, as the defendant seemed strange in his conduct, I had inquiries made. I was informed that a few weeks previously the

[1] *Feversham Report*, p. 73.

defendant had been convicted of a sexual offence and that his legal representative had stated that the defendant proposed to go at once to a nursing home for psychological treatment. The court thereupon had bound him over, directing him to do this. But the defendant had in fact bluffed his lawyer, for when he appeared before me, I found that he had been continuing his usual life and had had no treatment at all.

When a court sends a case for psychological treatment with the consent of the delinquent, the court should realize that once a delinquent passes into the care of a medico-therapist, the conventional and valuable doctrine of confidence between doctor and patient must apply. The practitioner should only be expected to tell the court or the probation officer such facts as will help in the general supervision of the case.

It is also important that courts should realize that a psycho-therapist can have nothing to do with discipline or punishment. His functions must be solely curative. If a delinquent has undertaken to have psycho-therapy and has been placed on probation with this object, the probation officer and the court must accept the exclusive responsibility for his obedience to the terms of the probation order.

We come now to the practical experience of those who have given psycho-therapy while the delinquents were on probation. There are many published reports of psychological clinics and child guidance clinics. As unfortunately my magisterial experience does not include work in juvenile courts, I cannot deal with child guidance clinics. I will deal only with the reports of the Tavistock Clinic (the Institute of Medical Psychology) and of the Institute for the Scientific Treatment of Delinquency, both working in London.[1] I have made use of the services of both these institutions for many years.

Shortly before the outbreak of the war of 1939 the Tavistock Clinic prepared for the use of a conference of

[1] Both cater also for children.

magistrates and psycho-therapists [1] a statement that gave a useful summary of such psychological disorders as may lead to an enforced appearance in a criminal court. In this statement it was explained that ' delinquent actions may result from various types of psychosis, especially when delusions are present'. The two terms psychosis and neurosis, both freely used in psychological work, give trouble to the uninitiated. The difference between the two is, I gather, that in a psychosis there has been a loss of reality, a retreat from reality into phantasy. The paranoiac, dominated by the idea that he or she is persecuted, suffers from a psychosis. There must be few busy magistrates who have not at some time or other been worried by this type of person. I had before me once an elderly man whose strong opinions that London Transport ought to issue season tickets on their omnibuses became so deep-seated that he persistently travelled without paying his fare, giving his name and address. As this had happened some sixty times and as in most cases the fares had never been paid, the Board took proceedings against him. He duly appeared before me. He refused to attend on a summons, and when I issued a warrant for his arrest, he wrote vigorously threatening me with a libel action. In court he told me with great indignation that the Transport Board had persecuted him for a long time. He was eventually certified. There are many people of this type who are not certified, as their delusions cause no harm.

The neurotic keeps in touch with reality, though his symptoms may seem to bear no relation to it. He may have the most intense obsessions, yet he knows that they are not realistic. In both psychotics and neurotics part of the emotional life is fixated. They have never fully grown up, but the psychotic is more backward than the neurotic ; his fixations are deeper seated. Both can usually be helped in some measure by psychological treatment, if it comes in time, but the outlook for neurotics is the more favourable.

[1] Organized jointly by the Magistrates' Association and the British Medical Association.

A point of real value to criminal courts, made clear in this statement of the Tavistock Clinic, is that in the case of psychotics the illness may well be unsuspected until a criminal act is committed. If courts would only realize this fact, they would hesitate to pass sentences without allowing delay for full inquiries to be made.[1]

This statement of the Clinic divided those whose conduct has a psychological basis into four categories. I have seen other classifications, but human conduct is very difficult to classify, and some delinquents come under more than one category. The grouping made by the Clinic is the simplest that I have seen, and I cannot do better than copy its description of the two types that cause most difficulty in the courts.

Reaction Character Traits. This is the commonest type of mental abnormality leading to anti-social conduct. The term ' reaction trait ' means a tendency developed in the mind in order to cover or mask an opposite tendency. Thus a dependent, weak boy may wish to ' show off ' his courage and manliness, or a child deprived of affection may repress this need by assuming a rebellious, ' don't care ' attitude of grievance against a harsh world. In this way he over-compensates for the feelings which he represses. Moral sense is present, but it is on the side of the rebellion, and the individual may be proud to be a ' public enemy '.

These reactions are usually formed in early childhood, so that the patient has no idea why he should be so affected. Such conditions constitute a definite psychological disorder and are probably the most recalcitrant and persistent of all types of delinquency, accounting for many recidivists. These delinquents are not improved, and are often made worse, by punishment. They often resist psychological treatment, but with understanding and a favourable environment, good results may be obtained.

Delinquents in this category constitute some of the most difficult problems of criminal courts. They are not easy to persuade to undergo psycho-therapy and are the least likely to

[1] See Chapter 6.

stick to it.   They require most skilful treatment ; yet harm
may result from punishment.   If a child comes within this
group, it is worse than useless to treat it as merely naughty ;
by so doing the chances are increased that serious criminal
acts may be committed later in life.   Punishment may easily
create a sense of injustice and prompt rebellious conduct.
These are the cases that are most likely to benefit from
institutional life wisely directed, but mere penal incarceration has little chance of securing any change for the
better.

The other classification of the Clinic was :

Psycho-neurotic Delinquency.   People whose acts fall within
this group have a strong moral sense with which their anti-social
conduct is entirely out of keeping.   In contra-distinction to
those who show reaction character traits, they are genuinely
ashamed of the tendencies which from time to time overwhelm
their better judgment.   These conditions also result from emotional difficulties in childhood, but this group differs again from
the preceding one in that the delinquent impulse is normally
kept out of mind but reappears at times of emotional stress.
The act satisfies some unrecognised childhood need appearing
in disguised form.   It is in this group that psychological treatment is most applicable, and the individual usually gives his full
co-operation.

Many sexual perversions, as well as addiction to alcohol and
other drugs, come under this heading.

Obviously cases in this group are more easily dealt with.
They are also more likely to benefit from probation, even
without any psychological treatment.

These opinions may be ignored, but they are difficult to
refute.   If we accept these views as scientific, as I suggest we
must, our present system of sentencing delinquents cannot
claim to be scientific.   How can a lawyer or a lay justice on
the Bench detect unaided whether a delinquent belongs to
either of these groups ?   A specialist in psychology can
usually diagnose in a short time to which group any particular
delinquent belongs and, therefore, what line of treatment will
be likely to prevent further criminal conduct.   But if both

juvenile and adult courts do not seek the aid of specialists, and allow the necessary time after the facts are decided,[1] then there must be serious danger that a recidivist is in fact created.

A statement of this nature could only come from those who have had much practical experience of treating delinquents. The Tavistock Clinic,[2] founded in 1920 as the result of the work. of doctors with ' shell shock ' cases in the war of 1914, did not set out to deal with delinquency, but circumstances forced delinquents upon them. Its main object was, quoting one of the clinic's reports, ' the study, alleviation, cure, and prevention of the disorders of mind which are not classed as insanity or mental deficiency, but which nevertheless cause profound and widespread suffering and economic disability in the community '.

When a delinquent was referred to the Clinic, either by a magistrate or by a probation officer, he was studied from both the physical and psychological points of view. The annual report of the Clinic for the year 1938, the last full report before the war, stated that most of the cases had been followed up for three years or longer. All of the Clinic's patients, delinquents or otherwise, were, of course, at liberty, so the follow-up must have been a big task.

On the results of treatment in adult cases the Clinic reported that 54·7 per cent were ' relieved ' ; of the remaining 45·3 per cent considerably more than half were ' slightly improved ', and we must remember that ' slightly improved '

[1] See Chapter 6.
[2] Some idea of the scope of the work done by the Clinic can be obtained from the sub-headings in one of its pre-war reports : Children's Department, Social Service, Educational Psychologist, Director of Studies, Research, Delinquency, Follow-up. It is obviously impossible for me to describe the work under all these headings, but it should be mentioned that valuable research work was carried on ' to co-ordinate physical and psychological findings in disease '. The uninitiated may think that psychological ailments and physical disease form two distinct categories. The Clinic has proved that this is frequently not so.

from a medical standpoint may well mean the cessation of further charges of crime. Of the adult cases followed up for three years or longer 55·8 per cent were reported as ' relieved '. As regards children 43 per cent were reported as ' apparent cure ', 29 per cent as ' improved ' and 28 per cent as ' not improved '.

The high scientific standards adopted by the Clinic are observable from the following statement which was sent to me when the above figures were supplied :

The figures quoted in this report are small and cannot be used for the formulation of statistical evidence as to the efficacy of psycho-therapy in the problem of delinquency. The results do, however, suggest that this line of treatment is helpful alone in carefully selected cases, and if combined with suitable environmental arrangements, can be effective for a still larger number.

This question of ' suitable environmental arrangement ' is of great importance in deciding whether treatment should be given in places of detention or while the delinquent is on probation.

The Institute for the Scientific Treatment of Delinquency worked on similar lines ; a few of its medical staff were also on the staff of the Tavistock Clinic. The development of the Institute is in a sense a history of the development of modern psychology itself in its relation to the problems of crime. It was founded in 1932. I attended its inaugural meeting at University College, London, on 29 November 1932, and was at first repelled by the propaganda literature provided. One leaflet included the statements : ' as the movement succeeds, as it must succeed with public recognition and support, so should our prisons empty. . . . The potential criminals will be useful citizens.' Though at that time I had been a magistrate for only eighteen months, this optimism was too much for me. But it was not long before experience made the Institute a practical and invaluable centre for treating delinquents. The following extracts from the annual report of the

Institute for 1938 show the realist attitude that was adopted :

By ' discharged as cured ' we mean that some fundamental cause of the delinquency has been discovered and treated satisfactorily ; for example, a mental disease of which the offence is symptomatic, or an unusual and specially severe environmental factor operating on a boy who otherwise would have remained honest.   By ' discharged as improved ' we mean that we regard the patient as having reached a stable, non-delinquent state, although the causes of his delinquency were of such a kind that we should not be justified in claiming a cure until a period of some years had elapsed.

But again it is desirable to emphasize that these latter cases, the majority of those treated by the Institute, may have been successes from the standpoint of criminal courts.

The report stated that ' all methods of treatment have been used '.   It also emphasized the value of combining sociological and psychological methods.   Of those treated, this report stated, about one quarter were sex cases and nearly one half cases of theft ; some were children ' beyond control ' ; there were also cases of attempted suicide and of wandering without visible means of support and refusing to enter a place of refuge.

When it is realized that in but a small proportion of the cases, both at the Tavistock Clinic and at the Institute, was any money forthcoming from the delinquent patients, even for administrative expenses, we obtain some idea of the difficulties of this work, and of the generosity of the doctors concerned.   Both these organizations are typical of English institutions ; they are built on faith, enthusiasm, and an ardent conviction that plenty of psychotics and neurotics, even when they are criminals, can be cured while they remain at liberty.   But it has to be said that these societies have on the whole received totally inadequate financial support from the charitable public.

This shortage of funds involves one serious obstacle in the way of psycho-therapy for delinquents placed on probation.   A psycho-therapist needs for his work full infor-

mation about the physical condition of his patient. He
also needs much social information about him, and possibly intelligence tests as well, before he begins treatment.
We have seen that similar information was collected before
Dr. Hubert began his treatments in Wormwood Scrubs
prison. Under the circumstances that originally existed at
these clinics, it is possible that the treatment given was
hampered by the preliminary investigations. The old rule
at the Institute for the Scientific Treatment of Delinquency,
for instance, was that the delinquent on probation first saw
a social worker. Usually another journey to the West End
was necessary for a visit to the physician. Ultimately he
saw his allotted psycho-therapist. These arrangements
were then necessary because the clinic was not sufficiently
well provided with funds to enable it to have its experts,
so to speak, on tap ; it had to utilize the spare time of busy
men and women. It was not, therefore, practicable for all
the interviews to take place on one day and at one place.
So no blame can be imputed. Since these days it has been
arranged that a patient sees the psycho-therapist on his first
visit. But for the guidance of new clinics it would be well
to look at this matter from the point of view of the delinquent. He has just had a nasty experience ; he has been
caught by the police and tried in open court. Probably he
has expected to be sent to prison ; he is relieved that the
court is trying to understand him, but alarmed that he has
promised to undergo something of which he has never
heard before. But he has screwed up his courage, promised
to co-operate, and sets out for the clinic after a day's work.
If he sees first a social worker who asks a lot of questions
about his home conditions, how many children, whether
any ancestors were ever insane, and so on (all necessary
inquiries), then he may lose courage. If at his second visit
he sees the physician, who, instead of talking about what is
uppermost in the delinquent's mind, examines him for flat-
feet or tonsils, or such like ailments, then the discouraging
process goes further. I have had cases where the good
intentions of delinquents evaporated after the preliminary

or second visit to a clinic and before they ever reached a psycho-therapist. In a high proportion of cases where consent has been given to psycho-therapy, there is much ' resistance ', conscious or unconscious, so if there is delay before the psycho-therapist is seen, however inevitable the delay may be, the curative process may fail before it begins. Such delay may also have the serious result of breaking the rapport between delinquent and his court and probation officer. For good results such rapport should grow stronger and stronger, quickly reinforced by a new rapport between delinquent and psycho-therapist.

Because of these earlier practical difficulties, I rejoiced when probation officers at the South-Western court, where I have worked since 1934, discovered that a psychiatrist of great experience, Dr. Alexander Court, was living in the district and was willing to help us. I have sent many scores of cases to Dr. Court, both for report on remand and for treatment, and it was never a difficulty that our delinquents had not time or energy to make the necessary visits. By sending cases to an individual and local doctor many difficulties were avoided. The same doctor could examine from both the physical and the psychological standpoint (probably at different times), and he could be supplied before the first visit of the delinquent with the social facts and history by the probation officers ; this made easier the path of the delinquent. The very fact that the delinquent had to enter a doctor's surgery, a type of place with which he was ordinarily familiar, minimized any fear of the unknown ; it requires more pluck to pay visits to a clinic than to see a doctor in his surgery, and pluck is not a conspicuous characteristic of most delinquents needing psychological treatment. The happiest results have come from Dr. Court's work, and this experience has convinced me that the ideal method of obtaining psycho-therapy for adults at liberty, when no expert is in the district who is able to help the court, is for the court to arrange with a clinic for the periodical attendance of a medical psychologist at the court or near by. This would only be

possible in big towns.   In London it is certainly practicable, all the more so because magistrates' courts in London
have Poor Boxes with large funds from which the necessary
expenses could be met.

If ever independent psychological clinics are adequately
endowed, or when under a new Criminal Justice Act public
clinics are established,[1] we may reasonably hope that the
difficulties just mentioned will be avoided.   Either the
clinics would send out their staff to courts as may be necessary, or delinquents would on visiting the clinic always pass
through the various experts and reach the psycho-therapist
on the first day of their attendance.   When either of these
conditions is general, it should be possible, except for the
most grave crimes, for most delinquents to remain free, but
under supervision, both for their preliminary examination
before the court decides their fate, and for any psychological
treatment that may be found necessary.

A problem that has to be faced when treatment on probation is proposed is the difficulty of giving long courses
of treatment to delinquents.   The analytical method is as
a rule, I am told, the best for the psycho-neurotic cases,
and also for many of those with ' reaction character traits ',
namely, where delinquency has been a reaction to an opposite
and repressed tendency.   The patient is encouraged for
three hours a week or more over a period of years to say
whatever comes into his head.   In this way the patient
gradually brings into consciousness, and thus within his
powers of control, what has been disturbing him in his
unconscious.   This is termed the method of ' free association ', a somewhat strange term to have been used by Freud,
who denied the freedom of human conduct.   (Freud realized
this.   In his *Autobiographical Study* he wrote that ' free
association is not really free.   The patient remains under
the influence of the analytic situation even though he is not
directing his mental activities on to a particular subject.
We shall be justified in assuming that nothing will occur

[1] I should value this much more than the establishment of the
special residential institution advocated in the East-Hubert report.

to him that has not some reference to that situation.' [1])
But whatever name for analytical treatment would be most
suitable, the fact remains that such treatment could only
rarely be given to delinquents on probation. Dealing with
ordinary non-delinquent people, Dr. Graham Howe wrote
that ' for most of us an hour a day for three years as a therapeutic method is out of the question '.[2] How much more
so for a delinquent who will ordinarily be earning his living
all day. The question whether it is possible to shorten
analytical treatment is one on which psycho-analytical
opinion is not unanimous. Most would firmly uphold the
necessity for the full-time treatment.[3] Dr. Graham Howe
wrote that ' perhaps there is the middle way ', and in fact
certain shortened methods of treatment have been evolved,
though the doctors who use them would not claim that
they are analytical in Freud's meaning of the word. The
report of the Tavistock Clinic for 1939 made reference to
war conditions having necessitated ' far more use of short
and rapid therapeutic methods '. So we can be hopeful.

There are, of course, many methods of psycho-therapy,
other than the psycho-analytical, which many therapists in
big practice have long used. Treatment by discussion and
suggestion has been favoured by many practitioners, and in
regard to delinquents it is often the only method that is
practicable. To quote Dr. Graham Howe again : ' There
are many cases in which the therapeutic method must
inevitably be limited, to a greater or lesser extent, to some
kind of persuasion. This method is particularly suitable
when time is limited or the patient has not sufficient intelligence to undergo the analytic or interpretive methods.' [4]
Dr. William Healy gave accounts of cases where good results
were achieved with juvenile delinquents from ' a couple of

[1] pp. 72–3.
[2] *Motives and Mechanisms of the Mind*, p. 250.
[3] In Freud's *New Introductory Lectures on Psycho-Analysis* he
deprecated strongly any shortening of psycho-analysis. But Freud
did not as a rule treat delinquents, so far as I am aware.
[4] Op. cit., p. 239.

prolonged interviews ', and from ' a single half-day '.[1] He employed a method of ' mental analysis ' that was not Freudian psycho-analysis.[2] In order to minimize our difficulties Dr. Court at times embarked upon quite short treatments, particularly with elderly homo-sexuals, who are usually more pathetic than criminal. After having had a series of such cases, I went to discuss them with Dr. Court. ' Is it any good sending these men to you ? ' I asked. Dr. Court pointed out to me that homo-sexuality is usually associated with loneliness, and that some talks with him might help to remedy the loneliness and thus restrict the desire for homo-sexual conduct. So I sent many of these old men to Dr. Court, and the results were always that at least a year went by without any further charges from the police against them.

No mere lawyer can say whether a short treatment is scientifically sound, but he can say that in most delinquent cases where the delinquents are at liberty, a short treatment is all that is practicable.[3]

When one realizes, as a magistrate must, that most of the people who come before us, whether for crime or because of matrimonial difficulties, have never in their lives had the working of sex explained to them in a natural, unemotional way, then one feels that a short treatment, even if not the best, must be of real assistance. Many adults, and even many juveniles, are sadly inhibited about what are commonly spoken of as ' the facts of life ' ; they have a definite sense of guilt about sexual matters. They are apt to regard all talk of sex as ' dirty ', even when their own language and conduct in matters of sex have been on a low standard. In

[1] *Mental Conflicts and Misconduct*, pp. 93 and 148.
[2] Ibid., p. 19.
[3] For long treatments in places of detention there would in many cases have to be a severe increase in the length of sentence ; but whether Parliament could be persuaded to authorize a three years' sentence for purposes of treatment for offences which have hitherto been dealt with by a maximum sentence of six, or in some cases three, months is a political question which I could not answer. But I have my doubts.

my court a youth pleaded guilty to an indecent assault on a child ; because there had been other assaults I asked the mother whether her son had ever been given any information about sexual matters. She replied : ' We thought he was a clean lad and didn't want to know about such things.' I was once obtaining the evidence of a girl of about twelve, the victim of a sexual assault. I had to ask the child where the defendant had touched her. The reply was ' on my rude '. These are everyday happenings in a magistrates' court.

CHAPTER 3

A FEW CASES

'The courts of summary jurisdiction are the most promising field of all. . . . Youthful offenders, whose minds are still plastic, can be helped, and can help the psychologist to learn more of the nature of criminal responsibility.'

HENRY T. F. RHODES.[1]

IN this chapter will be set out a few of the cases that have passed through my hands which illustrate some of the points made in this book, and especially the possibilities, advantages, and difficulties of non-institutional psychological treatment. These cases are in many ways typical; they are some which I have been able to follow up. The earlier cases all concern sexual offences, not because it has been only in sexual cases that I have enlisted the aid of psycho-therapy, but because it was in this type of case that my interest in psychology began. Most of us believe that we understand why a man or woman steals, why a gambler embezzles his employer's money, why an angry man does an injury to some one else, and so on. But such an offence as the exposure by men of their private parts with, as the law says, the intention to insult women or girls, is outside our daily experience and knowledge; so a resort to psycho-therapy seems the obvious course. As knowledge of psychological principles increases, we come to realize that our understanding of the thief, the gambler, etc., is not so complete as we thought. But it was some time before it dawned upon me that psychology could help in cases that were not sexual. The earlier the case, the more value has the statement that there has been no subsequent trouble. It also happens that all the cases set out here are of male offenders. I have sent some women to psycho-therapists, but they have been few, and unfortunately I have not kept notes about them.

[1] *The Criminal in Society*, p. 182.

It is worth while recalling that in the East-Hubert report it was stated that 'as a whole the exhibitionist group is a disappointing one from the psychological point of view'.[1] Psycho-therapists who have treated such cases sent to them by me have expressed directly contrary opinions. Some of the cases that follow were exhibitionists. They and the many others that have had psycho-therapy while on probation have usually been most successful. Perhaps this was due to the very fact that treatment was given while the exhibitionists were at liberty.

It will be noticed that in all my cases the services only of registered medical practitioners were utilized. It is in my opinion important that criminal courts should only enlist the services of medical men or women trained in psychiatry and psychology, and not make use of the services of lay psychologists. I have had offers from non-medical therapists, and without doubting the genuineness of the desire to help thus shown, I have always refrained from accepting them. To put the matter on its lowest footing : criminal courts assume a considerable responsibility in recommending delinquents to undergo psychological treatment, and, provided that the delinquent passes into the hands of a registered medical practitioner, courts would be in a strong position in the unlikely event that some complaint should be made against the practitioner or about the treatment. The fact that any such complaint could be referred to the General Medical Council gives security to all responsible for advising treatment. This is all the more desirable since the psychological treatment of delinquency is still in the pioneering stage and there are still many people who are hostile to modern psychology. It is undoubtedly a fact that valuable work can be done by properly trained and supervised lay therapists.[2]   Freud

[1] Paragraph 127.
[2] A useful book, *Psychology and Health*, is a good example of what can be achieved by a trained, non-medical psychologist. The author, H. Banister, was M.Sc. and Ph.D., and obviously had many patients.

himself, whose methods are more difficult than those of other schools, wrote that ' it is no longer possible to restrict the practice of psycho-analysis to physicians and to exclude laymen from it. . . . A non-physician who has been suitably trained, can, with occasional reference to a physician, carry out the analytical treatment, not only of children but also of neurotics.' [1] Adler also held this view.[2] But criminal courts are not in a position to estimate the efficiency of lay therapists ; nor can they easily distinguish between trained lay therapists and untrained quacks. So it is best to use only the services of doctors expert in psycho-therapy. Unskilled psycho-therapy can, it is well to remember, result in the mere suppression of unhealthy psychic energies, with the consequence that new symptoms may appear which may lead to a different, and possibly a more dangerous, kind of delinquent conduct.

The general standards of success need a little consideration. In the East-Hubert report there are these statements :

We do not believe that the word ' cure ' can be properly used until many years have elapsed during which there has been no further conflict with the criminal law. Perhaps not even then.[3]

In fixing a standard of cure, it must be pointed out that the primary object is to prevent further crime. To reduce the likelihood of the recurrence of any hysterical symptoms and to help general adaption in life, though important, must be regarded as secondary to this and may be more difficult or even impossible to attain.[4]

I fully agree. It seems to me that criminal courts are entitled to claim as successes those cases which for a period of years have not again been found guilty of criminal conduct. Such cases may not be cured according to the general standards of the medical profession, but in most cases complete normality would probably be impossible of attainment. Courts are not concerned with the complete cure of their delinquents ; so long as the delinquents are able

---

[1] *An Autobiographical Study*, p. 129.
[2] See *Alfred Adler, Apostle of Freedom*, by Phyllis Bottome, p. 241.   [3] Paragraph 57.   [4] Paragraph 73.

to live and work without again breaking the criminal law, courts have reason to be satisfied. The old men referred to at the end of the previous chapter were certainly not cured, but they ceased, at least for a time, to be public nuisances.

In some of the cases that follow it is obvious that no cure on strictly medical standards was attained. But if the motivating forces that have resulted in criminal acts have been so got under control that the individuals are no longer a menace to the community, then all concerned have done a successful job.

It should be remembered that all the events mentioned in the cases that follow took place during the years before the war of 1939, when unemployment was often rife. This added greatly to our difficulties and in some cases adversely affected the psychological conditions of the delinquents.

I have not attempted to follow up any of these cases beyond September 1939, for after the outbreak of war a statement that a delinquent has not again been convicted is ambiguous : it might mean that he is dead.

Body and Mind

E. F.[1] was charged before me for indecent exposure with intent to insult females. There were three charges, but I only tried one. He stoutly denied the charges and employed a solicitor to defend him, who conducted the defence on the usual lines that the insulted woman had imagined the alleged experience and that she herself was psychologically peculiar ; this woman was about 40 years of age. I found E. F. guilty and then learned that owing to numerous complaints, the police had been watching E. F., a fact that indicates that E. F. was only technically a first offender. E. F. was 23 years old, had both parents living, was in good work in a skilled trade, was a single man, but was ' walking out ' with a young woman. After conviction he was put back for an interview with a probation officer and I was

[1] Throughout the book the initials used are not those of the particular case described.

later informed that E. F. had expressed willingness to go for examination to the Tavistock Clinic. I remanded E. F. on bail for a fortnight and told him that I should much prefer handing him over to a psychologist to inflicting punishment on him, but that I could only do the former if it was reported to me that he had been frank and wanted to be cured.

After the fortnight I was given two reports from the Tavistock Clinic, one from a psychologist and one from a diagnostic physician. The latter reported some minor physical ailments, which, he stated, had no bearing now on his psychological complaint.

The following extracts from the psychologist's report are of interest.

This man was quite frank and open with me about his trouble and admitted it without any attempt at evasion. From his story his trouble began during last summer when he was out of work. Exhibitionism has occurred on a good many occasions since then.

It is not easy to be certain of the motive for his conduct ; he himself is completely unaware of it and can only describe it as a sudden impulse that frequently comes to him. He has always been a shy and diffident person, and I fancy that his facial acne, which he has had since he was 13, may have been partly responsible for this. His increasing fatness in the last couple of years (he has put on over two stone) has no doubt also made a difference because he does not very much like the nicknames he is called by his acquaintances. He is a man with very few friends, though his girl, with whom he is walking out, sounds as though she were quite the right kind of person, and she is sticking to him through his present trouble.

He was quite a clever boy at school, I gather, but seems in a most curious way to have lost ambition since then. I expect that his cleverness, and the fact that he was the only boy at home for five or six years, had something to do with his becoming self-conscious, and that, I fancy, has a good deal to do with his exhibitionism.

The psychologist stated further that, though he could not be certain, he thought E. F.'s conduct was ' a com-

pensation for an inferiority feeling '. He assured me that
E. F. was prepared to take the situation seriously and
sensibly, and added : ' I think that for the moment the
bump he has had through these court proceedings will be
sufficient to keep him from being a public danger for a little
while, though I am certain that the effect will not be permanent.' No immediate treatment could be promised, as
the clinic had then a considerable waiting list, but I was
assured that ' we can do quite a lot to help ' and that
psycho-therapy would assist E. F. to get rid of his inferiority
feeling.

On these reports and on the report of the probation
officer that, despite the original denials, E. F. seemed desirous of his help, I made a probation order for a year. The
probation officer had visited E. F.'s home and had formed
a favourable impression both of his parents and of his
young lady.

During the interval before psychological treatment could
begin it was arranged for E. F. to attend a hospital for
a minor operation on his nose. E. F. had lost his work
through the court proceedings, but after two months he
was in work again. He reported regularly to the probation
officer and all seemed to be going well. Some months
after his appearance in court he became formally engaged,
and after another three months treatment at the Tavistock
Clinic was begun. E. F. attended the clinic as directed,
and his psycho-therapist was put in touch with E. F.'s
panel doctor ; the latter advised a further attendance at
the hospital where the operation had been carried out.
Thus there was good team work between probation officer,
clinic, panel doctor, and hospital.

When E. F. had attended the clinic for three months,
the probation order expired. I had power to extend it,
but felt that E. F. would appreciate it if we showed trust
in him. He continued to attend the clinic just the same,
although he was no longer under any legal obligation to do
so. Nine months after the treatment at the clinic had
begun, I received through the clinic a report from the

psycho-therapist who was giving the treatment stating: 'The cause was a very great feeling of inferiority connected with sex. . . . He realizes that it was not pride that made him do it, but fear that people might think he was not potent.' In all E. F. had attended the clinic for treatment twenty-nine times. Midway in his treatment he had been married to his young lady, he had proved sexually normal, and when the probation officer last saw him, it seemed that the marriage was perfectly satisfactory. Unfortunately, E. F. did not respond to the follow-up inquiries from the clinic. But six and a half years after his appearance before me there had been no further trouble of a criminal nature.

A Childish Man

A case of greater difficulty was C. D., a young man 23 years old who had just completed his terms at a residential university. He had obtained an ordinary degree and was contemplating taking up teaching as a career. He pleaded guilty before me to a charge of indecent conduct. The facts might have resulted in a charge of homo-sexual conduct, but the police realized that there were practical difficulties in the way of such a charge; proof and corroboration are difficult in such cases. C. D. had undoubtedly been having undesirable sexual play with some small boys, and it sometimes happens that the only charge that the police can bring with any prospects of obtaining a verdict is one of indecent conduct under the London County Council bye-law, the maximum penalty for which is a fine of £5.

The distracted widowed mother of C. D. attended his trial, but, being fearful of the press, I advised her to talk privately with the probation officer and not in open court to me. Later in the day the probation officer reported to me that there was every sign of co-operation on the part of both C. D. and his mother. They both agreed to go to the Tavistock Clinic, so I made the usual remand on bail for a fortnight. An interesting report was available for me when C. D. appeared again in court. The following are extracts :

At the beginning of our interview he was rather inclined to be on the defensive·and anxious to explain away some of the things he had done, or at any rate to whittle them down. We very quickly got through this, however, and I think he was quite honest.

Undoubtedly he is emotionally homo-sexual. . . . I believe him to be telling the truth when he says that there has never been any overt homo-sexual action before, and that his other sexual activity, masturbation, has always been solitary and never with anyone else. When I enquired into his phantasy life, I find that he has had many phantasies about small boys. . . . He has had very occasional phantasies of friendships with girls of about seventeen.

He is very immature, both physically and psychologically. Apparently puberty was delayed. When he was a child . . . he had difficulty in holding his water . . . for that reason he was something of an outsider at school and made no friends. The inferiority was carried on into his life at . . . school, and there too he was very much out of things. His attraction to small boys was based partly on this inferiority, because it is so much easier to get the friendship and admiration of those who are younger than yourself than it is of your peers.

He has always been shy, shut-in, and solitary. He was the only child for five years and then was very jeaous of his sister when she was born. . . . His father died when he was five. . . . he is certainly worthy trying to help psychologically. Both environmental help and direct psycho-therapy are needed, and the latter is probably the most important. . . . He has a really inadequate appreciation of the anti-social nature of his conduct. . . . I think that some impressive and winged words from you would help quite a lot in making him face reality.

This report entirely confirmed our own impressions. C. D.'s spare-time occupation showed definite signs of regression into boyhood. The probation officer informed me at the second hearing that C. D. had during the fortnight's remand written some letters about appointments which showed that he had no doubts whatever that he would be a free man after his second appearance in court.

So I inflicted upon him, as the psychologist had suggested, some stinging words. I made it clear to him that there might have been a far more serious charge against him and that his conduct had not only done considerable harm to the boys, but also great harm to himself. A probation order for two years was made, and my usual term was included that he submit to medical treatment as directed.

The Tavistock Clinic had suggested that it would be beneficial if C. D. went to the Institute of Industrial Psychology for a vocational test, his original idea of becoming a teacher being now out of the question. This was arranged. It was also recommended that C. D. should stay in London for treatment, as an absence from home was considered advisable ; but as psychological treatment could not begin for several months, we allowed him to go home for a time. On advice he began to learn shorthand and typewriting. During these months at home his letters were typical of him, boyish and somewhat irresponsible. When C. D. returned to London, he obtained a clerical post and lived in a hostel recommended by the probation officer.

Owing to congestion at the clinic eight months went by before treatment could begin. After six weeks of treatment, during which C. D. attended the clinic three times a week after his work, his psychologist wrote that ' after four weeks rather resentful refusal to co-operate fully ', C. D. ' has now come round to a rapport which promises to facilitate treatment. . . . He has been carrying since childhood an enormous burden of anxiety.' Mention was also made of the fact that the relations between C. D. and his mother were in fact very different from what both conceived them to be.

Treatment continued for about a year, but for various reasons there were sometimes long intervals between the visits to the clinic. When discharged from the clinic, C. D. was judged to be ' improved '. His psychologist received a letter from him shortly afterwards and two years later C. D. called to see him ; he said incidentally that his sexual problems had ceased to trouble him. That was nearly four years after his conviction in court. After a further eighteen months I was able to ascertain that C. D. had had no more trouble with the police. He was still in the same work.

Lonely and Unloved

A serious crime was charged against J. K., namely, ' soliciting for immoral purposes in a public place '. Numerous complaints had been received by the police that a certain public convenience was a meeting-place of homo-sexuals and J. K. was caught as the result of a special watch by the police. He was a ' very respectable ' man of 35 who worked in a big shop for about £4 a week. He had no parents living and had been brought up by a foster-mother.

J. K. was stoutly defended by an eminent member of the junior Bar. But the evidence for the prosecution could not be shaken and I convicted. Being told by the police that there had been no previous convictions, I told J. K. and his counsel in court that I hoped to be able to avoid punishment, but that I could only take a lenient course if satisfied that J. K. was being candid. I said a little about the possibilities of psychological treatment. I remember the case well because while I was at lunch the defending counsel came to me to discuss what I had said and the advice that he would give to his client. This was a quite proper course, for I had publicly convicted J. K. I explained what was happening in some other cases that were in the hands of the Tavistock Clinic, but made it clear that before I could let J. K. be treated in this way, there would have to be an admission about the need for treatment. I gathered that counsel himself believed in his client's innocence. He had never heard of psychological treatment. Meanwhile the probation officer was having a private talk with J. K. and soon afterwards his counsel saw him.

When the court resumed work, J. K. appeared again. His counsel stated that J. K. was willing to go for treatment to the clinic, so I knew that all was well and remanded

J. K. on bail. Had counsel's further inquiries supported his view that I had wrongly found J. K. guilty, there would undoubtedly have been an appeal, for money was available. Unfortunately, the case was widely reported and some newspapers ' stunted ' it as the first case in which a magistrate had suggested psychological treatment.   This was, of course, absurd.   Long before I became a magistrate, Sir William Clarke Hall sent cases to psycho-therapists for treatment, and doubtless other magistrates had done so as well.

When J. K. appeared in court again after the fortnight's remand, an encouraging report was received from the Tavistock Clinic :

I came to the conclusion that his sexual aberration was in the nature of· a compulsion neurosis.   By this I mean that the impulse was motivated from deeper unconscious levels and was part of a defence mechanism against an intolerable feeling of deprivation and loneliness experienced originally in early childhood.   These feelings he has every time he gives way to his compulsion.   Indulgence is invariably followed by a sense of guilt and remorse, which is part of the typical clinical picture, and of the sincerity of which there can be no doubt.

In similar cases I have analysed the original situation has been an early childhood sense of frustration, followed by abject misery, for which there has been relief through withdrawal into self-love and masturbation.   The whole of this complex has then become repressed, to emerge again, as in this case, when some other homo-sexual person has made the first advances.   This man, like the others, only feels the impulse towards men resembling himself, looking, as it were, for a completion of himself in someone else.   The impulse is felt as something strange and abnormal, not belonging to the present personality, and in the sense of its being the repetition of an infantile situation, it does not.

There can be no doubt that J. K. is deeply anxious to rid himself of this abnormality (unconscious resistances apart), especially as he is ordinarily a man of healthy athletic tastes and normally fond of female company.   An additional factor in his condition may be the fact that a girl to whom he was very devoted died last autumn.

I should say that the outlook for a cure is quite promising.

The whole of this letter was, on the advice of the writer, shown to J. K.

Happily in this case it was possible for the Tavistock Clinic to arrange treatment without delay. After six months the probation officer was in a position to inform me that J. K. was still attending the clinic regularly and 'going on splendidly'. J. K. was voluntarily paying a small sum to the clinic for each visit. He was in regular work.

In the seventh month of probation a complication arose in a complaint from a young woman that her mother was wasting her money on J. K., who, she alleged, was having undue influence on the mother. This complaint was investigated. The mother was undoubtedly going to places of amusement with J. K., but she stated that she regarded him more as a son than anything else; she denied her daughter's statement that money had regularly been given to J. K. and stated that she had once given J. K. a loan of £2, which had been repaid. I advised the probation officer not to regard this situation as serious and that there had not been any breach of the probation order. The situation cleared up, and I was satisfied that no harm had been done. Probably good rather than harm had resulted from this association, for J. K. was greatly in need of maternal care.

Seven months after the making of the probation order the Tavistock Clinic reported that his work had recently prevented J. K. from regular attendance, but that he had 'been very co-operative' and had 'made substantial progress'. The report continued: 'At the present time he tells me that there is no sort of homo-sexual desire or interest and that he is quite confident that it is finished. Very likely this is true. I do not, however, feel inclined to accept this statement yet.' The report contained a reference to J. K.'s association with the married woman and this indicated that he was being candid with his psychologist. The last words in the report were: 'I have no doubt that at the present time he is quite safe from the

7

point of view of society. There is no serious likelihood at all of a resurgence of the earlier difficulties.'

Two months later the clinic sent a further report which stated that ' in view of the complete absence of symptoms, it was not considered advisable to carry treatment any further '. We were informed that :

The patient has been very co-operative and helpful and has worked hard. Although technically we still cannot feel that we have got as far as it is possible to go, there is no doubt that we shall have to leave things as they are at present. He has been warned to continue with treatment should he feel any symptoms whatever, quite apart from the type of difficulty which led him to come into contact with the police in the first instance. Since the patient himself is so well aware of the situation, I do not think we need fear that there will be any further anti-social activity.

I had bound J. K. over for three years, though I had made a probation order for only one year. This meant that any conviction within the three years would be reported to me by the police. At the conclusion of the year of probation the situation seemed so satisfactory that no prolongation of the probation order was necessary. Over four years after J. K's first appearance before me there had been no further trouble.

Afraid of Life

A difficult case was R. S., a rather miserable specimen of humanity who was charged before me for an indecent assault on a boy. He was a single man of 24. I found him guilty and then learned that two years previously he had been sentenced to six months' imprisonment for a similar offence. R. S. agreed to go to the Tavistock Clinic. The following statements were made in the report that I received :

I could find very little that would make me believe that this boy is really the established homo-sexual type . . . I believe that his difficulties in early life at home are responsible for his condition. He was the eldest boy in the family, scared of his parents, especially of his mother, and I think that that is why he has always had a certain fear of growing up and of the responsibilities of life. He has funked in his work. He should be in a very much better job than he has now; and, of course, he is afraid of marriage and the responsibilities of it. The result has been that he is something of a Peter Pan emotionally and so the schoolboy homo-sexual phase has persisted.

R. S. was working in a hotel kitchen at the time of the offence which resulted in his appearance before me. The probation officer confirmed that R. S. was undeveloped and that he had no real friends. The clinic's report continued :

I am quite sure that the boy is helpable, and I think he needs the right kind of environment, with interests of a healthy kind outside his work. He also needs, and I believe would make good use of, some psychological help. If you decide to put him on probation, I think that the probation officer's suggestion of a hostel for a time is an admirable one. He can be treated as a normal person and not as a pervert.

Residence in a hostel was arranged and R. S. continued at work. But two months later came a report from a doctor who had begun the treatment, not at the Tavistock Clinic. This report said :

This man has been seen here on several occasions. . . . His trouble is that of homo-sexuality. This condition can usually be greatly helped by treatment, although perfect cure is uncommon. The success of treatment, however, depends upon a real wish for cure resultant upon a sense of the discomfort and unsatisfactoriness of the condition. This is quite absent in in his case, although several interviews have aimed at eliciting it. . . . He has been discharged as unsuitable for psychological treatment.

I realized that the doctor who wrote this report had seen R. S. more often than the writer of the earlier report. But imprisonment having already failed to change R. S., I could not bring myself to admit failure. So I troubled the

Tavistock Clinic again. After some weeks a further report came from the clinic.

I still feel, as I did originally, that he is helpable, and am fixing up treatment for him here. . . . It is not much good asking a homo-sexual to give you his assurance that he wants to be cured : that is too difficult just at first. What he does recognise is that there is a general ineffectiveness and lack of grip which he wants altered. That, I believe, makes the surest approach to the situation. . . . At the present moment I certainly do not think he is safe, but I believe that something can be done.

There was inevitable delay. Then came regular treatment for two months. After that R. S. paid spasmodic visits to the clinic. When the year of probation was finished, the probation officer reported to me that ' I am sure he benefited by his treatment ' ; he referred to the difficulty of fitting in treatment having regard to the long hours that R. S. had to work in his hotel. I never heard anything more about R. S., but over seven years after his first appearance before me I found out that he had not been convicted again.

Five Times in Prison

A case of which the probation officer and I were rather proud was N. O., a single man of 58. From a first-floor window where he lived this man attracted the attention of a woman living in the opposite house by masturbating himself in full view. The woman so attracted happened to be the wife of a police constable ; on seeing this unpleasant sight, she went to the nearest telephone and told the police station what she had seen. Though some time elapsed, N. O. was still exhibiting himself when the police entered the room opposite. There was no doubt about guilt. Then I learned that there had been several previous convictions for this class of offence. N. O. had served five sentences of imprisonment of varying duration. Under the Vagrancy Act of 1824 N. O. was liable to be sent to Quarter Sessions as an ' Incorrigible Rogue ' and to receive a sentence of twelve months. The police pressed strongly that N. O. was incorrigible. It was not easy to resist this conclusion as two years before his appearance in my court he had been bound over on the plea of an alienist who was known to N. O.'s employer. But I discovered that that court had not made a probation order and had not taken any steps to secure treatment. I could not regard such a binding over as the giving of a genuine chance to N. O. We obtained a written report from the doctor who had been called in before and this gave me a little hope. Magistrates, like most people, have competitive instincts ; seeing that this defendant had learned all that there was to be known about prison and that another court had given N. O. what was doubtless regarded as a chance, I felt keen, and the probation officer was also keen, to try our own methods. So I made a probation order with a clause about treatment. N. O. agreed to this.

By this time N. O. had lost his job, so it was arranged for a hostel to keep him for a time, payment being made out of the court poor-box. N. O. was very willing to receive psychological treatment. He was sent to the Institute for the Scientific Treatment of Delinquency. Most unfortunately there was a considerable delay before treatment could be arranged. N. O. began to get very restive with the inactive life that he was leading. Later a report from the Institute was received and contained the following :

This man shows many pathological features in his make-up, although he does not show any more serious pathological condition than a fairly severe anxiety state. This is probably due to a very severe arterio-sclerosis from which he suffers. In view of the long history and his age it would be rash to hold out very much hope of psychological treatment curing him, but it is possible that some form of suggestion would enable him to gain control over his impulses, since he already has some degree of control.

The tendency would be for his arterio-sclerosis to increase the likelihood to abnormal sexual behaviour. . . . The outlook without any assistance is really bad.

The inevitable delay had the (for us) serious result that N. O. lost all keenness, and even willingness, to undergo treatment. The rapport had been badly broken. When the time came for treatment, the probation officer had to be distinctly severe. N. O. was presented with the alternative of attending the Institute or being brought back before me for a breach of his probation order. The threat was sufficient to make N. O. journey to the Institute, but he began treatment in a very unwilling spirit. The probation officer had to check up on every one of N. O.'s appointments and to use considerable pressure to keep him up to scratch. Happily about this time N. O.'s old employers were able to re-employ him. The return to work eased matters greatly. N. O. became happier and began to show an interest in his treatment and to appreciate the efforts made on his behalf. He improved considerably, both in physical health and in his attitude to life.

Treatment was continued for about six months and at the end N. O. expressed great gratitude to both doctor and probation officer. He said that he had complete confidence that he was cured and even added that he had made a will leaving half of his savings to the Institute. The probation officer by this time was full of hope. Two and a half years after his last offence there had been no further trouble.

A Failure

A case that illustrates the homely truth about the horse and the water was P. Q., a young man of attractive appearance, 22 years old. I convicted him of obtaining money by false pretences. He had obtained money from the mother of an old friend, who could ill afford to lose it, on the pretext that he was out of work (which was true) and of needing money for fares to a job that had been promised him (which was not true). He was the eldest of three children and his parents had married only a short time before he was born. I was informed that, as is not unusual in such cases, the father had visited on P. Q. his wrath at having had, as he saw it, to marry P. Q.'s mother. The mother had died of tuberculosis and at the time of his appearance before me P. Q. told the probation officer that his father was living unmarried with another woman and had turned P. Q. out. These statements were found to be true. P. Q. had been living with his grandmother, who was in very poor circumstances and had an invalid daughter to care for. P. Q. had been discharged from regular employment when his own tuberculosis had caused many absences from work. He had received a gratuity of £23, most of which his father had taken. P. Q. had attended a clinic for tuberculosis.

After a remand the probation officer reported that P. Q.'s father was definitely unhelpful and very untruthful. He had, however, been persuaded to contribute 2s. 6d. per week towards P. Q.'s maintenance. The probation officer considered that P. Q. was making an excuse out of his illness. He had been attending a tuberculosis dispensary on and off for nearly five years. The previous year he had been resident in a sanatorium for four months and later for a further month. A fortnight before his crime he had been seen by the tuberculosis officer, who later reported to the court that 'his general condition was fairly good and his pulmonary disease inactive'. But when this officer was asked by the probation officer, he stated that P. Q. was a very unsatisfactory patient and that constant complaints had been made about his non-attendance.

If Borstal had been legally possible, I should probably have sent P. Q. to Quarter Sessions with that object. But P. Q. was not qualified and it was doubtful if, even if he were, he would be passed as fit for Borstal training. So a probation order was made. That it was a speculation we knew. P. Q.'s grandmother had strongly resented a description of his case in a local newspaper and promptly turned him out. She was persuaded by the probation officer to keep him for a time. Heroic efforts were made to obtain work for P. Q. and after three weeks work was available as a learner in a hotel. The T. B. clinic was consulted and approved of the work as the hotel was in the country. A loan was given from the poor-box to tide P. Q. over until he received wages and arrangements were made for an informal supervision by a local probation officer. At first things seemed to be going well and P. Q. wrote to the probation officer : ' The job is quite permanent and I am really happy.' Six weeks later came a telegram from the local probation officer which was a veritable S O S. The young man had, we learned later by letter, been asserting that an aunt had just left him £18,000 ; fortified by this, he had acquired a young lady friend and had got control of three motor-cars, one for himself, one for his lady friend and one for her parents. On complaints from the motor dealer to his employers, P. Q. had been sacked. He was charged before the local court, but when the magistrates were informed that the case was already in hand in my court, they discharged him under the Probation Act. P. Q.'s performance being a breach of the general terms of his probation order, I issued a warrant for his arrest. On his appearance, a week in custody was ordered to give us all time to think. Then I extended the probation order for a year and inserted in the order a condition that for six months P. Q. should live where directed by the court. To all this he consented, his week in custody having been a bad rebuff to his vanity.

P. Q. was placed in a hostel and arrangements were made to transfer him to a T.B. dispensary near to the hostel. (The dispensary where he had been registered had been enquiring after him.) Open-air work was found for him, but he gave it up after a trial of a few days.

Then more troubles came. A solicitor from a country town wrote that five months before P. Q.'s original appearance in my court P. Q. had become engaged to a local girl, had entered into an agreement for a house, had ordered decorations and furniture. It seemed incredible, but the solicitor was not being fooled ; he had the bills for the work and goods. Apparently P. Q. had spread abroad the story that he had just been left £25,000. The probation officer brought to me his correspondence with this solicitor and I could only advise him to reply that we had the case in hand, but had no power to interfere with any proceedings that his clients might take. In fact no steps were taken in this disillusioned town. But P. Q. admitted the whole story to the probation officer. Meanwhile as P. Q. had found no more work, the hostel was after a month desirous of discharging him.

At this stage, seven months after my first acquaintance with P. Q., we consulted the Institute for the Scientific Treatment of Delinquency, although we feared that it was far too late for psycho-therapy. After going there for a preliminary examination P. Q. complained of the questions that had been put to him concerning sex ; he would play about with girls, but to talk about sex, even with a doctor, was not decent in his morality. We sent all our information to the Institute. Later a report came to the effect that P. Q. was ' of rather more than average intelligence '. It continued :

On the mental side he is to be regarded as pathological, and falls into a group of pseudologia phantastica, that is of pathological liars who, typically, show a tendency to boasting, posing and so on, which has characterised some of his offences and a great deal of his behaviour. The condition seems to have developed largely as a reaction to unsuitable home surroundings mainly in the form of parental quarrels. His tuberculosis is not in any way the cause of his mental condition, but would tend to aggravate it.

Such cases are treatable, though often difficult. . . . Psychological treatment would be prolonged, the more so as he is not altogether willing to be treated.

Faced with this situation, the probation officer, with the approval of the Institute, tried to get P. Q. into a ' Q Camp ', but we were unable to raise enough money for this. I doubt whether he would have stayed there, had he gone. We sent P. Q. to a London hospital for examination under X-rays and a report came that he was progressing as well as could be expected. Psychological treatment began at the Institute and shortly afterwards P. Q. obtained work at 25s. a week. The hostel was persuaded to keep him on.

But difficulties arose in a conflict between the ideas of the warden of the hostel and those of the Institute. This is one of our problems that often recurs ; institutional residence is required sometimes while psychological treatment is progressing, but we find that wardens of hostels are sometimes apt to be hostile to the whole idea of psychotherapy ; thus the delinquent lives in an atmosphere which actively discourages him in persisting with the treatment. This happened with P. Q. The Institute reported that he was not keeping his appointments and the warden replied that the treatment was interfering with P. Q.'s work. I was called in as referee and fully agreed with the probation officer that for P. Q. treatment was far more important than work. The warden wrote that ' a job to occupy the mind is the most beneficial form of treatment ' and emphasized that P. Q. was a most unwilling patient at the Institute. In fact P. Q. was both an unwilling patient and an unwilling worker. While these disputes were proceeding he obtained a job with higher pay (27s. 6d. a week), but gave it up after three weeks, complaining that the work was too heavy. In fact, P. Q. received but little psychological treatment.

Shortly afterwards the medical authorities decided that P. Q. should be sent to a sanatorium. He duly went. But just before he left London he gave us our biggest shock.

P. Q. calmly informed the probation officer that he had recently married. His wife had been working as a barmaid ; she was an illegitimate child with no home. It was some time before the probation officer could visit her, because when P. Q. went to the sanatorium, his wife moved to an address unknown to us. After a short time at the sanatorium P. Q. discharged himself against the advice of the doctors and he did not even have the decency to inform the probation officer that he had left or where he was going. The probation officer heard of the departure from the sanatorium because a letter which he wrote to P. Q. there came back through the post marked ' address unknown.'

After some time P. Q. called on his probation officer, who

promptly made a visit at the home. There it was ascertained that Mrs. P. Q. knew nothing about the tuberculosis. The probation officer consulted the tuberculosis officer who reported that P. Q. was ' suffering from tuberculosis of both lungs ', but that he had not attended for treatment since his voluntary discharge from the sanatorium. When Mrs. P. Q. was told of her husband's condition, she said cheerfully : ' It makes no difference.' All that could be done was to urge P. Q. to continue with his T.B. treatment ; he definitely refused to take up again the psychological treatment.

It was now the twenty-third month of a two-year proba-tion order. While we were still in doubt about the best course to take, a message came from the police that P. Q. was to be charged at another London court for stealing. He was found guilty. A full report of the case was sent to the other court and, as we felt exhausted, we decided that it would be best if another magistrate should survey the whole scene. So I asked the other magistrate to take into consideration the fact that P. Q. had broken the terms of the probation order made by me.

P. Q. was sent to prison for three months. The future, economically, morally and, more important, eugenically, seemed hopeless.

The Parents' Fault ?

Another case which illustrates the fact that psychology cannot undo the consequences of a bad hereditary endow-ment, combined with a poor upbringing, was A. B., a young man of 22 who pleaded guilty before me to a. charge of stealing. Nine months previously he had been found guilty of a similar charge by another London court ; a proba-tion order had been made. Two months after this A. B. had again been found guilty of stealing, but the first court had permitted the probation order to continue. A. B. informed me that all his thefts were committed because he wanted money for the purpose of going to the country to see his grandmother, who had brought him up.

I had no power to send A. B. to Quarter Sessions with a recommendation for Borstal training. He had pleaded guilty before me and by a then recent decision of the High Court he had to be sentenced by me. The law is the law and I had no power to commit him to Quarter Sessions and thus A. B. could not go to a Borstal Institution.[1]

Ā. B. had a bad impediment in his speech, not only in court. There was also a bad twitching of his right arm and leg. The magistrate in the other court had asked that I should take into consideration the previous breaches of A. B.'s probation order. Prison was the obvious course to take, but I felt that this wretched creature had not had a fair deal from life and that it was possible that he might respond to intelligent kindness.

Our enquiries elicited that the grandfather of A. B. was an epileptic and that most male members of the family had been unstable, especially in money matters ; one of the aunts made many complaints to the probation officer about her own husband and son. It was clear that A. B. had been unwanted by his parents at birth. So far back as A. B. could remember, he had been living with his grandmother. He told the probation officer, ' I was not told the reason why Mum and Dad did not live together and I forgot them for many years.' He had obviously been happy with his grandparents, especially when they moved out of London to the country. He said that when he was 13 he was caught stealing and that the result was that his grandparents sent him back to London to live with his father. He then saw his mother for the first time in his memory.

For five years A. B. had been in and out of unskilled work. Soon after he began work he left his father and lived in lodgings. ' I visited father now and again,' he said, ' but I never saw mother.' It was during these years that the stammering developed. He seemed to have had no companionship at this time and nobody who cared at all for him.

[1] *R. v. Grant*, 1936, 100 J.P., p. 319. Had A. B. been under 21, I could have done this in consequence of his breach of the previous probation order.

Shortly before the first time that the police caught him he had received a letter from his grandmother to say that she was seriously ill. In his own words : ' I began to worry and a few days later my boss went out. I saw some money lying about. I had been thinking of Gran and now I saw I could help, so I took the money [nearly £5] and rushed off to her. She never knew that I had taken the money. After a week I came back to London and gave myself up.'

Through his first probation officer A. B. had found work as a liftman. He lived in lodgings. But he did not do what he was ordered to do, to report regularly to his probation officer. After a few months he gave up his work of his own accord and was then out of work for three weeks. He got a worse job and abandoned that after six weeks. Then, he said, he badly wanted to see his grandmother again. He went into the room of the night porter at his late place of work and stole a wage packet containing £2 17s. He went towards, but did not go direct to, the grandmother. He spent the money in various towns and cheerfully explained that he got more money than his wages by occasional stealing. When supplies ran dry, he went to his grandmother, only to learn that the police had been enquiring for him there. He was found by the police and then came his second appearance in court.

This time the probation officer had wisely arranged for A. B. to go to the Institute for the Scientific Treatment of Delinquency. A. B. attended a few times and then came his appearance before me. A copy of the report sent by the Institute to the other court was obtained ; it included the following statements :

He· is in a condition of moderately severe hysterical instability, with symptoms which became acute during the interview. His delinquencies are connected with his mental condition and are deeply associated both with his difficult upbringing and his poor mental inheritance. He will be taken on for treatment. But this youth ought to get some sort of work to keep him occupied.

Both my probation officer and I were pessimistic. But I had made up my mind that A. B. was more sinned against

than sinning and had ruled out prison. It was obvious that
some attention should be given to his stammering and
twitching. Contact was made with the society that catered
specially for the physically handicapped which was commonly known as P.O.I.P.H., and through them he was
seen by eminent doctors in two hospitals. For some weeks
he received both psychological treatment and three times
a day electrical treatment to his arm and leg. His condition
showed no signs of improvement. He was kept out of
poverty during this period from the court poor-box. Suddenly the police informed us that A. B. was before another
court on a charge of stealing. We passed on the information in our possession, but had no power to do anything.
A. B. was sent to prison for two months.

Should A. B. ever have been born ? What if he ever
has children ?

Marital Failure

T. U. was a case that illustrates important points, but his
trial was considerably later than the other cases that have
been described. So the statement, which is true, that he
had not been convicted again by September 1939 has no
great value.

T. U. was charged with indecent exposure on a public
common. For legal assistance he went to a local solicitor,
who by frequent experience of practising before me, knew
my general line of thought. There was a plea of ' Guilty '
and the solicitor made a strong appeal for psychological
treatment ; he assured me that T. U. was willing to co-
operate in every way, that he realized the dangers of his
weakness and that he wanted to become normal. (Some
time afterwards this solicitor in private conversation told
me that it was only with considerable difficulty that he
persuaded T. U. to realize that the facts involved the
necessity for treatment.) T. U. had been happily married
for two years. He and his wife had decided not to have
a child for some time until his position improved ; at the
time of his arrest he was a clerk in safe employment earning

£5 a week; his wife was also in employment. T. U. was 26 years old.

When T. U. was challenged by the police, he had admitted not only the offence that had just taken place, but also that on many previous occasions he had exposed himself. His method was to sit on his bicycle outside a place where girls passed regularly and to expose himself when girls went by.

During a fortnight's remand on bail the probation officer ascertained two facts of considerable importance in the case. T. U. and his wife had been regularly practising *coitus interruptus* (withdrawal), a method of birth control that is widespread, but universally condemned by medical opinion. Secondly, T. U. had been greatly worried for a long time at his work; he considered himself persecuted by his departmental chief, who, he said, strongly disliked him. These two factors had, the probation officer reported, produced a morbid and nervous condition. Another interesting, but obvious, fact was that T. U. wore somewhat flashy clothes.

A probation order was made with the usual term. By this time the probation officers at my court had established contact with Dr. Court in the neighbourhood. Dr. Court was, as usual, willing to do his best for T. U., who seemed eager to be helped.

Unfortunately T. U.'s wife was not at all helpful. To the probation officer, she persistently asserted the innocence and wrongful conviction of her husband; she apparently preferred the role of the wife of an ill-treated man to that of the wife of a psychological patient. So the probation officer wisely refrained from further home visits, feeling that the home situation should be deferred until the doctor could report a definite improvement in T. U.

Happily T. U.'s conviction did not involve his discharge from employment, so one of the greatest difficulties in such cases at that time was non-existent. Luck was with us, for during the treatment T. U.'s departmental superior was promoted and no longer was the boss of our patient. This fact helped a great deal in the recovery.

After many treatments, taking several months, Dr. Court

was able to report that there now seemed a complete absence of desire in T. U. to repeat his offending conduct. The position at home had been frankly discussed between doctor and patient. The probation officer pointed out to T. U. that on his wages he and his wife could afford to have a child. We ascertained that Dr. Court had warned T. U. of the dangers of *coitus interruptus*. At the end of the probation period T. U. seemed happier and more confident. He professed gratitude for what had been done for him and even sent a message of thanks to me.

The last that we heard of him was six months after the expiration of his probation order. All was well then.

A Challenge

Many other cases could be quoted where the origin of sexual offences lay in unsatisfactory sexual relations between man and wife. One more must be described, mainly for the reason that it illustrates other practical problems mentioned in this book.

G. D. was a married man of 34 who pleaded ' Not Guilty ' to a charge of indecent exposure in a public park. When I had found him guilty on the facts, I learned that two park-keepers had been watching G. D. for several days in consequence of complaints from the public. There were two previous convictions for similar offences, one six years previously which had resulted in six weeks in prison with ' hard labour ' ; the other conviction was a few weeks after his discharge from prison and resulted in a sentence of two months in prison with ' hard labour '. So G. D. could have been sent to Quarter Sessions as an ' Incorrigible Rogue '. Both the probation officer and I felt that G. D. was a challenge to us.

In view of the previous sentences, I felt that we should have the opinion of the medical officer in the remand prison ; so G. D. was remanded for a week in custody. We sent such information as we could collect to the prison. After the week a report came to the effect that there was in G. D.

no trace of insanity or mental deficiency and that probably the unsatisfactory marital relations between G. D. and his wife were bound up with his offences.

It was difficult for the probation officer to get at the truth about the marital relations. Husband and wife gave inconsistent accounts. What seemed clear was that of the wife's three pregnancies two had been difficult and that the last one had caused some physical injury. Both husband and wife had wisely been trying in consequence of this to avoid another pregnancy, but, as so often happens, nobody had told them how this could be achieved without harm. G. D. told the probation officer that he had avoided sexual intercourse for some time ; his wife complained of his using withdrawal.

I was informed that the three children looked well fed but dirty and that the wife was untidy ; the home, in a poor neighbourhood, was not as clean as it might have been and showed signs of neglect. At the time of his last arrest G. D. was in work and through the efforts of the probation officer the employer continued the employment.

Obviously the only constructive course was to enlist medical aid. I was not optimistic, but the big fact was that prison had failed twice to make G. D. a harmless member of the community. I felt that cure was not likely, but that possibly the right doctor could strengthen G. D. sufficiently to make him reasonably safe. G. D. was willing to go to the Institute for the Scientific Treatment of Delinquency, so we fixed up the appointments. A probation order was made.

A preliminary report came to the effect that G. D. was of low mental capacity, capable of unskilled labour only. The urge to expose himself was stated to be so strong that ' the idea of prison never occurred to him '. Unfortunately there was pressure at the Institute and delay could not be avoided. Two months after the probation order was made, the probation officer came to me in distress. He had only been able to persuade G. D. with great difficulty to accept treatment and now such enthusiasm as had been generated

8

had evaporated. G. D. had been examined by three different experts, but there had been no psychologieal treatment. As I knew the authorities at the Institute personally, I got busy and two weeks later treatment began.

G. D. attended regularly for six weeks and then the psycho-therapist reported that owing to the 'limited intelligence and imagination' of G. D. the treatment had had to be one of suggestion and that he was 'more hopeful of some success than at first seemed possible'. The treatment continued for a little longer and the final verdict was that 'a repetition of the offence is much less probable than it would have been without treatment'.

While G. D. was having his treatment Mrs. G. D. was told of philanthropic birth-control centres. Their existence was news to her, but very welcome news. She was given an introduction to one such centre where the physical defects of women are also seen to. Mrs. G. D. duly went and appeared very grateful.

G. D. went through his year of probation without causing further trouble and I was hopeful that he would never trouble the police again. As prison did not stop him from repeating his offence within a few weeks of his release, I felt that we had had some success.[1]

A Persistent Thief

The crime of which X. Y. was charged was a minor one, the theft of 2s., but when I found him guilty, it was soon obvious that there had been innumerable previous thefts which had not resulted in criminal proceedings.

[1] Previous sentences to prison should never be regarded as a reason why psycho-therapy should not be tried. I have had many successes with such men besides those included here. Another is worth mention. D. B. was fined £5 in 1922 for exhibitionism, £20 in 1927, and was sentenced to 3 months hard labour in 1933. In 1942 he appeared before me and pleaded guilty. All his offences had been the same. Dr. Court gave a hopeful prognosis and undertook treatment. After a year the prognosis was still more favourable.

X. Y. was a lad of 18, employed for errands by a shop-keeper. He came from a respectable home in a provincial town and was the youngest of six children. He had done so well at his elementary school that he obtained a scholar-ship to the local Grammar School. Both his parents were living, but his father, an epileptic, had been in and out of Ministry of Pensions hospitals since 1915 after war service. X. Y. had been born subsequent to the appearance of his father's disability. Prior to the Great War the parents had kept a shop. There had been no trouble with any of the older children.

At 15 X. Y. had been expelled from school for dishonesty. His head master reported that he had ability and intelligence slightly above the average, that he was reasonably industrious, but utterly dishonest. In consequence of this he had been sent to a Boys' Home. There he remained for two years, earning a very good character ; there was no record of any stealing then. From the Home X. Y. obtained employ-ment (he was then 17), but was discharged within three months for dishonesty. In his next employment various complaints of small monetary losses had been made, but nothing could be proved. The theft for which he appeared before me was not in connection with his employment, but the employer refused to take X. Y. back owing to his sus-picions of earlier thefts.

To the probation officer, X. Y. admitted having been unable to resist the temptation to steal money since the age of 11 or 12 ; also that he had always taken small sums, even while at the Boys' Home. He said that in his last job he had had ample pocket money for himself and had used the stolen money for treating his friends to amusement.

I sent X. Y. for a week in custody while contacts were being established. On reception the medical officer, with-out any request from me (we had then no reason to ask for one), observed a psychological condition which needed further study. He wisely wrote to me about this and reported that X. Y. was suffering from a psychological abnormality for which treatment was necessary.

A twelve months probation order was made and X. Y. agreed to live for six months at a philanthropic boys' hostel from where he would go daily out to work. He would pay part of the cost of his keep out of his wages, and would come under excellent moral influences in the hostel. The superintendent of the hostel was told of the recommendation about psychological treatment and happily agreed to co-operate. It was arranged that X. Y. should attend at the Institute for the Scientific Treatment of Delinquency for examination. Shortly afterwards a report was received from the Institute which contained the following :

This patient has been examined both mentally and physically. There is no physical disease present. . . .
No evidence was discovered of psychotic or neurotic symptoms, apart from the impulse to steal money. This appears to be an abnormal manifestation in which the sight of money arouses an impulse to take it (not in itself an abnormal thing, but abnormal here because accompanied by an unusual degree of anxiety which is increased when he attempts to control the impulse). This suggests that he belongs to the group of obsessional neurotics, although no other signs of an obsessional neurosis were found. He is the type of case who should react well to psychological treatment, though it may need to be prolonged.

Treatment was accordingly arranged through the Institute. Meanwhile X. Y. had obtained work through the hostel and was earning £1 per week. He seemed to be very happy in the hostel. He was visited at the hostel by his mother and his brother.

Then occurred an event which may have had beneficial effects on X. Y.'s outlook on life. He experienced himself something of what for years he had been inflicting on others ; he had a suit stolen from him and also his Post Office Savings book, which showed a credit of £3 14s. Not long afterwards £3 was drawn out fraudulently, presumably by the thief. X. Y. and the superintendent did not see eye to eye about replacing the losses. The hostel provided a new suit, as that was necessary.

When X. Y. left the hostel, he was earning £1 15*s*. a week at his work. He went into lodgings recommended by the hostel and paid 25*s*. a week for his board and lodging. A few weeks later he was put on piece-work, which raised his weekly earnings to £2 10*s*.

After six and a half months a second report was received from the Institute that the doctor was satisfied with X. Y.'s regular attendances and that the thieving originated with his success in the elementary school; at the Grammar School X. Y. had associated with the sons of people in a much better financial position than X. Y.'s parents and he had stolen continually from his fellows in order to be equal with them. The report continued :

On admission he was rather graceless in manner, careless in dress, and had a very spotty complexion. He had one admitted lapse in the first six weeks of treatment, but showed much interest in the talks at interviews and seemed to gradually develop a much better ideal of life. He is now doing quite well . . . and, having lost his spots, is becoming a well-set-up young man. . . . He bids fair to become a useful and law-abiding young man. I should like to see this boy again in about three months time.

In the tenth month of probation X. Y. was earning on piece-work £3 6*s*. and was living in a boarding-house with other young men, greatly enjoying the companionship. He was becoming very keen on table-tennis and darts. Soon afterwards, however, his employers became slack and earnings dropped to 28*s*. a week. X. Y. then applied on his own to be trained by a big firm of multiple shops where the welfare work is good and where there are good prospects. Unfortunately he was not candid about the troubles in the past and when the replies to references came in, X. Y. was refused. If he had only consulted his probation officer, these difficulties would probably have been surmounted. Too late the probation officer heard of the situation and tried to put it right, but the firm, not surprisingly, took the view that, as X. Y. had not been candid at the start, others should be given the chance.

At the end of the year of probation X. Y. had acquired a girl friend and, possibly through her influence, expressed a desire to join one of the fighting services.   The services, while maintaining their high standards for recruits, are often willing to stretch a point by disregarding previous trouble if they are approached by a probation officer and, of course, told the full circumstances.   The probation officer got into touch with the recruiting authorities, told everything and was able to speak well of the progress that X. Y. had made. X. Y. was accepted and when we last heard of him he had served satisfactorily for about a year.   There had been no trouble.

About the time that X. Y. joined the service a follow-up enquiry was received from the Institute which was answered. An encouraging fact is that the file contains a very nice letter from a brother of X. Y. to the probation officer, thanking him warmly for all his care.

These cases illustrate a large number of points made in other chapters, but I shall make no attempt to point the moral.

CHAPTER 4

PUNISHMENT

The growing human being has to déform himself as well as form himself to fit into the world as he finds it, and he will often knock himself against some hard corners before the process is complete.

MISS MARGERY FRY [1]

No mere repressive measures for combating delinquency can possibly accomplish what a better type of general feeling for the values of socialised living might produce.

WILLIAM HEALY, M.D., and AUGUSTA F. BRONNER, PH.D. [2]

We should diligently read Samuel Butler's *Erewhon* and accustom ourselves to regard crime as pathological and the criminal as an invalid, curable or incurable. . . . If crime were not punished at all, the world would not come to an end any more than it does now that disease is not punished at all. . . . Punishment is a mistake and a sin.

BERNARD SHAW [3]

LESLIE STEPHEN recorded in his life of Sir James Fitzjames Stephen that that distinguished judge regarded it as right that the criminal law should be based on hatred for the criminal and that the judge regarded such hatred as a ' healthy, natural feeling '.[4]   That memory was justified, for Fitzjames Stephen himself recorded : ' I think it highly desirable that criminals should be hated, that the punishments inflicted upon them should be so contrived as to give expression to that hatred ; ' also : ' I think that the proper attitude of mind towards criminals is not long-suffering charity, but open enmity ; for the object of the

---

[1] From Miss Fry's contribution to *Penal Reform in England*, p. 130.
[2] *New Light on Delinquency and its Treatment*, p. 219.
[3] Preface to *English Prisons under Local Government*, by Sidney and Beatrice Webb.   [4] p. 423.

criminal law is to overcome evil with evil.'[1] Despite all the progress made this century in methods of dealing with delinquency, this is still to a large extent the theory of the criminal law and the attitude of public opinion. Throughout the centuries there has been a persistent endeavour to secure conformity with approved standards through coercion, fear, and punishment. This is the background and no one is likely to be a successful reformer of our penal methods unless he realizes that it is a modern conception that one of the functions of criminal courts is to try to cure the delinquents that come before them. Despite all the changes made during the present century, we are still far from the ideas propounded by Mr. Bernard Shaw in the quotation above, and are long likely to remain so.

Until the end of the last century only a few of those who studied the working of the criminal law scientifically were moved by any conception of reforming the guilty. Even so enlightened a student of criminology and penology as Beccaria (1738–94) wrote in his famous work *Dei Delitti* that ' another way to prevent crimes is to reward virtue ', thus assuming that criminal acts were always deliberate. Yet Beccaria expressed opinions so far ahead of his time that orthodoxy, both legal and theological, was outraged.[2] Other enlightened writers asserted that to deter people from criminal acts is the sole duty of courts. De Tocqueville (1805–59), an orthodox liberal of his day, wrote that ' the moral reform of the individual is a great thing for the religious man, but not for the statesman ; a political institution does not exist for the individual, but for the mass '. These opinions are well typified in the old story of the judge who said to a prisoner whom he was about to sentence to death for sheep stealing : ' You are not punished

[1] *History of the Criminal Law*, vol. 2, p. 179.
[2] Beccaria wrote this book at the age of 26 without any training in law or any experience of criminals ; he was much indebted to the ideas of others. In his *Three Criminal Reformers*, Mr. Coleman Phillipson said that *Dei Delitti* captivated the attention of Europe much more than did the voluminous lucubrations of theologians and publicists ' (p. 25).

for stealing sheep, but in order that sheep may not be stolen.' This was not only the view of the criminal law, but also of those who examined its working from a liberal standpoint. Thus Sir Samuel Romilly, though he devoted much of his life to penal reform, and in particular to the abolition of capital punishment for minor offences, declared in one of his famous speeches in the House of Commons, 9 May 1810:

They [the principles of punishment] may be divided into three classes. The principle of the first, is that punishment of the individual should operate on society in the way of terror ; the second is, to put it out of the power of the person offending to commit crimes in future, either for a certain time specified in the sentence, or for ever ; the principle of the third is the reformation of the offending party.[1]

Romilly believed that the reform of the offender could only be attempted when society had been protected against him ; this meant in his day that reform must be attempted in prison. But those who had practical experience of the effects of sentences to prison knew that reform in prison was doubtful. In 1847, twenty-nine years after Romilly's untimely death, Parliament appointed a Committee to investigate the everlasting subject of juvenile crime. The High Court judges were consulted and ' declared reform and imprisonment to be a contradiction in terms and utterly irreconcilable. They expressed a doubt as to the possibility of such a system of imprisonment as would reform the offender and yet leave the dread of imprisonment unimpaired.' Thus the deterrent effect of imprisonment was the essential, and the reformation of the offender was only to be tried so far as it was consistent with deterrence. This last quotation comes from the book, *The English Prison System*,[2] by Sir Evelyn Ruggles-Brise, whose appoint-

---

[1] Quoted from the *Life* by C. G. Oakes, p. 224.
[2] p. 89. This book was printed by prisoners in Maidstone Prison. The main life work of this great Prison Commissioner was to set up the Borstal system, which endeavours to combine deterrence and detention with a real education on constructive lines.

ment as chairman of the Prison Commission was a call from the Government of the day for the more constructive treatment of adolescent offenders. But even in the Borstal system the defence of the community is a prior consideration to the welfare of the individual.

The belief that criminal courts should make it a primary aim wherever possible to cure their delinquents arose slowly at the end of the nineteenth century. So however keen we may be to secure the widespread acceptance of this idea, it is desirable that we should realize that in putting it forward we are challenging opinions held and worked out at least from the time of Plato to the beginning of this century. It is right to refuse to be daunted by the fact that what is desired has not existed before, but it is also wise to appreciate the vastness of the change that we are advocating. For human nature differs little from what it has been for many centuries past. If we accept the doctrine of the inherited unconscious, then some modesty is called for in those who, like myself, want to see criminal courts devote themselves as much as possible to curative work. Courts cannot pursue a policy that would only fit a nation of highly civilized beings ; they have to wrestle with the fact that the unconscious urges of the vast majority of human beings are akin to those of the savage. This truth was well set out by Dr. C. G. Jung in an essay on ' The Spiritual Problem of Modern Man '.[1]

The man whom we can with justice call ' modern ' is solitary. He is so of necessity and at all times, for every step towards a fuller consciousness of the present removes him further from his original '*participation mystique*' with the mass of men— from submersion in a common unconsciousness. Every step forward means an act of tearing himself loose from that all-embracing, pristine unconsciousness which claims the bulk of mankind almost entirely.

Thus when the great Italian criminologist Cesare Lombroso (1835–1909) asked the question, in his famous work

[1] In *Modern Man in Search of a Soul*, p. 227.

Crime, Its Causes and Remedies : ' What sort of justice is
that which punishes a man less for the crime he has committed than to serve as an example to others ? ' [1] I fear
that the answer must be that this sort of justice is to some
extent inevitable in a world that is not generally on a sufficiently high mental or emotional level to appreciate a system
of purely curative justice. The community is almost
completely non-psychologically minded and could not either
understand, or refrain from abusing, a system of justice
wherein the needs of offenders were the sole consideration
of those who have to sentence them.

No definite rules can be laid down to indicate when
punishment is necessary. But it is certain that in our
time a criminal court will never be able to concern itself
only with the interests of delinquents. Courts, unlike
psychologists, are concerned with the community at large,
not solely with an individual delinquent. For instance,
if a boy is caught stealing, it may well be that a wise parent
is able to prevent further thefts by wise admonition coupled
with an increase in the boy's pocket money. Or if a young
man has such an urge to drive a car that he takes his father's
car without permission, the best cure may be a gift of a motor
cycle which will satisfy his urge for speed. But if that
young man takes somebody else's car, and that somebody
else complains to the police, a court cannot effect a cure
in this way ; in the interests of the public the court will
probably have to prevent the young man from driving at
all. Many unruly boys at school have been cured by being
made prefects by understanding teachers, but in criminal
courts when our sentence in fact results in a delinquent
being better off than before his crime, and these things
happen more often than is known, we take care to hide
our light under a bushel. We must do so, for we cannot
advertise rewards for crime. Our main function is to
safeguard as much as we can the welfare of the community.

Real danger to the community is involved in the operations
of such people as the fraudulent financier or solicitor, the

[1] American Modern Criminal Science Series edition, p. 383.

motorist who kills or maims when driving under the influence of alcohol, the maker of counterfeit coin, the postman
or railwayman who steals, and so on *ad infinitum*. Here
again is evident the clash between law and psychology.
Progress involves, not the immediate supersession of the
legal by the psychological view, but such a gradual improvement in the condition of society that by slow stages the
psychological view can be safely adopted.

The strongest argument against those who, like Bernard
Shaw, assert that criminal courts should concentrate upon
the needs of the offender, lies in cases of murder. In some
cases a psycho-therapist would find it easier to cure a murderer than, for example, a sexual pervert. Some murderers
could safely be placed on probation ; sometimes even the
supervision of a probation officer would not be necessary
to prevent a repetition of the crime. But society deals
drastically with murderers, regardless of their individual
interests, with the sole object that there shall be as few
murders as possible. Without entering into that somewhat minor question of capital punishment, which occupies
so much attention that would be far better directed to
more important penological problems, it is safe to say that
drastic punishment will long remain necessary in cases of
murder. But the arguments that apply to murder cannot
be excluded from many other serious crimes.

It has always to be remembered that penological theories
must be valid in foul weather as well as in fair. It was for
this reason that experience in criminal courts during the
war of 1939 was valuable ; those on the Bench who may
have had Erewhonian theories, if any, must have had
considerable difficulty in dealing with many of those who
committed crimes associated with war conditions. It may
be useful if I briefly set out some of the crimes which were
dealt with in the South-Western court during the earlier
war years, either finally or for committal to Quarter Sessions
or the Central Criminal Court : an organized gang who
looted from bombed premises ; a number of men and
women who obtained considerable sums of money from

Public Assistance funds by falsely claiming that their homes had been bombed ; several men who separately obtained from a ' black market ' forged identity cards and were thus able to cover up their desertion from the army for years on end ; men and women who, finding that their food rations were inadequate (owing to their own bad management and lack of imagination) stole large quantities of rationed foods ; men who obtained petrol for private use from supplies provided solely for use on war work, and so on almost indefinitely. Delinquents of this sort were utterly selfish, blind to national needs and the needs of others. To have dealt with them by any method other than severe punishment would have rendered abortive many of the restrictions imposed of necessity by governmental orders. So urgent did the necessity for severe punishment become in some cases that in March 1942 a special Order in Council was issued.[1] This even went the length of providing minimum fines for certain offences ' unless having regard to any special circumstances ' a court decided that the minimum penalty should not be enforced. The Order also extended the penal powers of magistrates' courts ; the maximum of six months' imprisonment for a single offence was raised to twelve for ' black market ' cases. Another drastic invasion of long-cherished constitutional principles was that in certain cases defendants were to be found guilty unless they proved that they did not know, or had no reason to believe, that a transaction was criminal. In a circular from the Home Office magistrates were exhorted to ' do all they properly can to eradicate the evil [of the ' black market '] by imposing on persons found guilty of such offences penalties of a deterrent character '.[2] Such experiences cannot be dismissed by the argument that war is essentially different from times of peace ; there is always a need to enforce the law, and law-breakers are often a menace to the community, even in the quietest of times.

[1] Order in Council, dated 19 March 1942, amending regulations 55 and 90 of the Defence (General) Regulations, 1939.
[2] Circular of 21 March 1942.

Anarchy would be the result of dealing with all delinquents in accordance with what is best for them. At all times experience shows that the standards set by the law would be extensively ignored without the sanctions which criminal courts impose. A useful example are those minor breaches of the law which lawyers term *mala quia prohibita*, in contrast to the actions which are inherently and among civilized peoples universally wrong, the *mala in se*. It cannot be disputed that the lesser breaches would be far more frequent if unpleasant consequences did not follow. The traffic laws are an example. When Parliament was forced by experience to re-impose speed limits for mechanical vehicles in built-up areas, probably the majority of motorists conformed because either they were convinced of its wisdom or because they did not wish to disobey the law. But powers in criminal courts to impose fines for breaches, to endorse licenses, and, on repetition, to forbid a motorist to drive at all, were essential, making reasonable motorists more careful and punishing the unreasonable minority. That this is so was also proved by experience during the war of 1939. At one time it was necessary, owing to air raids, for the police to ignore the minor traffic laws and concentrate upon more urgent problems. Results were lamentable, and as soon as possible it was necessary for police control, prosecutions, and punishments to be restored.

This principle applies also in another vital aspect of life. Social conditions would be strange indeed if the law refrained from some forms of compulsion, and punishment where necessary, to restrain men's sexual activities. If men could freely escape when they desert their wives and children, leaving them to be maintained by the community, or if no steps could be taken against the fathers of illegitimate children, then social conditions would inevitably deteriorate. Nature endows man with almost unlimited powers of procreation, so that any removal of restraints and punishments would play havoc with the interests of women and children.

It seems clear, therefore, that there are comparatively few who have yet reached such a stage of maturity that they can negotiate safely the stairs of life without the support of the banisters of law and punishment.

Wise punishment not only acts as a deterrent to those who are punished and to those who hear or read of the punishment, it often satisfies the unconscious needs of the delinquent. He understands punishment, and if his punishment is such as to win his approval, as it should, then he is on the road to rehabilitation. It is one of the elementary tenets of psychology that every one is fearful of his own aggressive urges ; this feeling is often unconscious. The absence of punishment for a proved or admitted offence can easily increase this fear. Thus delinquents may even resent the denial to them of the strengthening experience which punishment by a power stronger than themselves would involve. Among the women in Holloway Prison who were investigated by Dr. Grace Pailthorpe some definitely resented the fact that at the beginning of their criminal career no punishment was given them. ' I have seen many prisoners who had been put on probation who have declared that probation was the cause of their downfall. They feel that if at the very first they had been given a severe lesson, it would have stopped them, but being put on probation had made them think that it would not matter much what they did.' [1] Probation should not, I agree, have this effect, but in fact it often does. This is because the probation law was built on false foundations.[2]

It is the function of a criminal court to be the stern father. The probation officer should in effect be the kindly mother. Many failures among those placed on probation were, in my opinion, caused because the false sentimentality of the law of probation has tempted courts to act the part of the kindly mother. The probation system has done far more good than harm ; it provides the machinery, as has been shown, whereby psycho-therapy can be given to delinquents while they remain at liberty.

[1] *What We Put in Prison*, p. 29.
[2] Namely, the old system of ' binding over ' or, more strictly, of ' entering into recognizances '.

But the system would have done more good and less harm if from the beginning the law had combined constructive punishment with probation. When Mr. Herbert (Lord) Samuel [1] on 8 May 1907, introduced into the House of Commons the Bill that became the Probation of Offenders Act, 1907, he explained that probation 'was a milder form of punishment than imprisonment'. Thus he obviously intended probation to be a modern and humane form of punishment. But the language of the Bill was settled by those who had other intentions. They excluded all powers of punishment from the probation system. They were mainly in touch with those whose principal interests lay in juvenile crime. (Juvenile Courts were established by an Act of Parliament of the following year.) Had the Home Office been more in touch with those on the Bench whose experience lay with adolescent and adult delinquents, the great mistake of making probation and punishment mutually exclusive would not have been made. Whether it was wise to exclude from probation power to punish those under 16 (later 17) is a question that I cannot answer, being inexperienced in juvenile courts. I have my doubts. But I am convinced by experience that for those over these ages the separation of punishment from probation had most unfortunate results. Probation can by law only be given with the consent of the delinquent. The real explanation of the ugly fact that the use of probation for delinquents over 16 varied from 0 per cent to 24 per cent in different districts lies, in my opinion, in the quite intelligible belief in many Benches that probation given with the consent of the delinquent and without punishment is not suitable treatment. Such a view is encouraged by the further provision of the law that probation awarded in magistrates' courts does not even involve a conviction, an anomalous feature of the law that has been denounced by the High Court.[2] One most unfortunate result of this

[1] Lord Samuel was then Under-Secretary of State at the Home Office.
[2] In *Oaten* v. *Auty*, [1919] 2 K.B., p. 278.

non-use of probation has been that many young people between the ages of 16 and 21 got sent to ordinary prisons; most unsuitable places for them. In 1938 no less than 1,226 such delinquents went to prison, a third of them without any previous known offence. (In 1932, the similar figure was 2,653.) 120 of these young delinquents were 17 or under. I should not have slept at nights if any of these had been sentenced by me.

It would have been far better if from the beginning probation had involved a conviction [1] and if constructive punishment could have been given at the same time. Another unfortunate result of the absence of these possibilities has been that a dangerous idea has been spread abroad by the probation system in the areas where probation has been much used that every ' first offender ' (who in fact may be a hardened criminal) is entitled to probation. I have often heard such delinquents, confident of being released on probation, say that they have made plans for the week following their appearance before me. A woman probation officer at the South-Western court once told me that when she went to see two young women shop-lifters in the court cells and opened the conversation with the friendly remark, ' I'm sorry you are in trouble,' the reply was : ' Trouble ? This is our first offence.' People seem to believe both that every dog is entitled to his first bite and that every offender is entitled to a ' first ' crime without punishment. Both beliefs are false.

I agree that supervision for a year is an invasion of the private life of an offender that can be irksome ; also that some unpleasant things can be done in the name of probation, such as payment of costs and restitution, &c. But often there is no loss and no legal expense. It seems almost ridiculous that courts cannot fine delinquents and at the same time place them under supervision.

---

[1] Although technically delinquents placed on probation in magistrates' courts are not convicted, most of the consequences of conviction follow. Thus the police enter the case in their records and report the offence to the next court, if any, before whom the delinquent appears.

There are happily cases where it is wise for the court to use probation only with the consent of the delinquent. It would, for instance, be folly for a court to make a probation order containing a clause that the delinquent shall submit to medical treatment as directed, unless the delinquent has shown that he is willing to co-operate. Apart from the cases needing psychological treatment, there are some delinquents sufficiently mature to be given a free choice whether they will accept the responsibilities which probation involves or not. (Such delinquents, being more mature, are not likely to refuse.) In his book, *The Origins of Love and Hate*, Dr. Ian D. Suttie wrote that ' the efficacy of a prohibition is the greater, the more the prohibitor is loved, as well as feared '.[1] It may seem absurd for those on the criminal Bench to aspire to evoke the emotion of love ; but I have known cases where delinquents have developed a strong affection for their magistrate. Such affection is usually demonstrated to the probation officer ; messages of thanks to magistrates are often sent through him. In the fourth year of the war a young man called at the South-Western court and asked at the door to see me, as, he said, he wished to thank me. When I received this message, I told the police officer who brought it to bring the young man to my room, but to stay, in case it was not thanks that the young man wished to give me. But the young man was genuine. I cannot repeat all that he said, but he was candid that for over three years he had remembered me and the words that I had used to him, and that that recol-lection had helped to keep him straight. ' I'm on embarka-tion leave now, sir,' he said, ' and I don't want to go to the front without shaking hands with you and thanking you.'[2] I think that that was the proudest moment of my years as magistrate. I looked up the young man's papers, kept by the probation officer, and found that several

---

[1] p. 99.
[2] The young man had been before the war in a gang of car stealers and richly deserved six months in prison. It was doubt-less the probation officer who had led me to give him his chance.

times it was recorded that he had sent messages to me; also that on one occasion he had written to me. It is impossible for magistrates in busy courts to remember many individual cases, and I regret that I had forgotten this case. But whatever good I had done to this young man (he was not in the army when I dealt with him), he did far more good to me.

Dr. Suttie's standard should be the ideal of all on the criminal Bench, but my realist outlook prevents me from saying that the average delinquent is capable of benefiting from unadulterated leniency. Most delinquents placed on probation accept it mainly because probation means that there will be no imprisonment unless they misbehave further. Their 'consent' has little value. It requires a bigness of character, and of soul, to appreciate the absence of punishment for a serious crime. Forgiveness, conditional or otherwise, places a heavy moral burden upon the delinquent, and many of those dealt with by probation are not sufficiently mature to carry this burden. G. K. Chesterton once wrote in a newspaper article that nobody wants to be publicly punished, but that most of us would prefer that to being publicly forgiven. There was much psychological truth in that remark. I agree that punishment can be dangerous in that the delinquent may regard it as absolving his guilt to the extent that he can begin again with crime with a clear conscience. But such delinquents are probably irreclaimable, whatever steps are taken by their courts. It is my firm belief that if the teaching of modern psychology had been appreciated in the Home Office when the Probation Act was on the anvil, much attention would have been given (as it was when the Bill of 1938–9 was prepared) to working out constructive forms of punishment; but such punishments should be linked up with the probation system.[1] Shakespeare understood the dangers of leniency. The First Senator says in *Timon of Athens* that ' nothing emboldens sin as much as mercy '.[2]

[1] The Bill of 1938–9 did not propose to do this.
[2] Act III, scene 5.

Modern psychologists can explain why this is often true.

The psychologist or social enthusiast who condemns punishment is planning for an ideal world peopled by those who have attained standards of psychological maturity. When I meet such a one, my reply is to offer a day in court with me. It is a characteristic of most opponents of punishment that they have never had the responsibility of administering justice in a criminal court. A good example is the well-known American sociologist Harry Elmer Barnes. Though his activities are set out in one of the longest biographies in *Who's Who*, there is no indication that at any time he had to handle delinquents and decide their fate in public. Dr. Barnes's highly stimulating book, *The Story of Punishment*, has in it many diatribes against punishment, but he based his objections on theoretical grounds of determinism rather than on experience. Thus :

The human animal finds his conduct and his thoughts determined by the combined influences of his biological heredity and his social surroundings. There is not the slightest iota of choice allowed to any individual. . . . Conduct can be modified only by alterations in the organism or by the introduction of new or different social influences and forms of stimulation.[1]

When reading such expressions of opinion one can only wonder how on such lines the practical work of a magistrates' court could be carried out. Even so advanced a thinker of modern times as Havelock Ellis repeated with approval the ancient story of the English judge in a case of theft where kleptomania was set up as a defence. The judge said : ' Yes, that is what I am sent here to cure.' Havelock Ellis, who wrote from the point of view of anthropology rather than of psychology, added that ' we need not hesitate to accept this conception of the function of the court ' ; for it was his belief that ' self-control may be educated ' and that punishment, if ' scientific, effectual, and humane ', can be educative.[2] Modern psychologists of to-day realize

[1] p. 250.
[2] *The Criminal*, revised edition of 1900, p. 357.

this. Thus I once heard Dr. R. D. Gillespie of Guy's Hospital state that in his opinion it was wrong to ' say that in modern psychology punishment has no useful place. It has : but its method and place has to be carefully considered in each instance, and it should never be the only remedy prescribed.'[1] My personal contacts with psychotherapists have been sufficient to enable me to say that in expressing these opinions Dr. Gillespie can be regarded as representative of many modern psychologists who have been engaged in the actual work of trying to cure delinquents.[2]

One of the hardest tasks of any one sitting with authority on a criminal Bench is to decide when the interests of the offender can safely be regarded as paramount and when the public interest demands his punishment. This conflict between the interests of the individual offender and those of the community is not generally realized by those interested in penological reform. Thus Mr. Leo Page once wrote that ' the object of punishment in all cases is the protection of society ',[3] and that the reformation of the offender is but one means of protecting the community. I distrust all such generalizations and feel confident that Mr. Page would change this opinion if he could sit daily in a busy court. Any concentration on the protection of society would necessitate many sentences of permanent incarceration. For undoubtedly there are some men and women who will never accommodate themselves to the laws and conventions of human society. A large number of writers on penology have urged the permanent detention of the hopeless criminals.[4] Some writers on penology have even

[1] In a paper written for the Howard League.
[2] Dr. J. R. Rees, medical director of the Tavistock Clinic and a well-known practising psycho-therapist, once said that ' sometimes prison may prove a valuable and necessary method of treatment for older people '—*The Psychological Aspect of Delinquency* by various contributors, p. 40.
[3] *Crime and the Community*, p. 81.
[4] e.g. Lombroso, his pupil Baron Garafalo, Professor Saleilles, all of whose main writings have been re-published in the American Modern Criminal Science Series.

discussed the painless extinction of the hopeless.[1]   But as public opinion is not likely to accept such strong measures, the prolonged incarceration of many criminals cannot be avoided.

Amateur enthusiasts in penology have suggested that largely because of the Freudian doctrine of sense of guilt there should be a psychologist in attendance at all criminal trials.   This is going too far in the present stage of our development.   It needs to be realized that even qualified medical psycho-therapists are not necessarily better than experienced men and women on the Bench at quickly spotting during trials those cases which would benefit from psychological treatment.   Doctors have no more second sight than have magistrates or judges.   The presence of a psychologist at trials may be an ultimate ideal, but for a long time to come the great need will be that full inquiries after verdict shall take place, as urged in Chapter 6.

This difficult doctrine of sense of guilt is one into which I cannot go in any detail.   Suffice it to say that Freud taught that a strong sense of guilt can be the cause, as well as the result, of a criminal action.   Thus :

It was a surprise to find that exacerbation of this unconscious sense of guilt could turn people into criminals.   But it is undoubtedly a fact.   In many criminals, especially youthful ones, it is possible to detect a very powerful sense of guilt which existed before the crime, and it is not, therefore, the result of it but its motive.   It is as if it had been a relief to be able to fasten this unconscious sense of guilt on to something real and immediate.[2]

And again in regard to a case :

The analytic work then afforded the surprising conclusion that such deeds are done precisely because they are forbidden,

[1] e.g. Enrico Ferri in *Criminal Sociology* ;   George Ives in *A History of Penal Methods* ;   Albert Morris in *Criminology*.

[2] From *The Ego and the Id*, quoted in Rickman's Summary, p. 269.

and because by carrying them out the doer enjoys a sense of mental relief. He suffered from an oppressive feeling of guilt, of which he did not know the origin, and after he had committed a misdeed the oppression was mitigated. The sense of guilt was in some way accounted for.

Paradoxical as it may sound, I must maintain that the sense of guilt was present prior to the transgression, that it did not arise from this, but contrariwise—the transgression from the sense of guilt. . . .

With children it is easy to perceive that they are often naughty on purpose to provoke punishment, and are quiet and contented after the chastisement. Later analytic investigation can often find a trace of the guilty feeling which bid them seek for punishment.[1]

This psycho-analytical principle was expressly challenged by Adler,[2] but I am inclined to follow Freud here. There have been cases of mine where a psycho-therapist has satisfied me that the criminal act was the consequence of an excessive sense of guilt. Those who have charge of delinquents should not be ignorant of the possibility, to put it no higher, that punishment may be in fact the very thing that the delinquent is seeking, usually unconsciously. Where that is so, kindness and understanding should be more effective than punishment.

How strong the compulsion arising in an unconscious sense of guilt can be, according to psycho-analytical principles, is well illustrated by Theodor Reik, who maintained that it constitutes the reason why so many criminals make mistakes leading to their detection and arrest. It is a well-established fact that many arrests occur because of apparently trivial mistakes made by the criminal.[3] To the detective who takes advantage of such mistakes they may

Quoted, ibid., pp. 116–17.

[2] See *Social Interest*, pp. 138 and 218.

[3] The notorious murderers Browne and Kennedy, who passed through South-Western Court on their way to the gallows, were convicted mainly through the ‘ carelessness ’ of Browne in leaving in the stolen car the revolver used to kill Police Constable Gutteridge.

denote mere carelessness, but to Reik they were ' indications of hidden mental processes, unknown to the ego, which find expression ' in that way. ' The man ', he wrote, ' who commits a crime without witnesses is the only one who knows about it, and it seems as if he were obliged to share this knowledge, even to impart it, as if he were unable to keep it to himself because of the growing mental tension urging him to betray it at any cost.' This mental process would be a manifestation of the unconscious desire for punishment. In a similar way Reik explained another strange characteristic of some criminals, their return to the scene of their crime. Thus if a murderer does this, such apparent folly would seem natural to Reik, for he would expect that one of the hidden motives for the crime is the murderer's ' longing, unknown to his ego, to give himself up to justice '.[1] Such a theory seems attractive ; at least it would explain much conduct which would otherwise be inexplicable. If it contains truth, it would seem that the police, as well as those on the Bench, would do well to study the teachings of Freud. In fact this would be of great value, since the greatest weakness of the police, visible in their daily work in criminal courts and also in their text books, is their failure to be adequately interested in criminal mentality. They study intensely the methods of criminals in committing their crimes, but, as it seems to me, they do not concern themselves with the problems, why criminals commit their crimes, or how they can best be prevented from continuing to commit them. In all my efforts to utilize psychology to remove the causes of criminal conduct I have always felt that the police were merely regarding me as peculiar ; they do not seem to me to worry about the trouble that might lie ahead for them if I gave a sentence of imprisonment, which however long, must terminate some day, often leaving the criminal in a worst state than before. Many of the teachings of psychology would materially help the police to reduce the volume of crime.

[1] *The Unknown Murderer*, pp. 71–5 and 87.

If we accept the psycho-analytical teaching that real dangers arise from an excessive guilt sense, a new meaning is given to Hamlet's great saying : ' Conscience doth make cowards of us all.' But it is more than cowards that conscience, in the form of the guilt sense, can make ; it can make us invalids and delinquents, strange though that may appear. Once the guilt sense and its dangers become accepted, the maxim of pedagogy will have to be the homely saying :

Cultivate a little vice ; just enough to make you nice.
Cultivate a little virtue ; just as much as will not hurt you.[1]

This doctrine is difficult for those unacquainted with Freud's teaching. But until it is accepted, there will always be a danger lest education in virtues, whether at home, in schools, or in penal institutions designed for the re-education of their inhabitants, will in some measure have the reverse effect. Education or re-education founded on repression and an excessive demand for obedience can have this result.

None the less, penal or correctional institutions, whether for children, adolescents, or adults, can, even as they are, justify themselves in some measure. This is mainly because in recent decades our penal system has incorporated many modern ideas and methods in places of detention, a process which began in the creation of Borstal Institutions. In an official publication, unfortunately not on sale to the public, the Borstal method was thus described :

The task is not to break or knead him into shape, but to stimulate some power within to regulate conduct aright, to insinuate a preference for the good and the clean, to make him want to use his life well, so that he himself, and not others, will save him from waste. It becomes necessary . . . to infect him

[1] Compare :
They say the best men are moulded out of faults ;
And, for the most, become much more the better
For being a little bad.
Measure for Measure, v, 1.

with some idea of life which will germinate and produce a character, controlling desire, and shaping conduct to some more glorious end than mere satisfaction or acquisition.

On these standards there is little danger of the sense of guilt operating to produce the reverse of what was intended.

In founding correctional institutions on these lines England has been a pioneer. Shortly before the war of 1939 Dr. William Healy, famous child psychiatrist in Boston, U.S.A., and Mr. Benedict Alper, a social worker of Boston, came to England mainly to examine the Borstal system.[1] Their impressions were published later in their book, *Criminal Youth and the Borstal System*. Here these experts paid a great tribute to the merits of the staff in Borstal Institutions and to the whole system adopted there. Their verdict was that ' unquestionably the results of the Borstal System are relatively much better than those obtained by the reformatories '[2] of the United States. It is because our Borstal Institutions are such that they can earn the praise of such experts as Dr. Healy and Mr. Alper that they achieve so many successes.[3] Failures there are in plenty, and they receive excessive publicity. But even among cases that at one time seemed hopeless some prove satisfactory in the end, as the records of the Borstal Association, which supervises the young men after they have left Borstal, definitely show.

Happily the spirit of the Borstal Institutions is slowly infecting some of our prisons. There has been a definite

[1] Few circumstances in that grim year gave me greater pleasure than the fact that soon after their arrival in this country Dr. Healy and Mr. Alper sought me out and discussed with me the problems which they had come to investigate. They spent several hours with me on the Bench. I had arranged to go to the United States in September 1939 to see something of the work of such men as Dr. Healy and Professor Glueck in Boston, Dr. Ira Wile of New York, and of Judge Joseph N. Ulman in Baltimore.

[2] p. 236.

[3] The same official (unpublished) publication just quoted claimed that ' about three out of every four are reclaimed '.

improvement in the quality and training of the men and women employed in our prisons ; some governors of Borstal Institutions have been transferred to the prisons ; a school for the training of prison staff has been established. The principle has been accepted that such staff should be much more than turnkeys ; many members of the staff become unconscious psychologists. In another direction educational classes have been introduced, and, best reform of all, ' unofficial visitors ' have been introduced to befriend and stimulate the prisoners in their gloomy ' free ' time. Of course our existing prison buildings hamper these reforms, but many old prisons may be pulled down before very long and replaced by institutions on modern lines.

Statistics show that a first sentence to prison is more often than not the last. Since 1930 the Prison Commission has kept a record of the subsequent history of all prisoners received into prison on conviction for ' finger-printable ' offences for the first time. (Roughly this means all serious crimes.) In 1930 there were in all 4,006 receptions into prison of persons without previous proved offences. Of these 3,265 had not again been sent to prison by the end of the year 1938—82 per cent.[1] This is seemingly a good record. I agree that a possible explanation is that a high proportion of these men, women, and youths (especially the youths) need never have been sent to prison at all. Yet I have known it happen that a sentence of imprisonment could cure a case when probation had failed. A case of this kind was B. L., whom I first met in matrimonial pro- ceedings. His wife brought him to my domestic court because for several years he had failed to maintain her and their children. From the evidence I found that her com- plaint was proved and that B. L.'s failure had been wilful. As B. L. was not then in work, I made a nominal order for maintenance. Some months later the wife again brought B. L. before me on the ground that he had paid her nothing since the order had been made. B. L. pleaded that he could not pay because he could not work, and that he could

[1] *Report of the Commissioners of Prisons for* 1938, pp. 18 and 130.

not work because he had an anxiety neurosis.   He used this
technical expression.   He had attended hospital on that
account and was now under a local doctor.   I was not
impressed, for anxiety neurosis is one of those psychological
conditions which can be disabling but frequently mean
little.   I felt that it was most unfortunate that B. L. had
ever learned the name of his trouble, but that nothing but
seemingly harsh treatment would help him.   I decided that
he could work if he wanted to, told him that I would not
believe that he could not work merely on his account of
his doctor's advice, and I increased the order to an amount
that would be of real assistance to his wife and children if
he would pay it.   After more months the wife summoned
B. L. again.   Again he had paid nothing and had not done
any sustained work.   I adjourned the case for the attendance
of B. L.'s doctor.   I was not impressed by the doctor's
evidence—he was not a psycho-therapist—but his support
of B. L.'s statements prevented me from drastic action.
Many months later B. L. was charged before me with crime.
On his conviction I no longer felt bound to refer to his
own doctor, but sent him to the Remand Prison for a
medical report.   The prison doctor, expert in neurotic
ailments, reported the following week that there was no
evidence of insanity, mental disorder, or nervous disorder.
I felt that a sentence of several months in prison offered the
only hope.   Many months after his release B. L. was once
more before me about arrears on his wife's maintenance
order.   I found that he had been working regularly for
many weeks and paying his order and was delighted that
at long last I could be kind to him.   B. L. told me with
complete frankness that he had learned to work in prison.
    Though I am convinced that sentences to prison cannot be
avoided in many cases, I firmly believe (as I hope this book
will show) in the principle that every possible alternative
should be thought of before a sentence to incarceration is
passed.   These alternative methods need to be developed,
and as they are developed and improved, sentences to
prison should decrease.   I firmly believe in the probation

system, despite its defects.[1]   I have often placed delinquents on probation although I realized that I was not acting in the best interests of the community.   I have done so because the only practicable alternative was a sentence to prison.

Experience has made me confident that gradually more and more delinquents, and in an ever-widening type of crime, will be sent to modern correctional institutions, residential or non-residential.   I am confident also that gradually more and more delinquents will be placed on probation in charge of psycho-therapists.   All concerned in any way with crime can take courage from the thought that 'not so many centuries ago hysteria still belonged to a domain other than medicine; it was a phenomenon on which only the law courts were supposed to be competent to pass judgment.   The woman suffering from hysteria was called a witch and she was punished as such. . . .   It is not improbable that our treatment of the criminal will undergo a similar change in future.'[2]

To end this necessarily somewhat gloomy chapter on a hopeful note, I would recall that since I was appointed a metropolitan magistrate in 1931 I have used the probation law to send many scores of delinquents to medical psycho-therapists.   The results, typified in the previous chapter, have been on the balance most encouraging.   At the South-Western court we have long been careful to fetch back to the court those delinquents on probation who are not obeying the terms of their probation order.   Before the war hardly a month ever went by without some applications from a probation officer for further court action.   But I have never yet had to fetch back to the court, for either warning or punishment, any one who was undergoing psycho-therapy. I have never had a report from the police that a further

[1] When in 1934 I went to work at South-Western Court, London, the number of men and youths on probation was about 40, of whom 30 had been dealt with by other courts.   When war broke out in 1939, the number was about 250.   In 1934 we had one male probation officer, but in 1939 we had four.

[2] *The Criminal, the Judge, and the Public*, by Dr. Franz Alexander and Hugo Staub, p. xiii.

offence had been committed during the probation period by any such cases. The experience of a single magistrate must be slight when the numbers of delinquents are con- sidered, but I would submit that this absence of trouble has some significance. The results of my efforts to apply psychological methods have encouraged me to try, try, and try again.

CHAPTER 5

FURTHER OBSTACLES

We must not overlook the fact that the prevention and cure of criminality, and of sexual delinquency, will not be effected by individual therapy alone. The social and economic pressure which precipitates these manifestations must also become the object of our attention.

DR. ERWIN WEXBERG [1]

Despite of education, heritable constitutional conditions prevail in the making of criminals. . . . Crime in this country is only to a trifling extent (if to any) the product of social inequality, of adverse environment, or of other manifestations of what may be comprehensively termed ' the force of circumstances '.

DR. CHARLES GORING [2]

A man of a certain constitution put in a certain environment will be a criminal.

PROFESSOR J. B. S. HALDANE [3]

EVER since the use of psycho-therapy for delinquents became practical there have been some who have regarded it almost as a panacea against crime. They have urged that the problem of crime would be solved if only enough delinquents could be given psychological treatment. Such enthusiasts deserve the criticism once made by Florence Nightingale about one of her friends who proffered help : ' She does not want to hear facts ; she wants to be enthusiastic.' One can be enthusiastic for the principle of sending as many delinquents as possible for psycho-therapy without jumping to Erewhonian conclusions. There is indeed much need for enthusiasm in those who struggle to make penology

[1] *Individual Psychology*, p. 169.
[2] *The English Convict*, abridged edition, pp. 274 and 212.
[3] In a foreword to *Crime as Destiny*, by Dr. Johannes Lange, p. 14.

as scientific as possible, but harm is done by undiscerning enthusiasm, based on theories, not on experience. Such enthusiasm deters those on the criminal Bench from interesting themselves, as they should, in the possibilities of cure through psycho-therapy.

I have said that some criminals are irreclaimable. This is probably due in large measure to their hereditary endowment. Such a statement will not be widely accepted to-day when the influence of environment is widely held to be of greater importance than that of heredity.[1]   But to believe that crime is the product of social or economic neglect is to cease to search in human nature for causes of crime that are in fact much more powerful.   Professor Sheldon Glueck, a believer in sound remedial measures, stated in one of his later books that ' as the history of crime shows, there are very probably some persons who would be found in the criminal classes in almost any social system '.[2]   Professor Haldane's opinion, quoted at the head of this chapter, was to a similar effect.   One of the greatest English experts in the causes of crime was Dr. Charles Goring, a medical officer in the prison service.   At the end of a prolonged investigation his conclusion was, as stated at the head of this chapter, that ' heritable constitutional conditions prevail in the making of criminals '.[3]   This conclusion was forced upon Dr. Goring by the facts as disclosed in the investigation.   It came as a surprise to him and could not, therefore, be the product of preconceived opinions.[4]

[1] An example of much popular opinion can be seen in Mr. Dan Griffiths's ' Reservation ' to the report of the Departmental Committee on Persistent Offenders (1932).
[2] Professor Sheldon Glueck of Harvard University has done more than any other modern authority to ascertain the effects of the various remedial measures.   This quotation comes from his book *Crime and Justice*, p. 265.
[3] *The English Convict*, abridged edition, p. 274.
[4] The influence of heredity in forming character is well explained in a book, *The Biological Basis of Human Nature*, by Professor H. S. Jennings of Johns Hopkins University.   This important problem will be developed further in my next book.

My own impression, derived mainly from reading innumerable reports from physicians and psycho-therapists about criminals whose immediate fate I had to decide, is fully in agreement with these opinions.

Those born with a bad heredity are in many cases born into families with low standards. It frequently happens that such children come into the world unwanted, by the working of natural laws without any conscious desire on the part of the parents. ' A good many children are accidentally born,' wrote Dr. Rees.[1] No one knew better than he the fatal effect in a child's outlook of a feeling of having been unwanted at birth ; this feeling, whether conscious or unconscious, can prevent a child from ever accepting normal standards of behaviour, if there is no remedial treatment in the early formative years. Goring wrote also that ' upon the evidence of our statistics we find the criminal to be unquestionably a product of the most prolific stocks '.[2] Many magistrates of experience could say the same. The experience of Professor Sheldon Glueck was also similar,[3] and many other authorities could also be cited.

Of course it is not true that large families necessarily consist of unwanted children. Far from it. Large families are a blessing to all concerned, and there should be many more of them in all economic levels, provided that each child was welcome on its arrival and received adequate love and care from its parents.

Almost every book on the psychology of criminals that I have read emphasizes the deadly influence of the broken home,[4] which deprives young children of the feeling of

[1] *The Health of the Mind*, p. 203. This is, of course, not restricted to those with poor heredity.
[2] *The English Convict*, p. 272.
[3] e.g. *One Thousand Juvenile Delinquents*, pp. 77–8 and 82.
[4] It was because I realized this influence so keenly that I did all that was possible to secure better and more humane conditions for the hearing of matrimonial cases in magistrates' courts. The Summary Procedure (Domestic Proceedings) Act, 1937, would be of enormous value if only all courts worked it in its spirit as well as in its letter.

10

security that is essential for their healthy psychological development. Unfortunately broken homes are by no means the monopoly of those with poor heredity. But when this loss of security is the fate of children with poor heredity, the results can be irreclaimable delinquents.

Another characteristic of those of bad stock is that they often have less power of control over their sexual impulses. They often have illegitimate children. Such children are sorely handicapped psychologically. ' Feeling about father . . . is the basis of our unconscious attitude towards all authority and law ', wrote Dr. Graham Howe.[1] Can we be surprised that illegitimate children, who usually grow up fatherless, bulk largely in records of crime ? Many experts in psychology emphasize the importance of this factor.[2]

If the children of those born of parents with defective hereditary endowment, or of parents who disliked their coming, or of parents who were not married, could be brought at early stages in their development to Child Guidance Clinics, and at short intervals kept in touch with psychological experts, then the chances of their leading useful lives would be greatly increased. But it can scarcely be expected of psycho-therapy that it can often undo the effects of these early handicaps, when those so born become patients of psycho-therapists in mid-life, after perhaps years of anti-social activity. In some cases the initial handicap is, I believe, so great that no curative measures at any age are likely to prove effective.[3]

Let us now turn to other obstacles that check the progress of psychological treatment in criminal courts. These are of an entirely different nature, some of them matters of procedure rather than impediments inherent in the delinquents themselves.

[1] *Motives and Mechanisms of the Mind*, pp. 99 and 117.
[2] e.g. Dr. W. A. Bonger in *Criminality and Economic Conditions,* American Modern Criminal Science Series edition, p. 494 ; Dr. Ira Wile in *The Challenge of Childhood*, p. 293, etc. I should mention that Dr. Healy's investigations do not support this view— *Delinquents and Criminals*, p. 122.
[3] These matters also will be dealt with fully in my next book.

A practical obstacle arises from the indisputable fact that there are many offences which show a high degree of psychological ill-health which the law regards as minor nuisances. Sometimes even drunkenness may be the outward and visible sign of acute psychological tension, but the maximum penalty for it is ten shillings for a first offence and forty shillings for repeated offences. The maximum penalty when a ' common prostitute ' has been found guilty of ' loitering and importuning passengers for the purposes of prostitution ' is ordinarily forty shillings. Yet such a woman, especially if young, may reveal in her desire for prostitution an acute emotional conflict ; she may be ruining her own life and jeopardizing the lives of others and she may be heavily infected with venereal disease. When a man and a woman are found in a public place in circumstances that indicate ' indecent conduct ', then again the penalty is ordinarily the same. Yet the woman may be a prostitute and the man be reacting to an acute emotional conflict in his domestic life. All these and many others may well need psychological treatment, but in many of these cases one is compelled to ask the question whether the law could place ' nuisances ' on the level of serious crimes and thus make possible legal control for several months. Dr. Hermann Mannheim would apparently countenance this :

The classical school of criminal law . . . was, on the whole, content to make the punishment fit the crime, without paying much attention to the personality of the criminal, whilst the modern sociological school tries to adapt the treatment to the individual needs of the offender. This change, whilst often implying greater leniency, may sometimes, on the contrary, lead to the imposition of long-term penalties for comparatively petty offences which would previously have been visited with much shorter sentences.[1]

This is dangerous ground, for the first requisite of a penal law is that public opinion will accept it as sound. Public opinion is immature from the psychological standpoint and is, therefore, very sensitive if penalties should appear more

[1] *The Dilemma of Penal Reform*, pp. 98–9.

severe than the circumstances would appear to justify. I have occasionally wished that in the interests of defendants I had greater powers in ' nuisance ' cases and could set in train all the procedure which we use in cases of serious crime —remand for medical examination, home visits, examination by a psycho-therapist, and so on. But I realize that in this type of case the law must limit compulsory powers and rely on our securing the same result by consent. This we can sometimes do, but unfortunately some bad cases refuse to respond and continue in their ways.

For all these nuisance cases the probation law is technically available, and sometimes it is useful. But it is difficult to apply the sanctions behind the probation law in cases where the original offence is punishable by a small fine only. It is true that a breach of probation can be met with a money penalty, but I doubt if the higher courts would approve, when there is a breach of a probation order, the imposition of a heavy penalty in cases where the original offence was punishable by forty shillings.

In many of these cases, if the standard that courts should adopt were either the interests of the individual or Mr. Leo Page's ' protection of society ', then some of those who are now fined a few shillings might have their liberty restricted for a long period. In fact these problems are frequently insoluble. They illustrate the truism that every advantage has some drawback ; we rightly cherish personal liberty and severely restrict the powers of criminal courts. Far be it from me to wish things otherwise, but let us at least face the undoubted fact that liberty for all must mean that some will so misuse it as to jeopardize their own lives and be a danger to others. The only way to avoid this is to menace the liberty of all, and that is too high a price to pay. If a man has been found guilty of drunkenness and nothing else, he cannot be compulsorily treated for his real psychological complaint. The old saying *in vino veritas* can be psychologically true. Drunkenness can release the controls of human conduct and can also indicate what forces are being controlled in normal life. None the less the law cannot authorize a man's compulsory treatment, or any course other than his punishment for drunkenness and such voluntary measures as he may be persuaded to accept.

This leads to another, and very real, obstacle in the way of the psychological treatment of delinquents. All schools of psychology are agreed that for psycho-therapy to be beneficial the co-operation of the delinquent is necessary, and this applies both to treatment in places of detention and to treatment at liberty. While formal confession of the crime, or of the need for treatment, is not necessary, to himself at least the offender must admit his offence. He must want to be cured. Yet a large proportion of offenders steadfastly refuse to admit their offence, even to themselves and even when they have been assured that it is hoped to avoid punishment. Their pride is at stake. Their assertion of innocence gives them satisfaction and enables them to seek sympathy from those around them. They will refuse to see a psycho-therapist or to co-operate in treatment. Yet they seldom manifest any desire to appeal against their conviction.

The way that some of these delinquents will behave is illustrated by C. P., a case of indecent exposure. I found C. P. guilty, despite his vigorous defence of mistaken identity. He continued his denials after the trial to the probation officer, who told him of the arrangements for cure that could be made. C. P. said, in a nonchalant sort of way, to the probation officer that he was willing to pay a visit to the Institute for the Scientific Treatment of Delinquency. When this was reported to me, I regarded such willingness as hopeful and made a probation order, but without my usual term about treatment ; I did not want to hurt C. P.'s feelings. Later I heard that C. P. was undergoing treatment and could only wonder. There was no repetition of the offence, and the year of probation had almost expired when I received a letter from C. P. He desired to reassure me of his complete innocence and added that, as his double was still in the district where he lived, he had moved to another part of London. The probation officer and I could only smile and wonder again how the treatment had worked out. There had been no adverse reports from the Institute, so we could presume that the psycho-therapist had been satisfied. Some months later at a dinner I happened to sit next to the doctor who had given C. P. treatment ; I had never met him before. The doctor knew that I had been the magistrate in C. P.'s case and mentioned it. So I told him of the letter and asked whether at any time C. P. had admitted his need for treatment. The doctor informed me that at the first interview C. P. had informed him that I had ordered him to come (which was untrue, since I never order people to see a psycho-therapist). C. P. had insisted that there was no trouble to be cured and never at any time during the treatment had any admission been given. When I asked the doctor how under such circumstances treatment had been possible, he replied that, though periodically C. P. would repeat his assurances, he co-operated well in the treatment. Both sides accepted the denials as part of the game. C. P., the doctor said, was in a bad state when he first came, but after the treatment he was reasonably safe.

This is a useful case, for it shows that courts and pro-bation officers must never be satisfied with verbal denials ; they must get down deeper than superficialities. Some delinquents who at first appear unsuitable for treatment may soon overcome their resistance and manifest a desire to be relieved of their disorders. I have been told of cases where delinquents have become definitely uneasy when their earnest protestations of innocence have been accepted by their friends. If there is in fact willingness to be treated, that is enough ; courts see the ' penitent and contrite heart ' on rare occasions only.

The desire of an offender, especially in sexual cases, to retain his respectability by denying the offence is sometimes fortified by the calling of witnesses to his good character. In such cases people of eminence, and in particular clergy-men, will be called as witnesses to testify to the esteem in which the accused is held. There have been cases where courts have been so impressed by such evidence that they have acquitted the accused on the facts. Yet evidence of good character has little relevance in many sexual cases. Sexual offences, when they are manifestations of unconscious urges and inhibitions, are compatible with a virtuous life, even with sincere religious convictions and piety, though it is sometimes difficult to convince defending lawyers that this is so. But lawyers need to realize that there is frequently a possibility that a defence will injure a delinquent by intensifying his façade of innocence. There is an old story that a prisoner once burst into tears during his counsel's final speech to the jury. When asked later why he broke down, he replied : ' I never knew how innocent I was till I heard that fellow talking.' Such feelings are not conducive to reform.

A refusal to co-operate in treatment is sometimes due to a fear of being discovered insane. Public opinion is unhealthily ignorant about diseases of the mind,[1] and there is a widespread fear of insanity, which is regarded as something disgraceful. This fear was discovered during the East-Hubert experimental treatment : ' . . . in many personality types any attempt at modification . . . is felt as a threat to stability, sometimes expressed as a fear of insanity '.[2] In such cases only a doctor can reassure, but probation officers can help by telling of other cases where health and happiness have been restored through treatment.

Where offenders have no desire to be rid of the gratification obtained by their form of abnormality, treatment is seldom possible. In criminal courts this is a frequent obstacle. The East-Hubert report describes the case of one homo-sexual of this kind :

Although in many ways suitable for treatment . . . its application was quite impossible, as both his perversion and his other weaknesses were justified by him intellectually, and any attempt to change his attitude was regarded by him as an attempt to undermine his stability and, therefore, as something extremely dangerous.[3]

[1] See, for instance, *The Last of the Taboos*, by Dr. I. E. Hutton.
[2] Paragraph 89.   [3] Case XLIV.

Such cases are not rare. Often the delinquent who sees nothing wrong in what he has done is one who otherwise would greatly benefit from treatment. But usually nothing constructive can be done. We have to remember that what makes most of us go to a doctor is a consciousness of pain or weakness. A delinquent who finds no discomfort in his conduct is not often a good subject for treatment. Sometimes the criminal conduct may provide satisfactions unobtainable in other ways. If this attitude continues after conviction, psychological treatment is ordinarily ruled out.

Real co-operation may also not be forthcoming on another ground. There are some people who enjoy being a patient and have no real desire to get well, however much they may think they are co-operating with the doctor. Such people are usually the despair of the medical profession in all its branches ; they are specially hopeless cases in psychotherapy. They enjoy the companionship of their therapist, they love talking about themselves and receiving attention, but they have no true desire to recover. Such people were well described by Corneille :

> Ah ! qu'avec peu d'effet on entend la raison,
> Quand le cœur est atteint d'un si charmant poison
> Et lorsque le malade aime sa maladie,
> Qu'il a peine à souffrir que l'on y remédie.[1]

Similarly there are the cases, the backwash of improved social services, where people dread independence and like to be looked after by relief organizations ; they feel that they cannot stand on their own feet, and the more relief they receive, the more they want it to be prolonged. Such people do not make good patients for the psycho-therapist. In bad times they are seen in considerable numbers in criminal courts on charges for minor crimes. But as a rule little can be done to improve their outlook.

Sometimes a show of co-operation will be given during the first weeks after a court case, but it does not last. Several times I have made probation orders containing a clause that

---

[1] *Le Cid*, Act II, scene 5.

the delinquent shall submit to medical treatment—of course only after consent has been given,—but the first interview preparatory to treatment has been the last ; this not because of any fault on the part of the doctor. It is annoying when delinquents do not keep the appointments made for them and to which they have agreed, since the psycho-therapist is ordinarily a busy man or woman giving time voluntarily. Delinquents who behave in this way are usually of the low-grade type, physically and mentally.

In P. B.'s case the probation officer made four separate appointments with the doctor who had undertaken the case at the request of the Institute for the Scientific Treatment of Delinquency. P. B. had attended the preliminary interviews at the offices of the Institute, so had made some effort to carry out his promise to submit to treatment. But he failed four times to visit the doctor. He was a young exhibitionist greatly in need of treatment. Both probation officer and I were agreed that ordinary probation, without psychological treatment, would probably be useless, and the prison doctor, during the week on remand before my decision, had recommended treatment. When the fourth failure to attend the doctor was reported to me, I was in a difficulty. My legal alternative was to give P. B. a sentence, on the original charge, of three months' imprisonment. But what could prison authorities accomplish with such a type in three months ? When a weak-willed young man asked advice from a friend about the wisdom of his marrying, the friend gave the Socratic advice that whichever course he adopted he would regret it. That in fact was my position. In the course of a long discussion with the probation officer I learned that P. B. was now working in some subordinate capacity in a hotel ; the job was not an attractive one, but it was the first job P. B. had had for a long time. To bring him to court for his breach of the probation order would probably mean that he would be sacked by his employers. So we decided to take no formal action at all, to hope for the best and fear the worst. The probation officer saw P. B. and told him what we thought of him.

I hope that P. B. was impressed. Anyhow he committed no further crime during his year of probation. More I cannot say.

A worse case was that of G. L., a young man of 24 whom I found guilty of forging his Post Office Savings book. During the week of remand the probation officer discovered that G. L. was the son of a man in a good position and of superior type. The mother had been an excessive drinker for many years and had died of cancer two years previously. The father had married again, and the stepmother, a decent woman, had become definitely hostile to G. L. because of his persistent idleness. At 24, G. L.'s total work record did not amount to more than about twelve months in all. Both the probation officer and I felt that here was obviously a case for some simple psycho-therapy ; the drunken mother and the wrong relationship with the stepmother, which had spoiled G. L.'s relationship with his father, were factors that needed sorting out. We sent all the facts to the prison so that the doctor should know our perplexities. The medical report was to the effect that G. L. seemed quite rational, that there was no trace of mental defect, but that his perspective was somewhat childish. The probation officer and I agreed that without some contact with a psycho-therapist a cure through probation would not be likely to succeed. But G. L. was out of work and had been for some time. He had a girl friend of whom the probation officer was hopeful, but the affair had not been of long standing. With the help of the probation officer G. L. found work. While we wanted G. L. to see a psycho-therapist, we felt that the first need was to get him accustomed to regular work and to sort out the home situation, so I made a probation order and left over the question of psycho-therapy.

About two months later G. L. lost his employment and no fact detrimental to him was discovered. But, as is sometimes the way of romance, G. L. without wages was less attractive than before, and his girl threw G. L. over. The father had turned G. L. out of the home when he appeared in court ; the father stated that he was ' fed-up '

with the young man and refused all appeals to start life with
G. L. afresh. So at the end of two months' probation G. L.
was without home, employment, or girl ; scarcely the
moment to begin psycho-therapy. Help was given from
the court poor-box to tide G. L. over for a time, but soon
afterwards the probation officer discovered that, though
G. L. had been given money earmarked to pay for his lodgings, he had not done so. The probation officer, patient as
ever, proposed that G. L. should live in a hostel, and we
offered to pay the cost for a short time out of the poor-box
pending the finding of work. G. L. refused ; control of
any kind was unwelcome. The probation officer also paid
a visit to the home of the ex-girl friend, but there found that
G. L. had conducted his courtship under a false name and
definitely against the wishes of the girl's mother. G. L. got
into work again and soon lost it. Four months after the
making of the probation order several debts of G. L. were
reported to the probation officer, and G. L.'s landlady,
a woman known to the court for good, reported that G. L.
was both dirty and lazy ; he seldom got out of bed before
eleven o'clock in the morning. What hope was there that
G. L. would make the effort to attend on a psycho-therapist ?
As G. L. seemed unable to make any effort to find work, he
was given a letter of introduction to the Employment Department of the London Police Court Mission and an appointment made. After a fortnight the Mission reported that
G. L. had not turned up, and G. L. offered the, to him, conclusive explanation that he had lost the letter of introduction
and did not know where he was expected to go.

The probation officer then reported to me that G. L.
showed a complete lack of interest in the subject of getting
work. (The Unemployment Assistance Board was then
keeping him alive.) At this moment G. L.'s father, who
after all had been seeing G. L., reported to the probation
officer that he thought that G. L. was ' definitely mental '.
Before G. L. could be summoned back before me, G. L. had
to go to a general hospital on account of an ordinary infectious
illness. We accordingly asked the hospital authorities to

136 CRIME AND PSYCHOLOGY

take the opportunity to examine G. L.'s mental condition. Eventually the hospital reported that there was no mental illness and now no physical ailment. Soon after coming out of hospital G. L. had the impertinence to complain to the probation officer that the latter had lost interest. The probation officer recorded in his notes of the case : ' He has failed to respond to the efforts to rehabilitate him. He is still very much in the air and will not face reality. He is unstable and seems likely to get into trouble through incurring debts.' That prophecy was soon fulfilled. He was charged before me with three cases of obtaining goods by false pretences. When guilt had been established, the police presented me with a long list of similar crimes which G. L. wished to be taken into account. G. L. had since his first appearance before me repeatedly obtained meals in popular restaurants without paying for them ; the first of these was on the day after I had made the probation order. In despair I sent G. L. to prison for a substantial time and could only hope that prison would teach him to work. I do not know what his fate was. I can only hope that during the war he found his salvation in the army. From the outset there was a mere façade of co-operation. Because of this, probation failed and psycho-therapy could not even begin. In fact the case was hopeless from the start, though we did not know it. If he is alive, he may well be irreclaimable.

Perhaps this man could have been saved earlier by a Child Guidance Clinic. Perhaps also he was one of those of whom Miss Margery Fry wrote in her Clarke Hall lecture on ' The Ancestral Child ' :

There is also the unfitness of the abnormal for any place in such a society ['a system which gave a reasonably full and free life to the majority of its citizens ']. One meets them from time to time, the ' throw-backs ' to an earlier civilisation, the ' Dartmoor shepherds ', the rogues and vagabonds who are born some thousands of years too late, whom nothing will ever civilise, but who might have lived happily, and in their measure, efficiently, pitting their slender wits against those of other animals in a primeval world where tickling for trout or snaring rabbits would be as respectable as stockbroking is to-day.

A large amount of the law-breaking which swells the records of our juvenile courts [and of the adult courts ?] is an evidence not of youthful depravity, nor even of psychopathic conditions, but of the fact that we are applying to a primitive people the rather arbitrary laws of a highly sophisticated era.[1]

Another aspect of the genuineness of co-operation applies to psychological treatment in places of detention. In order that treatment may be possible in such places, a reasonably mild regime must exist for those to be treated. This fact will inevitably offer temptation to many in custody who see in a transfer to such a regime material advantages. Treatment will offer a way out from the severity of normal institutional life. Such difficulties arose when the experimental treatment was being given by Dr. Hubert. In the preliminary investigation of cases it was found that 'some prisoners have applied for treatment out of curiosity, some in the hope of avoiding work and to obtain preferential treatment in prison '.[2] Such difficulties will reappear when the 'special institution' recommended in the report is established.

Another practical obstacle in the way of courts anxious to secure psycho-therapy on probation is that the aggrieved persons, and sometimes local public opinion generally, expect severe penalties to be imposed and are apt to resent it strongly if the delinquent is not put in prison. This difficulty occurs mainly in cases of sexual crime. A woman who has been the object of the attentions of an exhibitionist, for instance, is a difficult person to handle. She would be satisfied with a sentence to prison and is not likely to pause to reflect on the risk that after his imprisonment the delinquent may be a greater menace to women and girls than before. According to the teaching of Freud, those who feel outraged by the offence of another are usually animated by

---

[1] Miss Fry was prevented from delivering her lecture by the outbreak of war in 1939. Her lecture was published by the Clarke Hall Fellowship. The above extracts are from pp. 16 and 18.

[2] Paragraph 39 of the East-Hubert report.

an unconscious feeling that they are being denied the rewards of their own virtue. There is comfort for them in the severe punishment of the offender. They regard such punishment as both a recognition and a reinforcement of their own powers of abstention from sexual excess.

The power of the super ego over our instinctive life is undermined . . . when the offender escapes punishment and thus fails to pay for his offense. Unwarranted acquittal means simply that the court permits the defendant to do things which we prohibit to ourselves. Under such circumstances the righteous member of the community finds himself facing the following dilemma : he must either give up his own inhibitions and give in to his own anti-social tendencies, or he must demand that the offender be punished. . . . The greater the pressure coming from repressed impulses, the more aware becomes the ego that it needs the institution of punishment as an intimidating example, acting against one's own primitive world of repressed instinctual drives. In other words, the louder man calls for the punishment of the law-breaker, the less he has to fight against his own repressed impulses.[1]

I have many times felt the truth of these theories. It has sometimes appeared to me that in such women their sex-morality and ideas have become somewhat ingrown, and I have wished that I could secure for them psychological treatment also, for were they not themselves in need of treatment, they would not have been seriously affected by the incidents complained of. I have seen such women in a state of collapse after they have given their evidence ; sometimes they have needed much coaxing before they will complete their story. Yet in psychological health there would be no trauma in a case of indecent exposure. But in the present state of society the law could not provide for any such treatment.[2] On rare occasions in my cases

[1] *The Criminal, the Judge and the Public*, by Franz Alexander and Hugo Staub, pp. 213–16.
[2] As Chapter 8 will show, the Children and Young Persons Act, 1933, made an attempt to deal with this problem in regard to child victims. But, as so often happens with official schemes, the plan failed.

a probation officer has succeeded in persuading a woman victim to see a psychologist in order, as he has put it, to avoid any unpleasant consequences of the whole affair. But courts have to be extremely guarded in giving such advice ; on no account must psychological reasons be explained when such advice is given. Public opinion is not yet ready for the idea that victims may need treatment.

Those closely associated with the victims of sexual aggression, as, for instance, the parents of a child victim of sexual assault, can also form obstacles difficult to surmount. I have on occasions found it impossible to convince such parents that the best course for everybody is that the offender should be rendered harmless for the future through treatment, and that imprisonment may make him a greater menace to children than before. The following is an extract from a local newspaper relating to a case of mine ; a man of 35 had been found guilty of indecently assaulting a boy in Battersea Park, and a psychological report had offered hope of cure.

The probation officer reported to Mr. Mullins, who afterwards said that he would bind prisoner over for two years and that a special condition of the probation order would be that he should submit to medical treatment as directed.

The father of the boy came forward and said : ' I want to make a protest.'

Mr. Mullins : ' What do you think should be done with this man ? '

' I don't quite know,' replied the father. ' I should leave that to you. I should like to be placed in a cell with him for about ten minutes. This is the third case of indecency against children in my street that I've heard of.'

' The father naturally has a grievance. But he thinks, apparently, that the community would be better protected by sending this man to prison for six months. This shows great ignorance about this complaint,' said Mr. Mullins. ' The public will be far better protected by endeavouring to cure this man of his habits.'

This is rather a short summary of what took place. In fact the father told me that it was becoming common knowledge in the district that in such cases I cared more for the offenders than for the victims.   I said a good deal more than was reported, with the hope of persuading the father to see how best these outrages could be prevented, but I was not successful in this.   All I could do was to ask the probation officer to have a talk with the father.

One cannot expect ' insulted ' women or the parents of boy victims of sexual assault to be psychologically minded. Nevertheless I have never had to be deflected from my intended course of action, and I usually find that probation officers in private talks can smooth the indignant ones down, even if they cannot convince them.

Severe sentences, regardless of the future possibilities for harm of the prisoners, are also favoured by public opinion and the popular press.[1]   Nothing can be done here, and a magistrate can only comfort himself with the Freudian doctrine just mentioned, that the critics may be criticizing because unconsciously their own desires are not fully under their own control.

One more practical obstacle is worth mentioning.   Courts in many cases can do little to alter the immediate environment in which delinquents live.   Crime may be a psychological reaction to a bad upbringing, a difficult domestic situation at home, unsympathetic parents, a stepmother, a nagging wife, a lazy husband, worry about children, and so on.   Usually alternatives cannot be arranged, and the delinquent on probation has to return during his treatment to his old surroundings.   Probation officers can sometimes have a remarkable influence for good in the homes of their delinquents, but often this is not possible.   Again, many reports that I received before the war from psycho-therapists contained the suggestion that suitable work should be found for the delinquent, and I fully realized the value of such work.   But in the pre-war years it was far from easy to place delinquents in work of any kind.   Probation officers

---

[1] I have often been criticized by a local paper for not giving prison without the option of a fine to those whom I direct to psycho-therapists.

did their best, and, though we kept the fact dark, delinquents were sometimes placed in a better position than many who had not committed crime. But unless society accepts Erewhonian theories, it is not possible to make the commission of crime a passport to congenial employment.[1] Most of us have had to struggle to get on in life, and that has been good for us. Much useful work is unattractive and boring ; so is much magisterial work. But it all has to be done, and delinquents should not be encouraged to pick and choose. Similarly with housing conditions : it is seldom possible to allow any preference to delinquents, even though defective housing may have contributed to the offence. But there is one service which courts can render without any fears of giving unfair preference to delinquents. Where ignorance about sexual life or the sexual side of marriage has been a cause of either crime or matrimonial breakdown, the services of a local medical man or woman, not necessarily a trained psychologist, are invaluable. Doctors always seem ready to help in court cases if they are asked. Fees seem to present no obstacle, though those sent to doctors on the advice of courts should be encouraged to pay fees to them if they can afford them. I have seen several cures of delinquents and many matrimonial reconciliations effected by the simple method of a few talks with doctors.

This chapter and the preceding one were necessary in order to place psycho-therapy for delinquents in proper focus. No service to the psychological treatment of delinquents is done by those who ignore the practical obstacles.

[1] In his book, *The Dilemma of Penal Reform*, Dr. Hermann Mannheim pleaded that what he termed the ' principle of less eligibility ' for prisoners should not be accepted. But there are many practical difficulties.

CHAPTER 6

THE NEED FOR INVESTIGATION

Trying a man is easy, as easy as falling off a log, compared with deciding what to do with him when he has been found guilty.

MR. JUSTICE MCCARDIE [1]

If a court decides . . . that imprisonment is the only way of dealing with any given case, it should not be allowed to impose sentence of imprisonment then and there. The case should be adjourned until such time as the court can be placed in full possession of all the relevant facts, including the results of a study of the offender's personality. To deal with a case in the absence of such investigation is equivalent to prescribing for a patient without due examination, and on the observation of a single symptom in his case.

DR. M. HAMBLIN SMITH [2]

IF improved methods of dealing with delinquents, of which psychological treatment is one, are to make headway in our criminal courts, a first and obvious essential is that when guilt has been ascertained there must be adequate time for investigation into the personality, health, and social circumstances of the delinquent. That sentences are usually passed without full information about delinquents is one of the worst features of our system of criminal justice; it is one of the greatest obstacles in the way of the scientific treatment of delinquents.

Lawyers have a saying that time is the essence of the contract. Time is also the essence of all wise sentences. All criminal courts have the power to defer sentence, and if they do not do this, and set on foot full investigations, there may be a danger that injustice will be done, or that after his sentence a delinquent may be a greater danger to the community than ever before. Much recidivism has its

[1] Quoted in *Life* by George Pollock, p. 152.   [2] *Prisons*, p. 138.

142

origin in a failure in courts to make full inquiries the first time that punishment was inflicted. Time is also necessary so that the delinquent, when all his defences have broken down, may have an opportunity to realize, not only the injury that he has done to society, but also the harm that he has done to himself. Many times have I seen delinquents who were originally full of bombast and rather absurd defences become genuinely reasonable, and occasionally penitent, after a remand for a week, either in custody or on bail, after conviction. During these remand periods, probation officers, fortified by the fact of conviction, can often work wonders.

Certain inquiries after conviction are, it is true, usually made. Thus the police, and sometimes probation officers, will tell the court what they have been able to find out about the delinquent before his trial. But it sometimes happens that the time between arrest and trial is too short to enable even these somewhat superficial inquiries to be made. So if time be not allowed when the facts are established, the court will sentence guilty people without knowing anything about them beyond the facts in the case that has been tried and possibly their police record, if any.

These conditions, so obviously wrong to those who approach the problems of penology from a scientific standpoint, do not shock the legal mind. I once spoke in the strain of this chapter at a meeting of the Medico-Legal Society in London after a paper had been read by an experienced barrister on the development of criminal law and penology. The lecturer replied : ' I am afraid I do not understand these complaints. . . . I always understood that the officer in charge of the case made enquiries before even the case came to trial. When the prisoner is convicted, the officer goes into the box and tells the Bench all about the prisoner.' [1] To me this seemed an extraordinary reply, but it appeared to satisfy the audience. How can the detective in charge of a case ever be in a position to tell the

[1] The curious will find these remarks in vol. iv of the Society's review, p. 304.

Bench ' all ' about a delinquent, especially when his inquiries have taken place before trial ? Often police officers are generous in their statements about their pre-trial inquiries and will refer to such matters as the influence over the defendant of somebody not in custody, bad home conditions, the unreasonableness of an employer, and so on. In the days of acute unemployment I more than once heard from a police officer that, as the defendant had been dismissed from his work, the police officer had persuaded another employer to take the defendant into his employment if the court approved.   On these occasions police officers are often seen at their best.   Their information, so far as it goes, is always of value, and, in cases with a bad record, is sometimes a useful corrective to the impressions of the Bench.   None the less, to rely solely on information obtained before trial is a survival from the days when the sole duty of the court was ' to make the punishment fit the crime '.   When considering police reports about delinquents, the limitations of the police mind have to be remembered.   As was said in an earlier chapter, the police are insufficiently trained to consider the effects on both themselves and the community of a term of imprisonment which may have by law to be too short for any cure in prison, as, for example, in the case of the maximum sentence on an exhibitionist (when first sentenced) of three months.   Police reports have of necessity to be confined to the past criminal record and present circumstances of the delinquent.   They cannot deal with internal causes.   Even probation officers can without a remand after conviction do little more in magistrates' courts than report on their first impressions of the delinquent.   (In cases to be tried at Assizes or Quarter Sessions obviously more time is available, but most of the objections to pre-trial inquiries still apply.)

The first question to ask, so it seems to me, is whether, on the principle that in our country accused people are innocent until convicted, any pre-trial inquiries can be justified, except a search by the police in their own records. I would maintain that with this exception no such inquiries are justifiable, whether by police, by probation officers, or, in the cases of children, by education authorities ; also that a pre-trial talk between accused and probation officer, while harmless, is only of value when the accused volunteers the statement that he proposes to plead guilty.   Then the probation officer can go further.   Pre-trial inquiries in past places of employment, or in the homes of accused persons, whether by police, probation officers, or education authorities, are in my opinion unfair and unconstitutional, for accused persons are in fact often acquitted.

How complacent legal opinion is on this subject is also well indicated by the following statement in the *Journal of Criminal Law* : ' It is not often that charges of indictable offences, not within the summary jurisdiction of justices, are dismissed, and so no harm is done by instituting inquiry provisionally on a committal for trial being ordered.'[1] Even Mr. Leo Page, who is usually on the side of the angels, defended pre-trial inquiries with a vigour worthy of a better cause.   ' Let us be realists and recognise honestly that the choice is not between pre-trial and post-trial enquiries,' he once wrote, ' but between pre-trial enquiries and no enquiries at all. . . .   As conditions are to-day it is simply impracticable to insist upon remands for enquiries in all cases.'[2]   Full inquiries are not necessary, I agree, in ' all cases ', for a few cases are so obviously hopeless or so obviously probation cases that a decision on the day of trial is possible.[3]   But reformers, among whom I include Mr. Page, should not frame their policy for conditions as they are to-day.   Present conditions need drastic alterations. Even so progressive a chairman of a juvenile court as Mr.

---

[1] January 1940.   The writer cannot have had much experience of the vagaries of juries.

[2] *The Magistrate*, September–October, 1940.   Mr. Page's court experience was mainly in courts in rural areas where, I agree, the difficulties of remanding delinquents after verdict are greatest. But these difficulties can be got over, as I will show.

[3] The effect of delay on a delinquent's work may sometimes justify the making of a probation order on the day of the trial.

John A. F. Watson accepted Mr. Page's apologia for pre-trial inquiries in rural areas.[1]

Pre-trial inquiries are seldom sufficient to save the Bench from the danger of forming conclusions from superficial observations in court; nor are they sufficient to save a probation officer from the snares of first impressions. In fact, it is often dangerous for any one, Bench, police, or probation officers, to form impressions of defendants while their trial is pending. The demeanour of defendants is a very unsafe guide to their inner personality; some appear truculent simply because they are shy; others may appear modest, even penitent, merely because they are good actors; others, again, have been cowed by the whole proceedings. I once heard from a colleague [2] the story of a highly truculent defendant accused of theft whom nobody could quieten, in court or outside. During later inquiries a probation officer discovered the cause of his truculence. He had listened attentively when the police officer read the formal charge in the police station. He agreed that he had stolen a motor car, a rug, and some parcels, but he was indignant at the statement, that he had also stolen ' divers objects '; legal phraseology had entirely misled him; he knew no divers, he kept reiterating.

Equally illustrative was a case of mine. During the court proceedings in a charge of theft we formed the opinion that the defendant was mentally deficient. So I broke off the trial and sent the defendant to the Boys' Prison for a medical and mental report. The medical officer reported the following week that the youth was in no way mentally deficient, but that he was seriously deaf. What I and others had taken for mental defect was in fact defective lip reading. My mistake was less striking than that of the police officer in charge of the case and the probation officer, who had seen the youth in private before the case began; nobody had spotted the reason for the youth's apparent slowness, and no doubt the whole proceeding since his arrest had, by

[1] *The Child and the Magistrate*, p. 61.
[2] Dr. F. J. O. Coddington, stipendiary magistrate at Bradford.

making him excited and nervous, lowered his lip-reading abilities.

About the same time a case was reported in the press where a young woman had been sentenced to prison for shoplifting. She appealed on the ground that if the court had known certain facts about her, a prison sentence would not have been passed. The appeal was allowed, as shortly before the theft, according to medical evidence given at the hearing of the appeal, the young woman had seen her father killed and was in a state of emotional upset. A remand after the facts had been proved would have resulted in her mental crisis becoming known before sentence ; all pre-trial inquiries had been inadequate.[1]

Pre-trial inquiries are a poor protection for a court against the good actor. Professor Cyril Burt told this delightful story in his book *The Young Delinquent*. He overheard the following dialogue at a children's remand home : Newcomer due at court the following day : ' Oo's the beak to-morrer ? ' Veteran : ' Old W.' Newcomer : ' What d'yer s'y to 'im ? ' Veteran : ' S'y it's the pitchers. 'E always makes a speech about it and nods at yer for provin' 'is point.'[2] The idiosyncrasies of magistrates, and of all who sit on the Bench regularly, are bound to become known, and the only safeguard against those who would take advantage of them is the remand for inquiries after verdict. My leaning towards psycho-therapy has long been known, and occasionally I have listened to pleas for psychological treatment from defendants, or their legal representatives, but later inquiries have shown a complete lack of any true co-operation.

I have always been grateful for the fact that early in my magisterial career I had a sharp lesson about the dangers of pre-trial inquiries. I had found a youth guilty of stealing. He was a miserable-looking lad, and when I asked him to talk about himself, he told me that he had been born in a caravan and had never known his father. The probation

[1] *Justice of the Peace*, 17 March 1934.
[2] *The Young Delinquent*, p. 143 n.

officer had accepted this remarkable story. I remanded the lad, a vagrant type, for reports by police and probation officer. A week later, the lad having been in custody as he said that he had no home to go to, the police produced his father and mother with whom he had always lived, about a mile from the court, until he left home a few weeks previously over some petty grievance.

In this question of remanding for inquiries after verdict the juvenile courts have less excuses than other courts, for the rules officially laid down for their procedure provide :

Where the child or young person is found guilty of an offence, whether after a plea of guilty or otherwise . . .

(ii) the court shall, except in cases which appear to it to be of a trivial nature, obtain such information as to the general conduct, home surroundings, school record and medical history of the child or young person as may enable it to deal with the case in his best interests, and shall, if such information is not fully available, consider the desirability of remanding the child or young person for such enquiry as may be necessary.

(iii) the court shall take into consideration any report which may be furnished by a probation officer. . . .[1]

These rules obviously permit the obtaining of full information before the facts have been ascertained by the court, but at least the minds of the magistrates in juvenile courts are directed to the necessity of having inquiries made. A little experience should teach such magistrates that inquiries after a finding of guilty are better than pre-trial inquiries. Unfortunately most juvenile courts, even in urban areas, are content with the latter. Thus in her careful survey, *English Juvenile Courts*, Miss Winifred Elkin wrote that ' in most towns the home enquiries are made and the school reports sent up before the case is heard, and unless there are special circumstances that make a remand advisable, the Bench reaches its decision on the child's first appearance in court '.[2] Happily in London,

---

[1] Summary Jurisdiction (Children and Young Persons) Rules, 1933, No. 11.
[2] p. 103.

where the juvenile courts have since 1937 been presided over by selected lay justices, remands appear to be the general rule. But that this is not so elsewhere is an illustration of the results of not making official rules mandatory, except for special reasons duly made public.

In 1939 the National Association of Probation Officers issued a questionnaire to its members asking about their practice in the matter of inquiries. The replies revealed a state of affairs that was profoundly unsatisfactory. Only 12 per cent of probation officers reported that home visits were made between verdict and sentence. Mr. Leo Page recorded in his book, *For Magistrates and Others*, that ' in courts of lay justices it is exceedingly rare to find any systematic remand for further enquiries '.[1] Most of such courts, whether in towns or country, are so organized that the same justices will not be sitting again for a considerable time. Therefore delinquents are disposed of finally, subject to appeal, on the day of trial. In the towns where magistrates' courts have the services of a stipendiary magistrate, whether he sits with lay justices as colleagues or alone, it is easier to remand cases for inquiry, since the stipendiary magistrate at least will be sitting at regular intervals.

The difficulty that the same magistrates may not be sitting again for a long time has been in theory overcome by a useful provision in the Children and Young Persons Act, 1933,[2] which permits one juvenile court to try a case and to record a finding of guilt and another court, differently constituted, to decide how best to deal with the case. During the debates on the abortive Criminal Justice Bill of 1939 an official amendment was moved and passed in the House of Commons to apply this provision to adult magistrates' courts. Such a change in the law would be useful, but it cannot be regarded as ideal that the court which tries a case, and therefore knows all the facts, should not have the responsibility of deciding sentence ; magistrates who have the duty of passing sentence must be handicapped if they have not heard the evidence. The only really satisfactory

[1] p. 96.   [2] Section 48 (3).

course would be to provide, in both juvenile and adult courts, that at least two magistrates must return at a later date to hear reports and decide the sentence. This may be difficult in rural areas, but difficulties should be overcome, not accepted as a reason for bad justice.

Adult magistrates' courts in London (Police Courts) doubtless have their defects, but as they are in session every working day, the remanding of delinquents causes no inconvenience and in fact is the general rule. This wise course is followed not so much because of any merit in the magistrates who preside in these courts, but because these courts are so organized that the remanding of delinquents after verdict seems the obvious course. The use of probation officers in the London courts long since became a matter of routine. Their predecessors, known as court missionaries, were at work in the courts soon after the movement to befriend Police Court cases began in 1876. A tradition has grown up that probation officers should be used and given an opportunity to report on cases before the sentences are fixed. So if, in fact, decisions about the fate of delinquents are given in London quickly after verdict, this is the deliberate choice of the magistrate and not an essential feature of the system.

Probably the reason why magistrates generally have not realized the gravity of this problem has been that in passing sentence quickly after the verdict magistrates' courts have been doing what is ordinarily done in the higher courts, Quarter Sessions and Assizes. To place the problem, therefore, in proper focus it is necessary to see what occurs in these higher courts.

In most towns outside London Quarter Sessions are presided over by a Recorder, a barrister of standing who is a member of the local Bar circuit and who continues in practice, except in the town to which he is appointed. In country districts Quarter Sessions have a chairman and deputy-chairman who are now as a rule lawyers. The duration of a sitting at Quarter Sessions naturally depends upon the volume of work. The busier Sessions may last

several days, but many Sessions last one day only, or a
fraction of a working day.   There is ordinarily an interval
of three months between sittings.   Into such a system it
would be difficult to graft any regular remanding of delinquents between verdict and sentence ; obviously the usual
practice must be to dispose of cases finally, subject to appeal,
on the trial day.   What is required is that every court of
Quarter Sessions trying delinquents (these courts have
much work of a semi-civil nature) shall be adjourned for
a week after all verdicts have been given, so that full inquiries
about the delinquents found guilty can be made.   But if
so drastic a reform were tried, it would quickly be found
that the existing system could not stand the strain.
Recorders would not find it easy to duplicate their sittings ;
many of them are busy barristers.   The legal chairmen
and deputy-chairmen of county Sessions might also find it
difficult to return after a week to consider reports and pass
sentences.

There are easy solutions for these practical difficulties,
once the will to recognize and solve them exists.   As,
however, plans to reorganize the criminal courts are only
indirectly relevant to the subject of this book, I have relegated
my ideas on the subject to an appendix.

The whole system of Assizes in all parts of the country
is still governed by ancient tradition.   According to this
tradition the function of the High Court judges on Assize
was to empty the prisons, which used not to be places of
punishment, but mainly places for the safe custody of
prisoners pending their trial.   As each prisoner was found
guilty, the judges, in the words of a witty modern writer,
' either transported him to the new world via the Atlantic,
or they transported him to the next world via Tyburn '.[1]
Thus the prisons were emptied.   In these more enlightened
days many of those awaiting trial are on bail, and the result
of the judges' Assize is often, not to free the gaols, but to
fill them.

Traditional customs are excellent when they do no harm.

[1] *Prisoner at the Bar*, by Arthur R. L. Gardner, p. 45.

Unfortunately traditional methods at most Assizes prevent the adoption of modern methods. The duration of Assizes, like that of Quarter Sessions, depends upon the number of cases, and there are many Assizes which are of such short duration that remands for inquiries are impracticable, unless cases are remanded from one Assize town to another, which is seldom done. So at most Assizes prisoners get sentences, even for psychological crimes, a few minutes after their trial and as a result of pre-trial inquiries.

That this system of sentencing at Assizes could be altered is indicated by the experience of the Central Criminal Court, popularly known as the Old Bailey. This court is the Assize court for London and certain neighbouring areas. There (as also at the London Quarter Sessions) the intervals between the sittings are short and the sittings last over many days. It is easy, therefore, for cases to be remanded after verdict, and the amount of work justifies the employment of probation officers in constant attendance on the court. The senior judge at the Central Court is ordinarily a High Court judge. At the Central Criminal Court there is a good record for placing delinquents on probation, but at the Assizes elsewhere there is a bad record. *Criminal Statistics* for 1938 showed that of the adolescent offenders found guilty at Assizes only 19 per cent were placed under the supervision of a probation officer, but that of those found guilty at the Central Criminal Court 42 per cent were so dealt with. The similar figures for adult offenders were: Assizes 4 per cent and Central Criminal Court 16 per cent.[1] These acute differences cannot be due to the quality of the judges, for, the judges who hold Assizes sit in turn at the Central Criminal Court. The true explanation is that the London court has a better record because it is so organized that probation officers can be regularly employed and can have adequate time to make their inquiries after the verdicts have been given. The Assizes have a poor record because there is ordinarily no time for inquiries after verdict, and because the infrequency of the sittings

[1] p. xiii.

makes the employment of probation officers for the Assizes difficult.[1]

Two short accounts of actual cases at Assizes will best show the need for time for inquiries between verdict and sentence. In his delightful book, *Stage and Bar*, Mr. G. P. Bancroft, who for many years was clerk of assize on the Midland Circuit, told the story how at an Assize Mr. Justice Avory was once greatly impressed by the plea of a man found guilty who had several previous convictions. The judge called up his clerk of assize. ' But can I, do you think,' he said, ' bind him over with all these wretched things behind him ? ' Mr. Bancroft encouraged the judge to follow his instincts and to bind the man over. The judge did so and the end of the story is not told. But would not the judge have been greatly helped in solving his doubts if the system had been that the ' old lag ' should be remanded for reports upon him by an experienced probation officer ? Assurances and promises from delinquents before they have been sentenced are always pathetic, but sometimes they have little real value. No one on the Bench, however great his experience, is in a position to know how genuine are professions of determination to reform. When the Bench passes sentence under the influence of sympathy or emotion, the situation is almost as dangerous as when the Bench acts in anger.

In that ultra-human book, *Notes of a Prison Visitor*, Major Gordon Gardiner told the story how once he was favourably impressed by a man serving his second sentence for warehouse-breaking. When the man was once more charged, Major Gardiner wrote to the judge. The case was remanded for Major Gardiner's attendance. The judge listened to what he had to say about the prisoner and then agreed to bind the prisoner over. But what if Major Gardiner had not taken the unusual course of writing to the judge ? It ought to be impossible, except in a rare case, for a term of imprisonment to be ordered, or for

[1] The solution for this limitation of Assizes in the matter of remanding for inquiries is discussed in the Appendix.

a probation order to be made, in any court without a remand for inquiry by the probation officer, his report being supplemented by police and medical reports as may be necessary.[1]

The greatest of many faults of the ill-fated Criminal Justice Bill of 1938–9 was that it made no attempt to tackle this difficult problem. Had the bill passed into law, sentences would still have continued to be passed within a few minutes of the verdict.

The more that those who know themselves to be guilty realize that they will be dealt with after a full investigation of their circumstances and conditions of health, the more ready will they be to admit their offences. This may at first sight seem a gloomy prospect for those barristers and solicitors who defend people accused of crime. As more scientific methods are adopted by the courts, more scientific knowledge will be required by those who defend delinquents. Lawyers handling crime can protect themselves against fears of unemployment by acquiring knowledge about why people commit criminal acts ; psychology and penology will have to enter the curriculum of young lawyers and this will be all to the good. Criminal lawyers will then be of even greater help to criminal courts than they are now.

The United States of America, having the same legal history as ourselves, is also confronted with this problem. Professor Sheldon Glueck wrote : ' Days, weeks and sometimes months are devoted to the trial ; minutes are usually given over to the solution of the difficult problem . . . of what to do with the defendant after he has been

---

[1] Another need is that courts should be placed under an obligation to consider any reports submitted by probation officers or prison governors or medical officers. Juvenile Courts are compelled by law to ' take into consideration any report which may be furnished by a probation officer '. In other courts probation officers and others are subjected to the rule of old-fashioned parents : speak when spoken to. Even a report recommending Borstal cannot be submitted unasked to a court by the governor of a remand prison.

found guilty.'[1] But in the Court of General Sessions for the county of New York, which corresponds to the Central Criminal Court and London Sessions combined, much progress in these problems had been made before the war. Every person who either pleaded guilty or was convicted of a crime in the Court of General Sessions was referred to the Probation Department for investigation. Sentences were adjourned for a period up to two weeks in order that the Division of Investigation might make a searching inquiry into the social, mental, and physical factors which moulded the defendant's personality and which conditioned him towards anti-social conduct.[2] In 1927 this Probation Department entered into 'a co-operative arrangement with the clinics of the various hospitals of the City of New York to conduct mental and physical examinations of offenders referred to them by the department '.[3] But in 1931 'the need for a separate clinic having become increasingly urgent, the judges and chief probation officer, aided by a group of outstanding authorities in the field of law, sociology and psychiatry, brought about the establishment of a Psychiatric Clinic of the Court of General Sessions as a branch of the Psychiatric Division of the Department of Hospitals of the City of New York '.[4] But one court, however eminent, cannot do more than improve the conditions under which its own delinquents are dealt with. There is reason for believing that penal conditions in

[1] *Crime and Justice*, p. 79.
[2] *A Decade of Probation*, by Irving W. Halpern, chief probation officer, p. 46.
[3] Ibid., p. 94.
[4] Ibid., p. 95. Would that a similar arrangement could be made by the London Police Courts. Money for such a clinic is available owing to many large and generous contributions and legacies to their Poor Boxes. I can visualize such a clinic, serving all the criminal courts of London, with, perhaps, two local branches where delinquents can be seen nearer their homes than at the central clinic. In November 1937 a tentative inquiry about the establishment of a special clinic for criminal cases was made by the London County Council to the then Chief Magistrate, but nothing came of it.

New York as a whole were not in advance of those in
London. In 1938 the Community Service Society of New
York published the results of an inquiry by its Committee
on Youth and Justice, and this report [1] makes sorry reading.
' A static penal code based on pre-determined amounts of
punishments for specific acts is working at cross purposes
with attempts at rehabilitation which at best are belated.' [2]
That is the general summing up of the report and the
specific complaint is made that ' the same crime committed
under almost identical circumstances by different individuals
can result in sentences differing from one another by a score
or more of years, the difference depending not upon the
crime charged and the law governing it, or the personality
make-up of the persons involved, or their social status,
but upon the judge's mood or feeling at the time '.[3] This
indicates insufficient inquiry after verdict.

Another advantage of remanding cases after the facts
have been decided is that justifiable anger in the judge or
magistrate about the proved facts will have time to cool.

Eager reformers have sometimes urged that every case
should on conviction be psychologically examined. This,
as just shown, is the rule at the Court of General Sessions,
New York, and was also the pre-war rule in Belgian courts
for ' more or less serious delinquents '.[4] But I have never
been able to picture the compulsory psychological examination of such ' serious delinquents ' as a fraudulent City
financier, or a motorist found guilty of dangerous driving,

[1] *Youth in the Toils*, by Leonard V. Harrison and Pryor McNeill
Grant.
[2] Ibid., p. 130.   [3] Ibid., p. 94.
[4] *An Introduction to Criminology*, by Dr. W. A. Bonger, p. 15.
In his earlier book, *The Psychology of the Criminal* (p. 168), Dr.
Hamblin Smith stated : ' It is of first importance ', he wrote,
' that mental examination should be made before final trial. . . .
Examinations made just after conviction are apt to be most misleading.'   Such a procedure is desirable when definite issues about
the sanity of an accused person have been raised.   But as a general
principle our legal system rightly frowns upon any compulsory
examination before trial.

much though they might be in need of the process. In England we are accustomed to proceed by stages, and the time is not yet for any wholesale scheme of psychological examination. A training of at least two years is necessary after a doctor qualifies in medicine, and it must not be forgotten that in the past there has been little prospect of adequate financial reward for psychological work by doctors among delinquents ; so the supply of such experts is limited. The scientific treatment of delinquency would not be advanced if there came into being a number of men and women doctors who had only had a superficial training in psychology and no experience with delinquents. Any mushroom growth, such as would be required for a whole-sale scheme of investigation, would be disastrous ; inadequately trained men and women might be tempted to develop unsound short and attractive treatments which might have serious consequences.

A useful plan would be for psychologists to work out a schedule of offences for which they would like to see a remand and examination in all cases. In such a schedule all sexual crimes of whatever nature would presumably be included ; also homo-sexual offences ; perhaps also repeated cases of theft. Arson would also deserve inclusion. At first it would be wise to hasten slowly, for it would be a big advance if the law accepted that certain crimes must result in a remand for inquiries and examination before sentence.

A proper system of remand and investigation would solve the problem, discussed in Chapter 1, of those delinquents whose mental state at the time of their offence does not come within the narrow limits of the McNaghten Rules, but about whom doubt exists whether they were not driven by some unconscious irresistible impulse to commit their crime. It was pointed out that strong legal prejudice exists against the widening of the Rules, and that other ways exist for doing justice to such cases. I would suggest that what has been written in this chapter offers the key to a solution in such cases. If after an ordinary verdict

12

of guilty on the facts there were full and adequate investigation, then these questions of 'impulse which the prisoner was by mental disease in substance deprived of any power to resist' could then be considered at leisure. Culpability would be thoroughly investigated and a wise sentence passed in accordance with the psychological evidence. There would then be no necessary stigma of insanity. If cure were possible without confinement, the probation system could be employed. Confinement would not mean Broadmoor. A verdict of ' Guilty but Insane ' is not an advantage to an accused person, except in cases of murder, where it avoids the death sentence.[1] The Atkin report well stated : ' Although a psychiatrist may not be in a position to declare an accused person irresponsible in law, which is a matter affecting the guilt of the accused . . . he may yet have evidence concerning abnormal psychological factors which may affect the prisoner's culpability and may be properly put before a court 'when determining the award.' If, therefore, it became the rule in all criminal courts to direct a full investigation in all suitable cases after verdict, it seems to me that without any extension of the McNaghten Rules the problem can be solved. The prolonged battle between psychologists and lawyers that would be necessary before the Rules were widened would become no more important than the battle between Tweedledum and Tweedledee.

[1] One day, I hope, our very stringent law of murder will be amended to provide degrees of murder, as exist in many other countries. Then only planned murders by sane people will result in a death sentence.

CHAPTER 7

PSYCHOLOGY AND CRIMINAL PROCEDURE

Psychology's primary contact with law lies in its possible substantiation or contradiction of the frequent psychological assumptions made by the courts in formulating legal rules of conduct. That is to say, when a court makes an assumption with respect to how individuals behave under particular circumstances, it is making an assumption which the data of psychology may corroborate or contradict. . . . In many fields of the law the courts are making psychological assumptions . . . which the present development of psychology makes it worth while for the law to collect and test in the light of such facts as psychology is now prepared to offer.

HUNTINGTON CAIRNS [1]

SO far we have mainly concerned ourselves with events in criminal trials after the facts have been decided, whether by plea of guilty or by trial of the issues between prosecution and defence. What has already been written leads to an examination of the methods of trial themselves. We must, in fact, face and answer the question whether the discoveries of modern psychology rob our historic methods of trial of their utility and their justification. To lawyers such a question may seem frivolous, but some psychologists have gone far towards condemning totally the methods of trial that have been laboriously evolved during the centuries. Thus we have the two extremes. There are those, mostly lawyers, who cannot see that our present legal and penal methods are in any way affected by the teaching of psychology. We have already had a glimpse of this mentality. There are also those who claim that psychologists should supersede judges and magistrates and concern themselves

[1] *Law and the Social Sciences*, pp. 173-4.

159

with both the ascertainment of guilt and the fate of the guilty. Happily the majority of psycho-therapists, through closer contacts with problems of delinquency, accept in principle the usefulness of our machinery of criminal justice, and on the other hand some criminal lawyers and some among those on the Bench [1] are beginning to realize that psychology can be of great assistance to them and that some of the maxims which tradition has handed down to them are not of such universal validity as they were brought up to believe. The latter discovery is, however, in its early stages.

No complete agreement about ideals is likely between on the one side lawyers and the Bench and on the other the Freudian school of psychology. But among psycho-therapists who accept Freud's teaching there are many who would accept in practice much that in theory they would criticize, this being a concession to the obvious fact that public opinion is psychologically quite immature. [2] The prospects of a progressive understanding between the Bench and psychologists would be advanced if it were realized that between the two great wars of this century some progress towards the acceptance of some psychological views had been achieved. We English people do not readily accept new theories, but we are masters in the subtle art of working new theories in practice without admitting them, or even realizing that changes have taken place. In fact much psychological progress has already been made.

The object of all criminal procedure is to ascertain whether the accused person has been proved guilty of the facts alleged against him. The English system does this by the combative method ; the state (or sometimes a private individual or corporation) accuses a defendant and has to

[1] By the word Bench I mean throughout this book all those who preside in criminal trials, whether at Assizes, Quarter Sessions or magistrates' courts. This definition includes, therefore, High Court judges, chairmen of Sessions and recorders and also magistrates, professional and lay.

[2] Freud would have agreed that society has every right to protect itself, but he would have regarded treatment and cure as the best protection.

prove the facts against him by evidence. In general the system of continental countries is by way of enquiry and investigation. Under both systems great forensic battles take place as to the nature of the crime that has been proved. It is axiomatic to a lawyer that this is the right, as well as at present the only practicable, method. The lawyer will be reluctant to admit that any other point of view is possible.

But in all schools of psychology the act is of less significance than the motive. The mental state at the time of a deed is what the psychologist would primarily wish to investigate. Hence everyone on the Bench, or engaged in practice in the criminal courts, would do well to read such a book as *The Unknown Murderer* (already mentioned in these pages) by Theodor Reik, which expounds the psychoanalytical point of view. Few among lawyers will be converted by it. To me certain parts appear extravagant, probably because of my psychological limitations. But the book is valuable as a help to understanding the Freudian point of view and it shows clearly how our long-cherished legal principles appear in the eyes of a psycho-analytical enthusiast. Reik concentrated on motive. He wrote complainingly about 'the enormous importance attached by criminal justice to the deed as such' and that this indicates 'a cultural phase which is approaching its end'. Modern psychology in his eyes 'shows that the concepts of guilt and innocence are inadequate'.[1] It is difficult to imagine a system of investigation solely concerned with motives when in fact a suspected person is denying his wrongful deeds, or when he has been subjected to accusations that are false. But at least it should be acknowledged that the psychological conception of responsibility is more thorough, and, I would say, on a higher ethical level than the legal.[2]

[1] p. 219.
[2] Here modern psychology acts on the same principles as the Christian religion. Both explore the spirit in which acts are done. Many psycho-analysts follow Freud, who in his book *The Future of an Illusion* claimed that religion is illusion and can be explained

This can be seen from examples. If two men are accused of a murder, lawyers will spend their energies in ascertaining which man did the killing or whether both took part. To the psychologist the important question is whether either man had an intention to kill and, if so, why. By law one of the men will be acquitted if it is proved that the other killed the victim without help or instigation. The psychologist will still want to enquire whether murder was willed by either man and, if so, the reasons why. In law there is a great distinction between killing by shooting and an attempt to shoot by someone who aimed badly or who did not keep his weapons in order. The psychologist will pay little attention to the result of the shooting ; he will want to explore the motive behind the desire to kill, and, if he is a psycho-analyst, he will want to know also, in the case of the man who failed to kill, whether this was the result of an unconscious wish not to kill. From the daily events of a magistrates' court comes another example. The differ- ence between dangerous driving of a motor vehicle, as defined by one section of our traffic laws, and careless driving, defined in another section, is of the utmost impor- tance to a driver. For the former offence he can be tried by a jury ; if convicted by either jury or magistrate, he will probably be forbidden to drive for a considerable period ; he may be sent to prison. Careless driving need not result in a suspension of licence and does not involve a sentence to prison. To a psychologist such a distinction is misleading ; his object would be to find out whether the driver is accident- prone, and, if so, the reasons for his condition. As Reik explained :

In psycho-analysis everything except psychological insight is unessential, while to the criminologist psychological events are accidental or unimportant compared with the reality which he has to elucidate.[1]

---

by psycho-analytical dogmas. Such analysts would not accept the statement that there is much in modern psychology, and even in psycho-analysis, that runs parallel with the Christian ethic. But I believe this to be true.   [1] p. 28.

However impractical a legal system founded upon this view may seem, can it be denied that this view is wider and more helpful to the community than is the narrower legal view ? All communities need protection against such people as those who would compass the death of another or accident-prone people who drive motor cars. The only protection which our present legal system offers is the punishment of those proved guilty in a trial conducted on rules which, however necessary, are arbitrary and which result in the frequent acquittal of those morally guilty. A psychological system, if one could image such in operation, would give a greater measure of protection, since its whole object would be to remove dangerous tendencies before they manifest themselves in dangerous acts.

As a magistrate I frequently find myself in the position of having to discharge accused persons, although I am morally certain that they did the acts complained of and that in future they will probably be a greater menace to the community than ever. I may feel strongly that they would benefit greatly from some form of treatment or supervision. But I have no choice. This is because magistrates, like all on the Bench, are working a penal system based on punishment. The psycho-analyst would have none of this. If he could accept punishment, he would only do so if it was a constructive part of the curative process.

The most conservative lawyer must see that our present system has limitations that menace the community. Sometimes this menace can be reduced by voluntary methods. Just as in an earlier chapter I mentioned that sometimes the victims in sexual cases have been persuaded in the private rooms of the South-Western court to seek psychological help, so similarly I have known many men, acquitted by me owing to lack of proof, who have been persuaded to seek such aid. In cases where I have been morally certain that the facts as presented by the prosecution in a sexual charge are based on solid fact, but have been compelled to acquit by defects of proof, I have many times added to my explanation why an acquittal is necessary a few carefully chosen words to the defendant.   I point out that only he knows the true facts and that, if in reality there is substance in the charge, he would be very well advised to have a private talk with the probation officer.   I sometimes add a few words of warning about the dangers of uncontrolled sexual forces, but I always end up with an assurance that if the defendant has any talk with the probation officer, the police will know nothing about it.   Such words may be unorthodox, but frequently they have been said in the presence of barristers and solicitors and no objection has ever been raised ; on the contrary, defending lawyers have sometimes advised their clients outside the court to respond to the invitation.   In fact, many acquitted defendants have frankly admitted serious troubles to the probation officer and have responded to offers of psycho-therapy by doctors, just as if they had been found guilty and had been placed on probation.   This experience is some evidence that both individuals and the community benefit when it is in practice possible for the psychological view to be adopted.

Analogous cases are where because of defects in the case of the prosecution defendants are charged, not with sexual offences punishable by imprisonment, but with indecent conduct in a public place under municipal bye-laws, the maximum penalty for which offences is usually five pounds.[1] I have known many cases where men accused only of the minor offence, whether found guilty or not, have co-oper-ated, of course behind the scenes, in receiving psycho-therapy—to their immense advantage.   Those found guilty of the minor offence have often acted just as if they had been found guilty of one of the major offences and were conse-quently in danger of a long sentence to imprisonment.   The threat of punishment has not been in such cases the driving force, but the realization that treatment is desirable in their own interests.   To the psycho-therapist it makes no differ-ence whether his patient was charged with exhibitionism, sexual assault or minor indecency in a public place ; it also makes no difference to him whether the patient was found

[1] The offence under the bye-laws is easier to prove.

guilty or not. He treats his patient according to his psychological needs, not according to his legal offence.

Those who are tempted to regard the psycho-analytical view as unsound should remember that Parliament has already taken the step of enabling juvenile courts to deal with the physical and psychological state of children, regardless of any question of criminal act. The Children and Young Persons Act, 1933, brought within the jurisdiction of the juvenile courts those under 17 who were not charged with any offence, but were 'in need of care and protection'.[1] Such children can, if necessary, be sent to an Approved School (where delinquent children are also sent), or they can be placed under the supervision of a probation officer for any period up to three years. This innovation has had invaluable results, but it has to be admitted that it is a step towards the psycho-analytical conception of the needs of both individuals and the community. Whether any analogous provisions can ever be framed for dealing with adults who manifest a condition which cannot be proved to be criminal, but is a menace to themselves and the public, is a difficult question. At least let it be realized that the present legal restrictions, limiting adult courts to the supervision of those who have committed an offence that can be proved, means that a large number of people who need help, and who may be a substantial danger to the public, are denied the curative facilities now available for proved or admitted delinquents.

Lawyers may find consolation in the fact that even Reik did not urge that psychologists should supersede the Bench as arbiters of fact. However low was Reik's opinion of criminal courts (it was those on the Continent which he knew), he was candid that ' in the present state of our science, psycho-analysis is neither suited nor competent to solve the question of guilt or innocence '.[2] He added :

The analyst may experiment with disconnected ideas, free associations, interpretation of dreams and faulty acts and other

---

[1] Sections 61 and 62.   [2] p. 56.

mental reactions ; he will contribute nothing of value to the question of actual fact.[1]

We do not know what Reik's motive for this admission was, but he may have realized that psycho-therapists have few weapons against those who persistently lie about their conduct. Possibly psychologists could extract the truth from an unwilling patient by injecting drugs or by hypnosis, for it is well established that when people are in deep unconsciousness they can reply to questions without any conscious censorship. But for the state to order the investigation of people's unconscious without their consent is a measure which in English-speaking countries would not as yet be acceptable. The legal method of trial admittedly creates inducements to lie, because of the fear of exposure and punishment, but at least it gives facilities for ascertaining facts without the consent of those in whose interest it is to lie. Our present methods of trial have been long accepted by public opinion as fair and as I have said, reforms must be such as to command public respect. Nevertheless there is no justification for complacency or for a refusal to inquire into reasonable reforms which in some measure can incorporate some of the advantages of the psychological approach.

I am convinced that some day trials for some offences will, with the consent of the accused, take place under circumstances where all possibilities of punishment are from the beginning excluded ; also that the usefulness of giving of some powers to adult courts analogous to the ' care and protection ' powers of juvenile courts will need to be investigated. In so far as it becomes the sole duty of courts to secure the right treatment for those before them, many of the elements of trial that are now rightly regarded as essential could be dispensed with. When this becomes possible, fewer guilty people would plead not guilty and many who could not be charged as things are, but who need assistance and who may be dangerous to others, would come under the

[1] p. 59.

jurisdiction of courts, since the only step that the courts would be able to take would be supervision and treatment. In this way it might be possible to use the psychological method to supplement the legal method of trial. If such steps became practicable, another advantage would be that persons aggrieved would to a large extent be spared the ordeal of giving evidence in a public forensic combat, an experience that can be far more distressing and psychologically harmful than is generally realized, especially where trial is by jury.

In this country psychologists have given comparatively little attention to these big problems. They have interested themselves mainly in delinquents after they have been found guilty by the courts. There is a real need for a thorough examination by psychologists into every step taken in our criminal system, from the moment when suspicion falls upon an individual to the passing of the sentence. I fear that at first they are not likely to receive much encouragement from the Bench or from lawyers, both of whom might be tempted to say of our present methods what a moderate left-wing member of Parliament once said to an extremist at a ceremonial opening of Parliament : ' This will take a Hell of a lot of abolishing.' But even in the absence of a legal welcome there are several important matters of procedure which psychologists should investigate.[1]

A rule of judicial procedure which lawyers value greatly, but which is contrary to psychological principles, is that those about to be charged with a criminal offence have to

[1] In the United States of America psychological interest has been diverted by Professor Munsterberg, an eminent American psychologist, who in his book *On the Witness Stand* proposed to subject witnesses to psychological examination before they give evidence in court. Though such a step might help a court to appreciate the value of witnesses, I agree with the criticisms made by Mr. Henry W. Taft, a leader among the lawyers of New York, in his books *Witnesses in Court* and *Legal Miscellanies*. For a long time it will be safer to rely on the cross-examination of witnesses, with all its limitations, to reveal any bias that witnesses may have.

be warned that they need not make any statement and that anything that they may say may be used in evidence at their trial. Criminal law insists that admissions by defendants can only be reported to the trial court if they have been voluntary and the well-known ' Judges' Rules ' have elaborated an involved system whereby alone the police can obtain and report admissions. Thus ' whenever a police officer has made up his mind to charge a person with a crime, he should first caution such person before asking any questions, or any further questions, as the case may be. Persons in custody should not be questioned without the usual caution being first administered. If the prisoner wishes to volunteer any statement, the usual caution should be administered.' It is probable that much ingenuity is shown by experienced police officers in interpreting these rules ; the anonymous but vitriolic critic of our magistrates who wrote under the name ' Solicitor ' stated that ' contrary to the Judges' Rules, a great deal of direct questioning of persons in custody goes on '.[1] Be this as it may, there is no doubt that, while the rules prevent what is popularly known as ' third degree ' methods, they also facilitate the escape from justice of many guilty persons. Even from the purely legal standpoint these judges' rules have been criticized. Thus Mr. Heber Hart asserted in his book *The Way to Justice*, a book which makes no reference to the theories and criticisms of psychologists :

All restrictions upon the interrogation of accused persons which can reasonably be considered necessary to prevent undue pressure or unfairness of any kind are no doubt desirable in the interests alike of justice and humanity. But that a policeman should be obliged to interrupt a prisoner, who appears about to make an incriminating statement, by administering a ' caution ' seems unnecessary from the point of view of justice to the prisoner and at the same time contrary to the interest of the rest of the community.[2]

---

[1] *Penal Reform in England*, p. 81, and see the same author's *English Justice*, pp. 102 et seq.   [2] p. 102.

Even in open court, where anything approaching 'third degree' methods would be immediately exposed and denounced by a free press, the Bench cannot question a defendant unless he freely elects to give evidence. This rule often operates to the detriment of a defendant, for there are many cases where a *prima facie* case has been established by the prosecution, but where explanations by the accused may well place a harmless construction upon it. This rule was also condemned by Mr. Heber Hart :

That at the present day a judge or magistrate should still be precluded from putting questions to the accused with the object of eliciting incriminating admissions or any other material information, unless he tenders himself as a witness, is a departure from rational procedure which cannot be justified by the interest of the innocent, while it involves grave mischief to the public at large.[1]

These rules are also a complete departure from the principles of psychology. Their basis is the legal theory that criminal offences are dealt with by punishment ; that being so, the law establishes a sort of sporting contest in which the accused is given definite rights. But in fact a large proportion of criminal offences are not now followed by legal punishment ;[2] more and more the court seeks the cure of the offender. There can, therefore, be no justification for the universal application of these restrictions. The moment that the treatment and cure of offenders become the object of criminal proceedings, the whole purpose and spirit of the judges' rules will cease to be relevant ; in fact, the rules will become obstructive to the purposes of the court. When the ultimate object of the law becomes cure through treatment, admissions of the facts will need to be encouraged by proper means from the beginning. Psycho-therapy has as

---

[1] p. 103.
[2] Of course the publicity of the trial can involve a stigma that can be in itself a punishment, sometimes a greater punishment than the one provided by the criminal law.

one of its essential features the facilitating of confession, but only of confession in private. Dr. C. G. Jung defined the stages of psycho-therapy as confession, explanation, education and transformation.[1] A therapist in tackling a delinquent would not begin by an abrupt request for confession ; he would probably begin by assuring his patient that there was no cause for fear and that complete candour will facilitate the treatment. Fear is the first obstacle in the way of psycho-therapy. In so far as courts can become psychological in their methods, they too must eliminate fear from their procedure.

Another weakness of legal method which psychology has revealed is that our methods of trial assume that ordinary people can if they wish give a clear and accurate account of their own conduct and also of what they have observed. Any serious contradiction, whether in explanation of personal conduct or in description of something observed, is apt to be regarded as evidence of deliberate lying. Innumerable honest witnesses have been reduced to bewilderment by this procedure. Yet psychologists of all schools would deny the assumption that people can be accurate or consistent when explaining either personal conduct or impersonal experiences. That human personality is inherently contradictory is almost an axiom of psychology. The psychological notion of unconscious mental processes means that we are unaware of the motives of our actions. Many of our actions arise from certain instinctive urges and tendencies. When we think we know about our motives, we are often adducing only proximate, and not ultimate, reasons, for our behaviour. The human mind is usually a bundle of inconsistent impulses. Certainly the witness is rare who gives the impression of being entirely objective and accurate ; plenty of witnesses who in fact are stating what is not true are telling the truth as they see it.

The emotions usually influence observation. On the happening of an event emotions tend to colour the impressions of observers. Thus when a motor car knocks

---

[1] *Modern Man in Search of a Soul*, p. 35.

down an unfortunate pedestrian, a spectator will interpret the facts according to his unconscious feelings. If he is a passenger in the car, he is likely to jump at once to the conclusion that his driver was not to blame. If he was not in the car, and certainly if he does not drive himself, he is likely to assume that responsibility rests on the motorist. Auto-suggestion is often at work when evidence about accidents is being given. Another example is the frequent assault case between two women neighbours in humble walks of life. Each swears, and believes, that the other woman was the first to strike, but the impartial magistrate can only seek refuge in his knowledge that at the time both women were so excited that their powers of observation were obscured.

Thus much of what lawyers are apt to denounce as deliberate lying is in fact the emergence of unconscious forces which disable a witness from truthfully recording what happened. This fact can rob cross-examination, that unique feature of the English method of trial, of some of its justification. That massive work Taylor on the *Laws of Evidence* states that cross-examination is ' one of the most efficacious tests which the law has devised for the discovery of truth '. It is true that sometimes through cross-examination lying is exposed and truth placed in proper perspective. But even apart from psychological considerations, it might be expected that the universality of this statement would be doubted, especially as other systems of justice have managed to reach a high standard of justice without cross-examination. In fact in magistrates' courts most of the work has to be done without it. The ability of average laymen in magistrates' courts to cross-examine is nil and much professional cross-examination is unskilled. When invited to ask his questions, the layman usually begins a rambling statement of his own case, or to abuse the witness. The unskilled lawyer often proceeds with sentences beginning ' I put it to you . . .' to invite the witness to agree that the contrary to what he has just said is true. The court benefits from neither proceeding.

This is an old problem. Sir James Fitzjames Stephen once said :

The prisoner, confused by the unfamiliar surroundings, and by the legal rules which he does not understand, tries to question the adverse witness and muddles up the examination with what ought to be his speech for the defence, and, not knowing how to cross-examine, is at last reduced to utter perplexity and thinks it respectful to be silent. . . . There is a scene which most lawyers know by heart, but which I can never hear without pain.[1]

I agree entirely about the pain. It is distressing to see humble people fumbling about when trying to cross-examine, sometimes giving themselves away badly in the process. But the law requires it. The law assumes that all advocates and all laymen have the ability in cross-examination possessed by a leading King's Counsel. What often happens was described by an anonymous doctor-magistrate : ' When told, as is the custom, that' he may ask the accusing witness questions, he begins a statement ; and, when ordered to shut up, as is also the custom, 'he subsides into mortified silence.'[2] Can this ' shutting up ' be avoided ? Mr. Frederick Mead, a metropolitan magistrate for a long time, wrote :

The defendant-in-person usually begins at once to make a statement. He should not be checked in this, but allowed to ' run on ' and so disclose the facts which constitute his defence, and the court by putting questions to the witnesses based upon the defendant's statement, will thus be able to achieve on the defendant's behalf a successful cross-examination.[3]

Sometimes this is a wise course, especially if the defendant's statement is short. But it is strictly illegal, as courts must not question defendants. If the statement is long, this method has the insuperable objection that what the defendant says when he is supposed to be cross-examining is not evidence and is not taken down by the clerk of the

[1] *Life,* by Leslie Stephen, p. 210.   [2] *Psychology in Court,* p. 117.
[3] *The Office of Magistrate,* p. 37.

court. A defendant usually tells his story best the first time ; if he is encouraged to pour it out before he himself gives evidence, his best points may be lost. I confess that in simple cases, I solve these difficulties by not emphasizing the right to cross-examine ; most defendants are content to have an opportunity of telling their story when their time comes. I often say to a defendant : ' You will have a chance of telling your story shortly, if you want to. You can ask this witness questions now, or would you like to wait till your turn comes ? ' The result is usually temporary silence.[1] But there is no satisfactory solution of this probem because psychologists have never examined and helped us lawyers to solve it.[2] The Departmental Committee on the Social Services in Courts of Summary Jurisdiction discussed this problem [3] and for husband and wife cases a new plan was provided in the Summary Procedure (Domestic Proceedings) Act, 1937. But the scheme, by reasons of the concessions to legal opinion, was useless. After the Act was passed, the Home Office tried in a circular to magistrates to make plain what was cumbrous in the Act, but they only succeeded in translating Greek into Latin. The problem remains, and will remain, until the requirements of both law and psychology have been considered together.

In the rules governing the procedure in juvenile courts a similar attempt was made. The rules for juvenile courts embodied the views of Mr. Mead, quoted above.[4] But in

[1] In wife v. husband cases I usually make no reference to the right to cross-examine.

[2] Legal aid in all cases would not be a remedy, for comparatively few lawyers are good at cross-examination and the problem arises in every case, however petty. No one has yet suggested that a lorry driver accused of passing a traffic light at red needs free legal aid at the public expense ; yet the problem of cross-examination must arise in his case.   [3] Paragraph 46.

[4] It is an open question whether some of the Rules in the Summary Jurisdiction (Children and Young Persons) Rules, 1933, would not be declared *ultra vires* if ever they came to be challenged in the High Court. This Rule in particular would probably not be upheld, as it authorizes the questioning of the defendant by the court.

13

fact they have not solved the problem and in my visits to juvenile courts I found much stumbling and unnecessary worrying of the child about the right to cross-examine.[1]

If a psychologist were invited to watch our courts at work, especially magistrates' courts, and to report upon their procedure, I feel sure that high up in his report would be a criticism of the physical arrangements of the court rooms. Courts are terrifying places for many people, far more terrifying than they need be. This applies to magistrates' courts, where no wigs or gowns are worn, just as much as to the higher courts. A psychologist would point out that it is clearly wrong, seeing that the real purpose of courts is that the truth may be elucidated, for the appointments to be such that fear and anxiety are created in those whose testimony will be wanted. The formal arrangement of the court, with the Bench high up on its dais, and everybody concerned placed neatly in an enclosed pew, has no fears for those defendants who have often been in such places before. But for the defendant or witness who comes for the first time, the very formality is frightening; and it is specially frightening for young people. Pomp and ceremony are useful adjuncts of justice in some cases and the ideal would be to have in the same building a formal and an informal court. But where that is not practicable, I would prefer that the sole court should be informal. Many modern churches have abandoned formal pews and it is time that they were abolished in magistrates' courts if a building has one court only. Chairs and tables, all movable, are desirable, being objects that everybody has seen before. It is undesirable for the Bench to be elevated high above other people. Architects could easily re-arrange our court rooms so that the Bench can see and be seen without being elevated high above those in court. Those on the Bench should rely on their own qualities, and not on their physical elevation, to

[1] In his book *The Child and the Magistrate* Mr. John A. F. Watson failed to solve the problem. His talks to the children, as printed, would seldom be fully understood. His real talks to children are, as I know by experience, much more suitable.

earn respect. The more like an ordinary room a court is, the more successful will the court be in most cases in extracting the truth from witnesses.[1]

Those who believe in the necessity for a formal structure of courts in all cases should ask themselves why it is that so few people in a magistrates' court can speak the words of the oath correctly. Personally I think it a pity that the oath includes the word ' evidence ', a word that is not in the vocabulary of a large number of witnesses ; it is shocking to see how many people stumble at that word. ' What I shall tell the court ' would be a practical paraphrase and I some-times give young children those words, in explanation of ' evidence '. But the main cause of the stumbling is not the word ' evidence ', but fear. The people who stumble when taking the oath can ordinarily read perfectly well, but they cannot do so in court. Again, many people are more deaf in court than they are outside, a fact upon which police officers and cross-examining lawyers sometimes comment adversely. But it is fear of their surroundings that intensi-fies deafness, not as a rule wilfulness. A feeling of anxiety is also the reason why such an exasperating lot of people say ' Pardon ' when they are spoken to in court. What they really mean is ' I am nervous. Give me time to settle down and think.' The question has usually been heard, and often an answer will eventually come without the repetition of the question.

A small but important matter from the psychological standpoint is the legal assumption that nobody will tell the truth unless he stands up. Some courts are so constructed that if a witness sits down, he disappears from view. Such absurdities need to be terminated and every witness and defendant who will occupy the court for more than a short time should automatically be asked to sit down. Nor should witnesses be worried by court ushers into doing every detail correctly—right hand instead of left, gloves off, &c.—when they take the oath. Our historic methods, as we have

---

[1] The next chapter will emphasize the importance of these factors when children have to give evidence in adult courts.

seen, are to obtain the truth through fear ; the very insistence on the taking of an oath has as its purpose to instil the fear of God. I do not think that our people are sufficiently advanced to justify the abolition of the oath, but at least witnesses need not be worried when they take it. The formality of a court and good drill by witnesses may flatter the court staff, but such things deter the very persons from whom courts need true statements. Ceremony has for so long been an integral part of the administration of justice that simplification for many cases will not be popular. But at least at magistrates' courts the aim should usually be, not the imitation of the pomp and ceremony of the Assize courts, but the most informal procedure consistent with dignity.

Another important detail is whether all evidence need be given in the witness-box. In my domestic court I abolished the use of the witness-box, save for independent witnesses, in 1935 ; the parties give their evidence seated in the place where they remain throughout the proceedings, standing only to take the oath. There seems no reason why defendants to criminal charges should not give their evidence from the place where they remain during the case ;—formal ' docks ' are relics of barbarism and should be abolished. Marching people about the court is disturbing to their thoughts and is not necessary. Once when I was visiting a juvenile court I was surprised to see that the father of a delinquent youth was moved some four yards from where he had been when he gave his evidence. When the court was finished, I asked the chairman why this was done. The reply showed a pathetic belief that things must always be done like that. In fact the father could have given his evidence just as well without moving.

There is one important matter of procedure concerning the interval between the decision on the facts and the decision about the fate of the delinquent, an interval which, as Chapter 6 has shown, is usually far too short. Where a delinquent has been examined by a doctor, in regard to his physical or psychological condition, or where a probation officer has made inquiries concerning his social surroundings and his general attitude to his offence, is it essential as a matter of principle that the delinquent shall hear or be informed of every statement made ?

The general legal principle is that a defendant is entitled to know what is being said about him to his trial court and to answer any observations that have been made. But there are many dangers in applying this principle rigidly. If written reports, after the verdict on the facts has been announced, are excluded, much essential information will be withheld. Prison doctors and other experts cannot attend every magistrates' court dealing with delinquents whom they have examined, and in sparsely populated areas even probation officers cannot always attend, as they serve several courts and distances are great.[1] So the case for the admissibility after verdict of written reports is strong. Must every statement in such reports be revealed ? If an arbitrary rule is made to this effect, as is often the case, harm will be done. For instance, it may have been discovered in the course of inquiries that the delinquent is in fact an illegitimate child. This fact has in many cases been concealed from the delinquent by those responsible for him. Or a medical examination may have revealed the symptoms of an incurable disease ; or a psychological examination may have suggested that some event in the delinquent's earlier life, of which he is now not aware, has relevance to the offence. In principle people should know the truth about themselves, but if there has been secrecy in the past, it cannot be right that revelation shall take place in a criminal court, when the delinquent may be in a very emotional state. Without, therefore, rejecting the general principle that information in reports should be passed on to delinquents, I would plead for some discretion.

Rule 11 (iv) of the juvenile court Rules gives discretion to juvenile courts. If these Rules are worked properly, they

---

[1] In some rural areas the number of probation officers is too small. This will continue until the national exchequer pays most of the cost of local justice in rural areas.

must be of the greatest value.   I would suggest that an
inquiry might well take place to see whether this Rule can
usefully be adapted and made available through legislation
in all criminal courts.   Courts must, I believe, be trusted
in this matter of written reports after verdict.   Parliament
had sufficient confidence in our criminal courts to give them
in nearly every case an unfettered discretion between
a sentence of imprisonment and complete forgiveness.   It
is asking little more that courts shall be entitled to receive
written reports and be trusted to give in public such information as will not do harm to the delinquent.

In such written reports, as also in evidence given before
a court, medical psychologists should always realize that
they are addressing those who are not acquainted with their
technical terms.   This applies, of course, to all expert
witnesses, but the lesson needs to be learned by psychologists especially.   It is always difficult to paraphrase
technical terms, but with care it can be done.   I have read
of a psychologist who wanted to explain that boys and girls
cannot produce any original work unless they really want
to do so ; what he actually wrote was that ' the urge towards
creative ideation in the adolescent must be primarily
volitional '.   A doctor once told me that by inadvertence
he once told a court that an offender was suffering from
a ' congenital convergent strabismus '.   He found the Bench
becoming anxious and hastened to correct himself and say
that the offender was born with a squint.   These stories
have a moral which psychologists should heed in their
contacts with courts.   Nor is it desirable that psychologists
should give the full reasons for their conclusions.   Psychology is so contrary to ideas generally accepted that studied
moderation is necessary if cases are to be explained to courts.
It is easy to bring psychology into contempt in the minds of
the Bench.   Once I even heard a High Court judge, of
immense experience of criminal courts, pour scorn on
psychology and show a lack of appreciation for the fact that
in his work psychology could be of immense help.   A psycho-
analyst of great reputation once sent me a report about

a difficult lad who was before me for the theft of a bicycle. This lad, said the report, made a ' love-substitute ' of bicycles ; he had lost his brother, to whom he had been devoted, through blood-poisoning derived from some game with him with a rusty bicycle wheel. The lad felt in some undefined way, I was told, responsible for his brother's death. The ' love-substitute ' theory may have been true, but a certain scepticism was justified, because according to police reports the lad had only stolen bicycles when confined in places of detention and attempting to escape. But whatever the explanation of the lad's unconscious motives, it was unnecessary to elaborate them in a report for the use of a criminal court.

It would also be well if psycho-analytical writers of books for popular consumption, like all other specialists writing for the general public, would heed this warning. For popular expositions will be the ones that legal beginners in psychology will read. Most psycho-analytical theories must seem extravagant to the uninitiated and detailed explanations may easily provoke derision. Dr. R. E. Money-Kyrle's book *Aspasia*, for instance, contains many terse statements which would really require many pages to explain to the uninstructed mind. Thus ' while most sociologists attribute our social ills to the economic system, we [psycho-analysts] have reduced them to the Œdipus Complex '.[1] Such a challenging remark, and the tone of facetiousness which characterized the book, cannot help to inspire confidence. Professor Flügel of the University of London wrote in his ' An Introduction to Psycho-Analysis ' (part of the book *Outline of Modern Knowledge*, a popular work), of ' the symbolization of coitus by means of climbing or walking upstairs '.[2] The meaning would be clear to those who have proceeded far in psycho-analytical studies, but others might think that the professor was trying to draw a distinction between the emotional life of those who live in houses and those who live in bungalows. Psycho-analysts writing books for the general public, like those writing reports for

[1] p. 62.　　　　[2] p. 59.

the use of the Bench, would be well advised to confine themselves to conclusions and general theory and to give only such explanation as can be understood without any deep knowledge of psycho-analytical theory. They need to remember the advice said to have been given to a newly-appointed judge by a colleague of much experience : ' Never give your reasons. Your decisions will probably be right. Your reasons will probably be wrong.'

CHAPTER 8

CHILDREN IN THE COURTS

We know that a shocking experience can produce a psychic trauma which will so disturb the psychic mechanisms that, under certain conditions, delinquency will result.

AUGUST AICHHORN [1]

THE preceding chapter dealt with desirable and possible changes in the procedure in our adult courts. But psychology shows also that many changes in procedure are urgent, both in adult and juvenile courts, when those under seventeen [2] are brought into courts of law, either as witnesses or defendants. We have seen already that in childhood psychological traumas can easily arise, unbeknown to those in charge, and that such traumas can have serious results in later life. Yet even now our present methods of handling such young people in courts could not have a worse effect upon them if they had been specially designed to create the danger of serious traumas.

It is desirable first to deal with juvenile courts themselves.

Juvenile courts were first established in this country in 1908. That until then delinquent children and youths were taken to the ordinary courts and were in legal theory dealt with according to the ordinary procedure should be remembered by those who are prone to expatiate upon the glories of our legal traditions.

While it was obviously necessary to remove delinquent children from the conventional magistrates' courts, the criticism has often been made that it was not desirable to establish criminal courts for them at all ; it has been urged that there is an undesirable element of class justice in juvenile courts, since parents in the world of salaries and

[1] *Wayward Youth*, p. 55.
[2] The age will, of course, vary with the type of child or adolescent.

nurseries usually manage to deal with their children's peccadillos without the attentions of magistrates. There is much to be said for this view. It might perhaps have been better to remove the delinquencies of those who are regarded by the law as children (those aged from 8 to 14) from criminal procedure completely and to have established for them some procedure to be worked by the education authorities.[1] Then those who are legally known as ' young persons ' (those aged 14 to 17) might have been dealt with by the ordinary magistrates' courts, but under a different and separate procedure.[2]

It is certain that juvenile courts in general have never come up to the high level expected by those responsible for their creation. Considerable light was thrown upon the defects of many juvenile courts when in the early days of the war of 1939 many thousands of children were evacuated from towns into the more sparsely populated areas.

In general it may be said that such failures as have existed in juvenile courts have been due to the fact that in a large number of areas the courts were never constituted according to the law, which requires that juvenile court magistrates should be drawn from ' a panel of justices specially qualified for dealing with juvenile cases '.[3] What was intended was well expressed by Mrs. (Dame) Barrow Cadbury in her book *Youthful Offenders Yesterday and To-day*: ' The magistrates should be chosen because of their understanding of children, should know something of the schools they attend and their various activities and recreations, including the cinemas they love. They should know of Sunday School brigades, scout and guide companies and clubs . . . Some-

[1] There is now a movement among education authorities to obtain control over child delinquents. But it comes rather late.

[2] The plan evolved by the American Law Institute emphasized that it is ' undesirable to extend the scope of the juvenile court to the older youths. Those courts utilize an informality of procedure wholly unsuited to the trial of older youths.' Such an opinion from a most progressive body of experts in America should be heeded by enthusiasts for juvenile courts in this country.

[3] Clause 1 (2) of the second schedule to the Act of 1933.

thing should be known too of hospitals, school clinics, convalescent homes and child guidance clinics.'[1] A point that has received far too little attention is whether it is possible for a magistrate to be good in his approach to both children under fourteen and youths between fourteen and seventeen. In my opinion much harm has been done by placing youths in the hands of magistrates who have the mentality that is excellent for children only. I would add that the most desirable quality in juvenile court magistrates is an appreciation and understanding of those hopeful children who are at least sufficiently alive not to obey blindly all the precepts of their elders. Despite considerable efforts by the Home Office, there used to be many courts where the only apparent special qualification of the magistrates was their seniority; there seemed to be the widest possible gulf between the ages of the delinquents and those of their judges. In 1936 one member of a juvenile court was at least 90 years old and over a hundred were between 80 and 90. Steps were taken by Parliament during the war to prevent magistrates from sitting in court when they could not, by reason of age or health, efficiently perform their duties, but there is no doubt that the average age of magistrates in a juvenile court should ordinarily be considerably lower than in an adult court; this has not yet been achieved. In some areas the whole of the magisterial Bench was included in the juvenile court panel, a policy which defied the Act or else indicated an estimate of local ability which verged on the absurd.

In the years between the wars, and since, a great deal was said and written about the volume of juvenile crime. The figures were certainly bad, but in this respect England was better off than the United States of America; in England 13 was the age at which most crime is committed, whereas in the United States 19 was the age of maximum crime. I regard this contrast as a tribute to the English juvenile courts; the fact that as ages increased from 13 onwards, less crime is committed, points to at least partial success in

[1] p. 114.

the methods adopted.   But statistics of juvenile crime can be
misleading, since, as the courts become more humane and
intelligent, more prosecutions are brought.   From the
psychological point of view dangers lie for those who commit
crime and are not brought to court, rather than for those
who are prosecuted, provided that courts make full inquiries
and act in accord with psychological principles.

In discussions about the volume of juvenile crime the fact
is apt to be forgotten that several modern developments
have invited juvenile crime.   We who are middle-aged may
flatter ourselves that we were less criminal than the children
of to-day,[1] but we should remember that in our childhood
shops were utilitarian places where on entering customers
were asked what they wanted ;   there were no open-counter
shops where cheap and attractive goods were within touch
and where much stealing went undetected, thus offering
a perpetual challenge to our morals ;   there were no cinemas,
no funfairs, few slot machines where we could spend our
pennies, and possibly other people's ;   and those parents
who made bets, did not send their children with their weekly
flutter to the bookmaker.   Much of the juvenile crime
to-day should be placed at the doors of those who for
commercial gain provide all these facilities for children,
thus giving continuous opportunities to the young for
giving vent to their more debased sporting instincts.

We shall never be able to claim that juvenile crime is
being adequately handled until every juvenile court has
available the services of a child guidance centre, staffed by
experts in child psychology.   The play-therapy which child
psychologists have devised can do marvels with children
suffering in reality, though this may not appear on the surface, from emotional strain.   Provided that a child's intelligence is not too low, such therapy can do much by relieving
the strain to rectify dangerous situations and thus remove
the impulses to delinquent conduct.   Through play,
psychologists can bring children to express their difficulties
and to release their fears and repressed emotions, and to

[1] I make no such claim for myself.

acquire an appreciation of the true proportions of their troubles. Up to 1939 child guidance centres were few and were dependent on charity. They received quite inadequate support, as did all agencies for providing psychological treatment for those who could not afford professional fees. No one would wish that children's hospitals and other places where physical ailments receive attention should be supported less, but there is a great need that institutions offering psychological help should be better supported. It has been unfortunately true that a child with a psychological disorder that may eventually result in serious crime, even in murder, has so far received less public sympathy than a child with a spinal complaint or defective eyesight.

An important feature of psychological work among children is that usually the parents, as well as the child, attend the psycho-therapist. In a most tactful manner the sins of the child are visited on the fathers and mothers, who receive both therapy for themselves (unconsciously) and advice how best to handle their child. The advice about their child may well seem revolutionary to the parents, but experience has shown that a good proportion of parents are educable. By thus working on both parents and child, the possibilities of further troubles arising from the child's psychological disorders are minimized. Juvenile courts can sometimes do this without the help of expert psychologists. Probation officers, when they have natural abilities in psychology, can achieve great success with parents and child. On one of my visits to a London juvenile court I heard a probation officer speak of a ' real miracle ' effected in the home of a delinquent child who had been under her care ; this was confirmed by the representative of the school authority. The delinquency of the child had set in motion all the forces of social inquiry and betterment, the parents had responded and the future of the child and of his home seemed bright. But for certain types of cases a juvenile court, like an adult court, cannot be really efficient without facilities for psychological investigation during a remand, after the decision of the facts, and for psychological treatment where this is recommended. The London juvenile courts increased greatly in efficiency when the services of Dr. J. D. W. Pearce became available at the Remand Home.

Progress in rectifying the defects of juvenile courts will be gradual. What is even more urgent is that attention should be directed towards certain matters affecting children in the courts that have received comparatively little attention. The first is the question of the trial of children and young persons by jury at the higher courts. The second is the question of the methods employed when young people are either the victims or witnesses in the trials of adults for sexual crime.

I have no hesitation in saying that no humane system of justice would under any circumstances permit any child or young person (8 to 17) to be tried by jury. I have already indicated my lack of faith in the general principle of trial by jury, but I realize that in regard to adult delinquents we who criticize trial by jury are voices crying in the wilderness. But when considering such trials for those under 17, a demand for their total abolition is both reasonable and practicable. The presence of a jury adds twelve (in war time seven) people to the number of those who must be present at the trial and Parliament has already accepted the principle that juveniles should be tried in the presence of as few people as possible.[1] The presence of a jury also renders impossible any abolition of that formality and awe-creating ceremonial which English people have been brought up to regard as essentials of criminal trials, but which are both meaningless and harmful when young people are being tried. Yet the law compels trial by jury in three sets of circumstances. The first is that in all charges against those from 8 to 17 for homicide our historic methods of trial at Assizes are in full force,[2] except for minor concessions to modern ideas, namely certain optional

[1] Section 47 of the Children and Young Persons Act, 1933.
[2] Third schedule to the same Act.

restrictions on publicity and the presence of spectators. Juvenile courts in homicide cases can only hear the evidence and decide whether a case has been made out which Assizes should try.

It is happily rare that murder or manslaughter is committed by anyone under 17, but where this happens, it is obvious that the teachings of modern psychology should be fully grafted on to our legal procedure. But in fact strict legal procedure is applied to such cases with a minimum of concessions to psychology. In 1938 a grim case occurred which amply illustrated the dangers of such strict legal procedure. A child of 13 was tried by jury at the Central Criminal Court for the murder of a little girl of 4. The methods employed were those applicable to the most depraved adult murderer, save that the name of the child was never revealed. I was told by some one present at this trial that even the option in the court to exclude spectators was not exercised. A City dignitary in full robes sat on the Bench with the judge. Both judge and counsel wore their robes and wigs. A child of 13 would have been less than human if he did not take pride in the fact that all this display was on his account.

As so often happens in juvenile cases, the facts were not seriously in dispute. The defence relied on an ancient presumption of law that a child between 8 and 14 is incapable of criminal intent (*doli incapax*). This needs a little explanation. The Act of 1933 extended to 8 the age at which the law declares that ' it shall be conclusively presumed that no child can be guilty of any offence '.[1] Between 8 and 14 this presumption still applies, but it is no longer conclusive ; it can be rebutted by evidence that the child was conscious of guilty knowledge at the time of the offence.[2] That these

[1] Section 50.
[2] This presumption applies, according to legal theory, even in juvenile courts, but in fact these courts do not take it seriously. In one juvenile court the presiding magistrate took this legal presumption seriously with the result that nearly every child delinquent was acquitted, to his or her immense surprise and detriment. It is all wrong that this ancient presumption still exists ;

188 CRIME AND PSYCHOLOGY

ancient doctrines still apply to those over 8 years of age is
an illustration how modern law has been unable to shake
itself free from ancient fetters. The presumption had
meaning in the days when children were executed or transported, but is irrelevant under modern conditions. However, the presumption exists and it constituted the main
point of those defending this child of 13. It was around
this issue of guilty knowledge that the trial centred. The
facts of the crime were well summarized in the *Medico-Legal
Review* : the little girl's body ' was found tied up in a sack
in a conservatory communicating with the boy's bedroom.
A gag had been pushed into the child's mouth and her neck,
arms and legs bound with rope and linen. The crime was of
a sexual nature '. The jury had to decide whether these
facts and the evidence generally proved the existence of
guilty knowledge, a matter totally irrelevant from the
psychological point of view. The speeches were made and
the judge summed up, and all the time the lad sat in lonely
eminence, probably wondering what it was all about. The
jury brought in a verdict of Not Guilty, so nothing remained
but to discharge this strange lad.

Could any procedure be more likely to make a lad worse ?
To be acquitted of a killing that in fact had been committed
is dangerous for any one, but for this child of 13, who doubtless knew that he was in some way in disgrace, an acquittal
must have been a startling revelation. Whatever this child
was at the time of the killing, he was probably in a worse
condition when all this paraphernalia ended in his discharge.
The very fact that the whole court, judge, jury, counsel,
solicitors, court staff and spectators, were all there because
of him must have had psychologically dangerous results.
To be acquitted after all that must have seemed a triumph
to this child.

There have been plenty of warnings from experts against
the dangers surrounding children when their crimes are

The more that delinquent children are found guilty by juvenile
courts, the better for them. Survivals from the handcuff age
should be abolished.

made the subject of elaborate proceedings. To take one only :

For them [uncontrolled and selfish children] the first court trial means the first step towards independence. In spite of his mental and physical immaturity, the child feels himself to be grown up from then on, for he has been treated as an adult by the court. He has been the hero of an act of which the State has taken notice, and with a feeling of self-importance he waits for the newspaper reports of the trial. This feeling of having played a part in public life is not restricted to the child himself. His comrades regard him with a certain respect, varying in degree, it is true. His particular chums admire him. But it would be a mistake in child psychology to believe that his example only frightens and repels still innocent children. . . . The damage that the presence of such a child in a school does is beyond estimation.[1]

I have no means of knowing how this strange child took his ordeal, whether he was terrified, which I doubt, or whether he was proud of the attention bestowed upon him, which is more likely. But I am confident that psychological injury was done. In my view the whole proceedings were both farcical and dangerous. They showed legalism in a luridly harmful light. The trial, as well as the acquittal, probably made the lad feel a hero. The sequel was almost bathos. Bewildered by the verdict, the authorities brought the child again before the same juvenile court, six days after the trial, as a child being ' in need of care and protection ', placing him thus in the same category as neglected and homeless children. After the fine display at the Central Criminal Court, these further proceedings must have seemed derogatory to this child, who could not possibly understand the necessity for them ; he probably considered them as a monstrous injustice after his acquittal. In the end he was confined in an Approved School and may well have resented this, since the jury had acquitted him. One

[1] *Crime and Its Repression* (1903), by Professor Gustav Aschaffen-burg. American Modern Criminal Science Series edition, pp. 301–11.

14

cannot help feeling that if the law can do no better than provide such a trial and sequel for such a child, it is time that psychologists spoke frankly.

As so frequently happens in the annals of crime, other charges of murder against children quickly followed, one quite soon after this child's acquittal. In these later cases the age limit of 14 had been passed, so the defence of incapacity to commit crime was not available. But these other young people had in their turn to appear before judge and jury at an Assize court.

The remedy is simple. All crimes of whatever nature alleged against those who are under 17 should be dealt with finally, unless there is an appeal, in juvenile courts without a jury, and, where the crimes alleged are serious, like homicide, a judge of the High Court should act as president of the court, the other two magistrates being his colleagues, taking the law from the judge. The procedure should be that of ordinary juvenile courts, and thus all the ceremonial, so harmful to a child, would be avoided. I know our King's Bench judges sufficiently well to be confident that they would willingly co-operate in such a scheme ; they would probably welcome an opportunity to administer justice to young people without any of the conventional trappings. If such a scheme were adopted, all presumptions of incapacity to commit crime in those over 8 years old should be abolished ; they have no meaning when trials are conducted on modern lines.

It would be necessary to abolish at the same time the other two circumstances under which young people between 14 and 17 can be tried by jury. At present delinquents over 14 are under the same law in all essentials as adults in regard to trial by jury. They can only be tried in a juvenile court for indictable offences, and for offences (other than assaults) punishable on summary conviction with imprisonment ' for a term exceeding three months ', if they give their assent when formally asked by the court. Such cases probably constitute the bulk of the criminal work of juvenile courts in connection with those over 14. All stealing, even an apple from a coster's barrow or a sweet from Woolworth's, is indictable, and therefore the young delinquent has at the outset of the proceedings to be asked whether he will be tried by jury or by the juvenile court; similarly a lad driving his motor-cycle dangerously has to exercise his option. If consent is not forthcoming, the case has to be committed for trial by jury. The explaining of this option by the court disconcerts the unhappy youth, who can seldom understand the situation that is being laboriously explained to him. Whenever present at a juvenile court as spectator and learner I have been impressed with the futility of giving this option. The situation is often pathetic and sometimes ludicrous. The confused and bewildered expression on the face of the young delinquent, his reluctance to answer, and the appealing look round to see whether his parent can help him in the predicament thus presented to him, these always seem to me as unnecessary as they are cruel. I deal ruthlessly with these requirements of the law when I have a youth under 17 charged before me for an offence committed with an adult. I say something like this : ' Don't bother about this, but I have to ask whether you would like to go to another court and have a jury. Are you content for me to deal with you ? ' I have never known a youth choose to be tried by jury. In principle I am opposed to any delinquent having an option of court ; it should be the function of Parliament to decide which offences shall be tried by magistrates and which by juries, assuming that juries must continue. But it is absurd that young offenders between 14 and 17 have to make this choice. The Act of 1933 abolished the choice for children. It is time to abolish it at least for those under 17.

Let us turn from youthful delinquents to youthful witnesses. Here also the existing situation is profoundly unsatisfactory. Why considerable reforms should have been introduced for young delinquents without at the same time giving attention to the unfortunate lot of those children and youths who are either the victims or the witnesses of unpleasant crimes is a mystery that can only be understood by those who know how legal reforms have to be on the catch-as-catch-can principle ; subjects are taken up under restricted terms of reference as opportunities offer, and only rarely is any subject given a thorough overhaul.   So far almost no official consideration has been given to youthful victims and witnesses in court, save that they may only be in court when required to give evidence,[1] and that there is an option in the court, which should be a duty, to clear the court of spectators when they give their evidence [2] and to keep their names out of the newspapers.[3]   These are valuable minor reforms which otherwise leave young people as they were decades ago.   The problem that cries out for consideration now is the giving of evidence by young people in charges against others for ' an offence against, or any conduct contrary to, decency or morality '.[4]   This problem again involves the demerits of trial by jury.

In the Children and Young Persons Act, 1933, is set out a list of offences against young people in respect of which the precautions enumerated above must, or may be, applied.[5] This list includes such charges as the abduction of an unmarried girl under 16, indecent assault on a girl, homosexual assault on a boy, ' carnal knowledge ' of children, incest, causing prostitution of a girl, and so on, none of them charges from which children are likely to escape without psychological injury unless they are most carefully and scientifically handled.   It would seem elementary that when children have to give evidence, either of such offences against themselves, or of such offences against others, there ought to be stringent precautions to protect them.   In fact the only precautions have already been mentioned.   Apart from them, children have to appear as witnesses in ordinary courts in the ordinary way ;   they frequently have to give evidence on such matters before juries.   Such a state of affairs deserves the old description ' methods of barbarism '.

Some of these charges can be tried before magistrates if

[1] Act of 1933, section 36.   [2] Section 37.   [3] Section 39.
[4] These words are used in section 37 and 39 of the Act of 1933.
[5] First schedule to the Act.

the accused persons give their consent; for instance, indecent assault. When this happens, magistrates can, if they are psychologically minded, minimize the terror which the giving of evidence must cause to children who have, it must always be remembered, had an extremely unpleasant experience. I was once present at the trial, before lay magistrates, of a man charged, and later found guilty, of an indecent assault against a girl of 10. I was greatly impressed by the care taken by clerk and Bench to make the proceedings as homely as possible; everything done was fully legal. Only three magistrates were on the Bench, a small court was used, all the optional powers to protect children were used, and after the proceedings I carefully watched the child who had been the principal witness. There was no trace of immediate psychological injury, and I learned later that in fact none had been caused. In many cases, however, the absence of immediate injury could be no indication that later signs of injury would not show themselves.

In magistrates' courts informal methods are easy to arrange. In such cases there should never be more than three magistrates on the Bench; this should be necessary by law. The only other people who need be present when children give their evidence are the clerk of the court, the accused and his legal representative, if any, one police officer in charge of the accused—he can sometimes be dispensed with—the prosecuting lawyer, if any, and one press representative; the child should wherever possible be accompanied by a parent, and the woman probationer officer should be present, if possible. At most a dozen people are necessary. The smallest possible court should be used, preferably one with only movable furniture. The witness-box should never be used by child witnesses, but a chair should be provided with another chair close to it for the use of the parent or probation officer. All these arrangements are legal; they should be compulsory by legal enactment.

When I first became conscious of the importance of these factors, I did what judges frequently do, namely, bring the chiid witness up to the Bench for the giving of evidence. I found a great drawback in this method. The child was then facing both the court and the man who was charged with the offence. This tended to make some children tongue-tied. I have seen children terrified when they once more saw the man who assaulted them ; I remember one child who burst into tears and tried to run from the court when she saw the man about whose conduct with her she had complained. I solved this difficulty by placing the child on a chair with her back to the accused, asking the child to turn round only when it was necessary to identify the accused man. If the accused has no lawyer (ordinarily he should be granted legal aid when he cannot afford to pay professional fees), he must be given his legal right to cross-examine, but I sometimes invite him to agree to tell me his questions so that I can put them to the child ; an alternative method is to invite the accused to write his question down. Of course such methods of cross-examination are only possible if the accused agrees to them, but I have never known an accused refuse. If there is a defending lawyer, he is sure to co-operate in informal methods when children give their evidence ; such has been my experience.

Some years ago I resolved never to take the evidence of a child in these cases from the dais. If there is a convenient room, I invite all necessary people to accompany me there and take the children's evidence in the room. If there is no such room, I come down into the well of the court and sit near to the accommodation provided for lawyers. The child sits on a chair near me. It is of great importance to be on a level with the child. Nobody enjoys speaking to some one who towers above. Another important point that I have learned from experience is to ask every one to remain seated, even lawyers when they are examining or cross-examining a child witness ; human voices are always more restrained when people are seated ; lawyers when seated are always less formidable. Should these informalities result in the child's voice not reaching the press (every effort must be made so that the defendant hears what the child says), then I ask the clerk to read the evidence over when the child has left the court.

To those with hide-bound opinions all this may seem sentimental, perhaps funny ; but magisterial dignity lies in doing a job well, not in behaving on a dais as everybody has behaved for hundreds of years. I have heard children's evidence in this way for many years, and have never had any complaint. Many members of the Bar have seen me conduct proceedings on these lines, and some have publicly expressed their approval and gratitude. By such methods I have often seen timid and crying children converted into comfortable witnesses ; in this way I have obtained evidence which would have been refused if ordinary methods had been adopted.[1] There is no reason why some such method should not be made compulsory when children give their evidence in unpleasant cases.

Before a child takes the oath and gives evidence, it is well to begin with a little chatter about trivial things. I usually ask about home and school, compare the child's age with that of one of my children, or comment on the child's dress ; anything that momentarily diverts the child's mind is useful in establishing confidence. With such an introduction, evidence flows more easily. If, as sometimes happens, the child sticks when difficult incidents come to be explained, paper and pencil are useful, but, of course, what is written down must be read or shown to the accused, the prosecution, and the press. Such informal methods are in the interests of the accused as well as of the children. If in fact a child has invented the whole story, an event that is rare but does happen, the real facts are more likely to emerge through informal methods than otherwise.

In disputes between husband and wife the evidence of children is often necessary. As these cases are not criminal, even greater latitude can be permitted. My practice has long been to invite the agreement of both parties to my seeing the child in private, accompanied by the clerk and

[1] On these methods I once successfully obtained evidence from a child of 2, where a man was charged with indecently assaulting her.

a probation officer. I take the child and the others to my room and later report in court what has been said. I have never had consent to this course refused. The clerk of the court records in his notes both the fact of the consent and my summary of what has been said. Children have often come into my room crying and saying, ' I want Mummie ' ; such children would seldom tell their story in a formal court. But they usually settle down, and, after their story has been told, they are often full of smiles. A golden rule for magistrates who do this is never to see a child alone ; the presence of a probation officer and the clerk of the court is essential.

Magistrates can also adopt such methods as these when they are dealing with a case that has to be committed for trial at a higher court. Here the law provides that ' the room or building in which such justice or justices shall take such examination . . . shall not be deemed an open court '.[1] This section of an ancient Act of Parliament has fallen into disuse, but it applies to all witnesses and needs to be revived when children are required to give evidence.

But what happens when these cases reach Quarter Sessions or Assizes ? The answer is that present methods render the adoption of informal methods impossible.[2] How can young children be expected to tell their stories about frightening experiences when facing a formal court in which many people are in wigs and gowns ? When perched aloft in a high witness-box, even adults feel nervous, especially if they have to stand. Even under the best of circum-

[1] Section 19 of the Indictable Offences Act, 1848.
[2] In sections 42 and 43 of the Children and Young Persons Act, 1933, an attempt was made to provide informal methods when children give evidence in the higher courts in this class of case. But as is usual with official attempts to secure relaxation of hoary legal methods, the attempt completely failed, because of the legal limitations introduced to prevent legal opposition. The law, as so often happens, has provided a quite ineffectual remedy for a glaring evil, thus making matters worse than before, because since 1933 the authorities have doubtless been convinced that they have legislated the evil out of existence.

stances, it can scarcely be anticipated that young children, telling of an event about which they have told before at least twice, will give exactly the same details. When giving evidence in an ordinary criminal court, they are extremely likely to get muddled about dates and other details ; possibly they will be so scared that they cannot speak at all. A frequent result of old-time methods in court is, therefore, that accused men are acquitted against the weight of the facts ; when this happens, children-witnesses, who have already suffered severe psychological injury, have these injuries intensified by their experiences in court and all in vain.

I have consulted experienced counsel, magistrates, and police officers and found much support for the view that those guilty of sexual offences against children are all too often acquitted by juries when the evidence would have justified conviction. In this way dangerous men are set free, possibly to prey upon other children, whereas their conviction might have led to their treatment and cure. In this connexion we cannot ignore that there is a strange tradition in the legal profession to the effect that to secure a verdict of ' Not Guilty ' when the facts point the other way is a professional triumph. Justice, one would think, demands that the guilty shall, whenever possible, be found guilty. But our English criminal procedure places a premium on the acquittal of the guilty. Forensic agility often counts more than the truth. Lest this statement be challenged, I would cite the facts given by the first Chief Metropolitan Magistrate under whom I served, Sir Chartres Biron. In his memoirs there are several stories which support the statement that I have made, though possibly the author would not have realized their effect. Thus referring to an old-time barrister well known in the criminal courts before my days, Sir Chartres Biron wrote that, ' without any material, he would manage to create an atmosphere of suspicion round your case, which, as it was entirely baseless, was very difficult to dispel '. This barrister, Geoghegan by name, was often employed for the defence in cases where Biron acted for the prosecution. Another case is described

in this book : ' to the evidence there seemed no answer ',
wrote the ex-prosecuting counsel. But Geoghegan was
astute enough to introduce some quite irrelevant issue, and
he did this ' with such skill that he made this fact seem an
essential point in the prosecution '. The prosecution had
made no attempt to prove or deny the point that Geoghegan
was so laboriously stressing, but the jury were completely
taken in by these tricks of advocacy : ' all the prisoners were
acquitted. It was an amazing verdict, a legitimate triumph
of advocacy at its best.' [1]   I cannot recognize the triumph.
Many verdicts of ' Not Guilty ' are obtained in such ways,
but to me they seem to flout justice. Be this as it may,
such acquittals are surely serious perversions of justice
when the essential witnesses for the prosecution are young
children, the victims of sexual assaults. So experienced an
advocate and criminal judge as Cecil Whiteley once wrote
that cases of indecent assaults on young girls and boys are
among the types of case ' in which although the evidence of
guilt is quite clear, acquittals are far more numerous than
in any other class of case and in which juries do not " a true
verdict give according to the evidence " '. Whiteley also
showed why these things happened : ' The unfortunate
child has made a statement to a police officer, which has
been taken down in writing, has given evidence on oath at
the police court, and on entering the witness-box in the
crowded court of trial, has to face a judge and counsel in
wigs and gowns. It is not very difficult for an experienced
counsel to obtain some answers in cross-examination which
are inconsistent with the previous statement or evidence.' [2]
Any such inconsistency is manna to an astute advocate, and
on such a foundation he can often work on the passions or
prejudices of the men and women who constitute the jury.
It almost seems sometimes as if juries get so worked up that

---

[1] *Without Prejudice*, pp. 126–7.
[2] *Brief Life*, pp. 95–7.   Cecil Whiteley served in the important
judicial posts of Chairman of first the Surrey and then the London
Quarter Sessions and later as Common Serjeant at the Central
Criminal Court.

they will not let the prosecution win, whatever the facts and whatever the judge may say in his summing-up. But in private talk advocates who act thus will often admit that verdicts so gained were a defiance of the facts.[1]

These important matters have not received much attention. Apart from the brave words of Cecil Whiteley, I have in all my reading only come across one other reference to them. Mr. Archibald Crawford, K.C., of the Scottish Bar, once wrote that ' readers can realise how revolting it is for counsel to have to ask questions of a little innocent girl having as their objective ' details about a charge of rape of which the girl is alleged by the prosecution to have been the victim. ' Not only counsel ', continued Mr. Crawford, ' but all concerned are harassed almost beyond endurance. It is as if all in court were in conspiracy to rape the child again.' [2]   That simile should be born in mind when at long last these problems receive adequate consideration.

Much more than sentimental regrets is required.   In planning action the question of the total abolition of trial by jury in this type of case must be faced.   No informal procedure, which will set the child at ease, is possible so long as trial by jury is the rule.   No amount of kindness in a robed and bewigged judge can place a child at ease in a crowded court.   When at the Bar, I saw judges do all sorts of human and unconventional kindnesses to child witnesses.'   But kindness alone cannot succeed, for fundamentally the circumstances in which judges do their work with juries are wrong when children give evidence in cases of sexual assault.   What is the remedy ?   All the sexual offences set out in the schedule to the Children and Young Persons Act, 1933, should be tried, when they are too grave to be tried in magistrates' courts, in a new kind of court.

[1] Verdicts of Not Guilty in jury trials about driving motor cars when under the influence of alcohol are often obtained through clever advocacy rather than on the merits of the case.

[2] *Guilty as Libelled*, p. 127.   The title of the book refers to a name in use in Scottish courts.   It is noteworthy that Mr. Crawford also lamented that in these cases judge and counsel are ' dressed up in costumes which alone terrify the young mind '.

There could be a High Court judge as chairman (at Quarter Sessions the Recorder, chairman or deputy-chairman) and two magistrates. Cecil Whiteley went further : ' There are such a large number of acquittals in these cases ', he wrote, ' that serious consideration should be given to the suggestion that they should be tried by a court consisting of an experienced magistrate as chairman, a doctor and a woman magistrate.' [1] Whiteley's proposal was intended solely for the lesser cases of sexual assault, but I should prefer the reform to include the gravest sexual assaults, such as rape ; for these the presence of a High Court judge would be desirable.

In a tribunal such as I have suggested all the informalities described earlier in this chapter would be possible, to the great benefit of child witnesses. The fair trial of the accused would in no way be jeopardized. To deprive them of the unfair and harmful advantages which they now enjoy is not to treat them unfairly. Guilty men cannot complain if they are found guilty. The tribunal suggested here would be fully capable of sifting the evidence, so that those who are in fact innocent would be in no danger ; in fact they would be in less danger than now, since it is always possible, though in fact it is rare, that a jury of men and women inexperienced in criminal matters may convict merely out of sympathy for distressed children.

Since I first put forward the ideas that I have just elaborated, I have had much support from psychologists,[2] but very little from the legal profession. This fact illustrates the need that lawyers practising in criminal courts should study the teachings of psychology as well as the criminal

[1] *Brief Life*, p. 97.
[2] I set out some of these ideas in the *Law Journal* of 23 January 1937. There quickly followed an indignant, but anonymous, letter from a barrister, but later a strong letter from Sir Walter Langdon-Brown (6 February 1937), who mentioned ' the psychological injury inflicted by the ordinary procedure on the innocent party '. When war broke out in September 1939, definite action by a group of psychologists was on the point of being taken to pave the way for reform in these matters.

law.   On all the matters mentioned in this chapter the voice of medical psychologists should be heard, rather than that of criminal lawyers, for these are primarily psychological matters.

There is one more point of importance in connexion with the handling of children in the courts.   In an earlier chapter it was stated that the victims of sexual crimes often need psychological treatment as well as the perpetrators.   I have had as witnesses before me children under 14 who, far from being shocked by the assault upon them, met the man repeatedly and allowed him to repeat his conduct many times.   There is a section of the Act of 1933 which attempted to provide for this need where the victims are under 17.[1] It provides that any court which convicts a person of any of the sexual offences enumerated in the list mentioned a few paragraphs back may ' direct that the child or young person be brought before a juvenile court ' as a child needing care and protection.   The intention was excellent.   But the purpose of this section was frustrated by the use of this much-abused word ' conviction '.   Delinquents dealt with under the Probation Act in magistrates' courts are not, as we have seen, legally convicted ; I have already said that this piece of legal sentimentalism is inherently bad.   The result is that, if a magistrates' court places the offender in this class of case on probation and directs psychological treatment, the best constructive course, no use can be made of this well-intentioned section.   This is much to be regretted, since it is often difficult to persuade the parents of the young victim that special care needs to be taken to prevent lasting harm to the child.   Such parents are apt to be so consumed with indignation against the offender, and no one would blame them, that they resent any suggestion that their child needs the attentions of any one.   If magistrates could freely use this section, good might result, but in practice I for one usually ignore these powers and work through the probation officer behind the scenes to try and persuade the parents to take a wise course ; if necessary, we

[1] Section 63.

place the matter before the local education authority and suggest that they bring the child victim before a juvenile court under the ordinary section concerning children in need of care and protection.

One of the reasons why it is desirable that child victims of serious sexual crimes, and their parents also, should come under the supervision of some psycho-therapist is that it is an almost universal human tendency in grown-ups to take the line that the sooner the child forgets the unpleasant experience the better. It seems so natural to say to the victimized child, when the prosecution of the offender is over, ' Now you can forget all about these horrible matters.' So widespread is this attitude that even the Departmental Committee on Sexual Offences against Young Persons (1926) adopted it. (That Committee, mainly composed of lawyers and magistrates, considered very little the matters discussed in this chapter.) Thus when discussing the pros and cons of trying this class of case in magistrates' courts, the Committee's report stated that one of the drawbacks of committing these cases for trial at a higher court is that ' the details have to be kept in mind during a waiting period . . . the child being thus obliged to remember what in its own interests it should be allowed to forget '.[1] A very human point of view, but one completely at variance with psychological principles. As was said in the first chapter, it is fundamental in psychology that to forget is not necessarily to obliterate ; what is forgotten may still have a lasting influence upon the personality and at any time in life may be the cause of serious trouble. Children who have undergone this class of experience should never be permitted to forget it ; the need is rather to keep the experience alive, but gradually to get it into reasonable proportions. If the incident is prevented from entering the unconscious, it should do no permanent harm. This depends, of course, upon the degree in which the child has been brought up free from harmful repressions and inhibitions. A child wisely brought up, from the psychological point of view,

[1] p. 27.   Another statement of a similar kind appears on p. 60.

should suffer no more permanent injury from a sexual assault than from the recollection of having once missed a train or from having seen somebody else's house on fire. Where damage is done, the real cause is not the experience but the defective upbringing. The life-style, to use a favourite expression of Alfred Adler,[1] decides whether a bad experience does lasting injury.

Such being the teaching of psychology, it may be as well that at present almost no children are sent to juvenile courts when their aggressors have been convicted, for a juvenile court would need to have a good knowledge of psychology to handle such cases wisely. But this question of the careful handling of the victims illustrates once more the great need for co-operation between medical psycho-therapists and those who lay down our laws of criminal procedure. The section of the Act of 1933 is a bad illustration of how not to introduce reforms.

All the matters discussed in this chapter are illustrations of this need that medical psychologists should criticize our legal tribunals and make themselves ready to assist the work of reforming them. Whenever I have been in contact with psycho-therapists and have talked about our criminal courts, I have invariably observed an attitude of criticism. Such criticism needs to be made openly, so that the authorities may know what reforms are desired by those in the best position to suggest them. Psychologists should, in fact, be less respectful to our criminal administration. If there were more vocal criticism, the Bench, as well as Whitehall, would hear it and in time would realize the need for changes.

---

[1] ' No experience is a cause of success or failure. We do not suffer from the shock of our experiences—the so-called trauma— but we make out of them just what suits our purposes. We are self-determined by the meaning we give to our experiences ; and there is probably something of a mistake always involved when we take particular experiences as the basis for our future life. Meanings are not determined by situations.' *What Life should Mean to You*, by Alfred Adler, p. 14. Adler went much further than I could accept as regards human power to determine life, but here one can accept his reasoning.

Many of those on the criminal Bench, though they cannot be expected to run after every new theory, are ready to accept what has been proved, and by now many psychological principles have passed from the stage of theory to accepted truth. The matters discussed in this chapter would make a good starting point for the reform of our criminal procedure on psychological lines, for where the interests of children are concerned, the most conservative are usually ready to listen to pleas for reform.

CHAPTER 9

THE BENCH AND THE DELINQUENT

With all that is at stake in the treatment of young human beings there are ordinarily less training requirements for those who are expected to alter the conduct tendencies of delinquents than there are for those who treat sick cattle.

DR. WILLIAM HEALY [1]

An ' experienced ' judge means one who is well used to trying c fendants and who, generally speaking, makes an excellent job o) that side of his duty. But when we come to the passing of sentence, our ' experienced ' judge is experienced merely in making up his mind and delivering sentence with complete composure.

DR. R. M. JACKSON [2]

The large majority of judges and magistrates do not possess the necessary training or experience to qualify them to prescribe the best treatment. Psychology, the science of human behaviour, forms no part of a legal education.

E. ROY CALVERT [3]

IT would seem obvious that the more scientific the treatment of delinquents becomes, the more scientific knowledge will be necessary in those who have the tasks of receiving reports about delinquents and of deciding what is to be done with them. The previous chapters have been mainly concerned with alterations in the organization, procedure, and conduct of criminal courts. Now we must turn to the thorny problem of desirable changes in those on the Bench.

In this country the professional Bench has earned the general respect of the public, and only occasional criticism

[1] *New Light on Delinquency*, p. 221.
[2] *The Machinery of Justice in England*, p. 178.
[3] *The Lawbreaker*, p. 81.

is heard. The lay justices who sit in magistrates' courts have in recent years received much criticism, some of which should fall upon the cumbrous, archaic laws that they have to administer and upon the unsatisfactory and almost feudal system by which lay justices are appointed.[1] But many of the lay justices have the advantage that they have a closer acquaintance with the problems of the people whom they judge than have the professional Bench. To defend the system of lay justices would be outside the scope of this book, but at least it may be said that more sympathy with progressive ideas,[2] and in particular with the psychological treatment of delinquency, has hitherto been shown by lay justices than by professional magistrates and judges.

Both the professional and the lay Bench receive much criticism from those who study the sentences of our courts from the psychological standpoint. Psychologists have so far shown themselves more willing than lawyers to make concessions and to admit that no complete execution of their ideas is possible. Lawyers, and here lay magistrates copy their example, have failed to realize that historic methods are to a great extent unsuited to modern requirements. I see some danger that the public respect for the administration of criminal justice may be in some measure undermined through the growth of knowledge and interest in psychology. Dr. R. D. Gillespie expressed the opinions of a large number of experts and students when he said : ' The impression that a psychiatrist is apt to get of court proceedings is that of a " fact-finding commission ", . . . a commission whose scope of reference is unsatisfactory and limited and whose recommendations as to treatment in consequence are likely to suffer from as grave defects as would the prescriptions of a doctor who is forbidden to have any

[1] The report of the Royal Commission on the Selection of Justices of the Peace, 1911, contained many severe criticisms of the methods of appointment, but only the feeblest of recommendations. The reforms made in consequence of this report have made little practical improvement.

[2] Only a few professional magistrates have taken part in the proceedings of the Magistrates' Association, a progressive body.

knowledge of his patient's constitution.'[1] Countless criticisms to a similar effect could be quoted ; three from varied sources have been set at the head of this chapter. I am convinced that fundamentally such criticism is justified. Delinquents in this country are in fact sentenced by those, whether professional or lay, who have undergone no training in the subjects essential to the adequate understanding of human conduct. Training in law is no better qualification for decisions about the fate of delinquents than is life in business, in the army, or on the land, &c. A long legal experience of criminal trials is no sufficient qualification for that most difficult task of the Bench, the sentencing of delinquents. Experience has shown that the best judges in criminal causes are sometimes those who before their appointment to the Bench had no experience at the Bar of criminal work.[2] This is a portent that needs investigation. Our present system is well illustrated by the following story told by Mr. R. C. K. Ensor :

During the latter half of the late Lord Alverstone's long career as Lord Chief Justice [1900–1913], the present writer once asked him at a dinner whether he was interested in books on criminology and penology. He replied that he never read any, adding in his downright way, without the slightest suspicion of its absurdity, ' I prefer to rely on common sense.' What would now be thought of a doctor who, when asked about books on medicine, answered that he had never read any, but that ' common sense '

---

[1] *Medical-Legal Review*, April 1939.
[2] In a former generation Sir James Willes (judge of Common Pleas 1855–72), Sir Robert Lush (judge of the court of Queen's Bench 1865–80) and Lord Lindley (judge of Common Pleas 1875–81), were all great judges in criminal causes, but none of them had any considerable experience in the criminal courts when at the Bar. In our own day Lord Atkin (judge of King's Bench 1913–19) was a successful judge in criminal matters after a forensic career mostly in the Commercial Court. The reason for the judicial success of these great lawyers may have been that they knew little, on appointment to the Bench, of the sentences customary in criminal courts. Realizing their ignorance, they may have studied.

was his guide ? In the eighteenth century, no doubt, such a doctor would have been at least conceivable.[1]

Common sense has always been a strong feature of our Bench. It, like impartiality, is an essential virtue in those who deal in any way with delinquents ; it is shown by both professional and lay Benches. A training in common sense is given by practice at the Common Law Bar, but also in non-legal walks of life from which most lay justices come ; work in trade unions, for instance, soon separates those possessed of common sense from those who lack it. It would be a bad day if ever the fate of delinquents passed into the hands of those not well endowed with common sense. That once happened. That great and witty barrister Theobald Mathew once described in his inimitable way what happened when, after the passing of the Judicature Act, 1873 (which brought many different courts together in a ' Supreme ' Court of Judicature), judges inexperienced in the frailties of mankind began presiding over criminal trials :

The trying and sentencing of a prisoner for stealing a pair of boots involved, in the opinion of Lord Cairns and Lord Selborne, no great intellectual strain. But strange stories began to be told when Equity [2] judges and the judges of the Probate, Divorce, and Admiralty Division began to deliver Her Majesty's gaols. One, determined to stamp out crime, thought that malefactors would be deterred if he were to pass in every case the maximum sentence allowed by the law. Another, summing up in a murder trial, dwelt upon the significance of the evidence that the prisoner had requested his wife, on the morning after the crime had been committed, to hand him his bloody shirt. The same learned judge, having heard from the constable that the alleged burglar had greeted him in the back garden at 1 a.m. with the words ' Hullo, Robert ; so early in the morning ! ' commented to the jury upon the fact that the accused was familiar not only with the

---

[1] *Courts and Judges in France, Germany and England*, pp. 89–90.
[2] For the information of those without legal training, Equity courts dealt with such matters as trusts, wills, company law, and so on.

Christian name, but also with the ordinary habits of the police officer, for he had expressed surprise at finding him abroad when the day was so little advanced. A judge of Admiralty training expressed the opinion that a verdict of 'guilty but insane' amounted to an acquittal, and was with difficulty prevented from releasing the prisoner.[1]

In the days when the choice of the Bench after the verdict was merely between sending a delinquent to prison and binding him over, or between a long sentence of imprisonment and a short one, common sense went far in the judicial equipment. But the position now is very different. More and more scientific evidence and reports are being submitted to the Bench, and for the understanding of the issues raised in this way, common sense, though still invaluable, is not enough. With the younger delinquents adult courts have the choice between supervision by a probation officer, training in a Borstal Institution, fines, and prison ; there are other possible courses. To make this choice wisely requires considerable understanding of the personality and environment of the delinquent. It is an eighteenth-century conception that common sense alone can qualify either lawyers or laymen to settle the fate of delinquents.[2] Those who handle delinquents, in prisons, Borstal Institutions, and on probation, are more and more receiving definite training. This welcome process seems to demand that those who have to decide the sentence should receive training also.

If those on the criminal Bench have some knowledge of psychological principles, the benefit is not confined to those whom the Bench has to sentence ; those on the Bench will themselves benefit, for then the task of dealing with people, not only with defendants but with witnesses and others as well, becomes infinitely more interesting. There is much that is wearisome in the work of those on the Bench, especially in magistrates' courts. The daily round becomes less dreary to those who have some psychological knowledge,

[1] *The Nineteenth Century*, December 1933, pp. 705–6.
[2] It is also an anachronism that penology has to be learned by practising on delinquents.

for they can see more than what is apparent to all. When deciding their verdicts on the facts, judges and magistrates must make up their minds solely on what has been given in evidence. But between verdict and sentence a wider field is open, and there is ample opportunity for efforts to understand defendants, their relations, and the witnesses in the case.

It will be worth while to consider from this point of view a few of the types of people seen in the magisterial kaleidoscope. Thus the mother of a youthful defendant found guilty of crime may seem a very tiresome person, but to those with a little psychological insight she may appear less tiresome and even interesting. Her words, ' He's such a good boy at home,' so familiar and so unhelpful, may reveal her as a fond mother (in the Shakespearian meaning) who may be the real cause of her son's downfall. She may have always allowed him to have too much his own way, and have thus deprived the young man of that strengthening and educative experience that his parents are stronger than himself. Or the indignant and outraged father who makes the task of both court and probation officer so difficult by his constant assertion that owing to the disgrace he ' has done with the lad ' may intrigue the court by unconsciously revealing much about his son's emotional life. There may have been perpetual conflict in the lad's home between this overbearing father and a weak but stubborn mother. The defendant may have lived at home in a state of acute emotional disorder, caused by both fear of the father and anger at his treatment of the mother. Such a conflict may easily be the psychological cause of a criminal act by young people who will ordinarily be entirely unable to explain their conduct. A young woman in her late ' teens ', found guilty of theft, may appear at first sight to be a very boring defendant, merely one of innumerable cases of petty shoplifters. But to the psychologically-minded the very absence of any motive for the theft (she may have stolen something of a kind with which she is already well supplied) may reveal a great deal about her upbringing. The young woman may have been so guarded by her parents, so repressed and protected, that there arose an unconscious urge to hurt them and thus to express the feeling of hostility that must arise in all who are deprived of what is adventurous. The stealing may have been nothing but the expression of this urge to hurt. I remember an apparently meaningless theft of this kind ; a young woman had stolen something in a shop in the actual presence of the mother, and the mother had not at all enjoyed the fuss and bother following upon the detection of her daughter's theft. But the daughter seemed to have enjoyed the experience and the humiliation of the mother that it involved. To have punished the daughter would have been to intensify her unconscious hatred of the mother. I could not punish the mother, as she had not been charged, but she was the person really responsible for the young woman's act. Through the probation officer, however, I could let the young woman understand her own situation and also warn the mother that the time had come when risks must be run and free experience gained by the daughter. Another type that is psychologically interesting, however annoying the individual may appear, is the delinquent youth with a stepmother. In the youth's unconscious there may well be a bitter hatred of the step-mother that is utterly irrational and unjust, for the step-mother may have done everything possible to show kindness. But in the unconscious lies the conviction that the step-mother has usurped the place of the real mother. This happens even when the real mother has died. When the stepmother comes into the family by reason of divorce, the unconscious hate may well be worse. A criminal act can be the result of this conflict.

There is no end to the psychological interest obtainable out of the most ordinary people. Magistrates who sit in domestic courts are familiar with the deserted wife who has no responsibilities, but who assures the court with ardent conviction that her errant husband must support her because she has bad health and cannot work. In a high proportion of such cases the illness exists, but it has a psychological origin. It is to her a welcome means to escape from the necessity to cope with life. Her unconscious desire to escape from life's burdens may well have been the underlying cause of the matrimonial breakdown. Even minor motoring offences can set up trains of psychological thought ; the motorist who admitted to the police constable at the time that he never saw the traffic lights at all becomes an irritating defendant, but an interesting psychological case, when he pleads not guilty in court and gives evidence on oath that the light was green when he passed it. Almost in the same breath he will sometimes agree that what the constable recorded about the conversation at the time is correct. Similar psychological interest can be derived from many prosecutions where two motorists who have collided at a cross roads are brought before a court on a charge of careless or dangerous driving. Small tradesmen prosecuting their roundsmen for embezzlement are equally interesting. Often the roundsman-defendant is a patently honest man, however stupid and bad at keeping accounts. The trouble may well have arisen because of the excessive good nature of the defendant in giving credit to customers. But the worse the supervision by the employer over his roundsman's accounts, the greater will be his belief that the roundsman is guilty of deliberate crime. Such men are psychologically of great interest.

The truth is that the majority of those who appear before a criminal Bench, whether as defendants or witnesses, become greatly more interesting when they reveal their psychological situation. Thus work in court becomes less dreary in the same way that a dull play would become interesting if one could peep behind the scenes and watch the actors when they retire from the stage. Those on the criminal Bench, therefore, can by making some studies in psychology, both render themselves better able to do justice and also protect themselves from that boredom which is sometimes the lot of those who sit hour by hour listening to the troubles and crimes of other people.

As the discoveries of psychology have become established, a demand has arisen that the duty of sentencing delinquents should be taken away from our criminal courts and transferred to some administrative body of experts. It would be wearisome to give quotations, but this reform has been discussed by, amongst others, Mr. R. C. K. Ensor,[1] Mr. Albert Morris,[2] Hans von Hentig,[3] and Professor Sheldon and Eleanor Glueck.[4] Dr. Hermann Mannheim only refrained from supporting this reform because he maintained that the criminal Bench should be trained in penology.[5]

In 1929 Mexico passed a law which ' eliminates the traditional court sentence and provides instead for a diagnostic council . . . to prescribe treatment for the guilty '.[6] A similar plan has been worked out in the United States of America ; the American Law Institute, composed of a number of leading lawyers, judges, and professors of law, called together in 1934 a group of experts in law, sociology, psychiatry, and other sciences to consider the revision of the criminal law in its application to those between 16 and 21. In 1937, an Advisory Committee was constituted to consider the reports and to make recommendations for improving court methods. Prominent on this committee were Dr. William Healy, Professor Sheldon Glueck, both of whose writings are quoted in these pages, and Judge Joseph N. Ulman of the Supreme Court of Baltimore ; he had already declared in his book, *A Judge takes the Stand*, that ' the imposition of sentence by judges is merely an historical survival that probably will be discarded if ever we begin to deal rationally with crime '.[7] To this conclusion also the working group of the advisory committee came after prolonged examination of the problem. They recommended that judges should only be empowered to

---

[1] *Courts and Judges in France, Germany and England*, p. 90.
[2] *Criminology*, pp. 295 and 471.
[3] *Punishment, Its Origin, Purpose and Psychology*, p. 238.
[4] *Later Criminal Careers*, p. 208.
[5] *The Dilemma of Penal Reform*, p. 204.
[6] *Criminology*, by Albert Morris, p. 495. [7] p. 254.

sentence offenders where (*a*) the law gives no judicial discretion, as in cases of murder, (*b*) in trivial cases punishable by small fines.   In all other cases they recommended that judges should hand delinquents, when proved guilty, to a Correction Authority, organized by an executive department of the State Government.   It was suggested that the Authority should be composed of experts and should study delinquents physically, psychologically, and socially.   Probation work and the supervision of released prisoners were also to come under the supervision of the Authority, as well as new institutions for the younger delinquents, such as remand homes, observation centres, &c.

This inquiry is significant of the trend of thought among those who study delinquency as a science.   Similar demands will assuredly be made in this country.   But dissatisfaction with existing conditions will have to go much further than it has hitherto before such a scheme becomes a practical proposition.   One of the members of the working group of the American inquiry wrote to me saying that no easy victory was expected ; another member wrote that the American Law Institute had 'a specially built and very capacious waste paper basket '.   In this country any such proposal would be met with widespread opposition.   I for one believe that there is a better way to achieve the desired end, namely that the criminal Bench should educate itself in penology and psychology.   But it will be folly to dismiss the idea of some form of treatment tribunals, if no attention is given to the defects of existing methods and to the need for training those who have to sentence delinquents.   We are not likely to continue indefinitely with mere ' common sense '

In his remarkable survey of our general educational needs, *The Future in Education*, Sir Richard Livingstone wrote :

We need to become familiar with the idea that everyone engaged in routine or practical work, especially if he occupies a directing position, needs periods of systematic study in order to refresh and re-equip and reorientate his mind.   There is no occupation or profession in which the resumption of systematic education in later life would not be profitable, and there are few human beings who would not greatly profit by it.[1]

This was not said with any direct reference to the Bench, but it is difficult to see any reason why those on the Bench are exempt from this need. Indeed there are reasons why especially those on the Bench need this continuation of education, for psychology teaches that men and women on the Bench are prone unconsciously to visit on their victims their own personal difficulties. To quote Dr. Healy :

The best example of the man in power who can allow his personality characteristics almost full sway is the judge . . . During thirty years I have had the opportunity to recognise a very wide range of beliefs, attitudes, prejudices and manners displayed on the bench. Such differences in leanings are exhibited that the psychiatrist almost aches for the chance to unravel the mystery of unconscious bias.[2]

If this view of an eminent psychiatrist is accepted, psychology comes very close to the Bench, for it teaches that those who sentence delinquents are subject to the same inescapable conflicts and unconscious tensions as those who appear before them. When John Bradford saw some victims being taken to Smithfield to be burnt at the stake he cried out : ' There, but for the grace of God goes John Bradford.' Similarly the judge and magistrate need to understand that they, like the delinquents before them, are moved by unconscious situations. It is fundamental with psychologists that it is just as necessary to inquire into the psychological state of those who make and enforce our laws as it is to investigate those who break them.[3]

[1] p. 93.   [2] *Personality in Formation and Action*, p. 173.
[3] Many psycho-analysts maintain that wars are largely the consequence of the unconscious emotions and instincts of those who rule and even of those who are opposed to war. See *War, Sadism and Pacifism* by Dr. Edward Glover : ' Only when we can measure our own charges of aggression and defensive hate can we expect the problem of war to become a mere academic or scientific issue ' (p. 45). See also *War and Peace* by Dr. William

Those on the criminal Bench need to understand the motives that animate them, their feelings and their reactions to the crimes with which they deal. They need to realize that whether prompted to anger, sympathy, or indifference, something in them, rather than the conduct of the delinquent, may be the motivating force. It seems obvious, therefore, that co-operation between the Bench and psychotherapists is something more than the receiving and giving of assistance about delinquents ; the Bench needs psychological assistance in the handling of itself. The very position of authority held by the Bench has its dangers.

Authority over delinquents involves the danger that there may be unrealized satisfaction in the infliction of punishment. Those on the Bench, being human and, therefore, psychologically immature, may even be animated by entirely unconscious sadistic forces ; such forces exist in most human beings. There is also the danger of projection ; to punish another may be to project upon him the punishment that those on the Bench unconsciously feel to be deserved by themselves. Repressed aggressive tendencies in judge or magistrate may achieve their outlet in the infliction of punishment on delinquents ; the more severe be the sentence, the greater may be the relief to such tendencies. In a similar way unconscious forces may result in sentimentality and in an unwise eagerness to be lenient.

Unconscious forces of this kind may also direct the reactions of spectators to criminal trials, of those who write about trials and of those who read their accounts. ' With what pleasure we read newspaper reports of crime. A true criminal becomes a popular figure because he unburdens in no small degree the consciences of his fellow men, for now they know once more where evil is to be found.' [1] People find in the evil doings of the criminal a

Brown and Part One of *War and Crime* by Dr. Hermann Mannheim. The forces that unconsciously produce wars are similar to those that produce bad sentences of criminals.

[1] Dr. C. G. Jung. *The Integration of the Personality*, p. 70.

comforting, but possibly false, assurance that they could not possibly commit such deeds. The same phenomenon was well described by another authority : ' Society in dealing with his [the criminal's] delinquency appears often to use it as an excuse for wreaking on him those violent aggressivities which we are just civilized enough to restrain ourselves from manifesting towards people who are reasonably well-behaved.' [1] In all kinds of people, those on the Bench, journalists, and readers of newspapers there is an unconscious feeling: ' the criminal must not get away with his deed for I cannot get away with my temptations '. That this feeling exists is no reason why punishment should not be inflicted ; but it is a reason why those who pass sentence should realize that the psychological gulf between them and the unfortunate in the dock is not so wide as may appear.

It is well that psychologists are giving attention to the psychology of the Bench. Respect for the Bench is fully compatible with this study. In 1938 and 1939 much evidence for such a study was afforded by many on the Bench, in all ranks, in connexion with the proposal in the Criminal Justice Bill to abolish flogging and birching. Those who were loud in their protests against this humane and psychologically sound reform, gave much food to those studying judicial psychology. Further psychological studies come from the widely differing attitudes adopted to particular offences ; for instance in regard to the crime of abortion. Even differing judicial policies in regard to bigamy, motoring offences, and cruelty to children reveal much to psychologists.

Under the English system, whereby the professional Bench is recruited in mid life, or later, from the practising Bar, it is more difficult to work out a system of training than it would be under the continental system, whereunder lawyers decide at the outset of their professional lives whether they will practise or seek a judicial career. But

[1] Dr. Pryns Hopkins in *The Psychology of Social Movements*, p. 113.

once it is realized that such training is essential, the practical difficulties could be overcome without much difficulty. A beginning might well be made with magistrates, both professional and lay. Before either a practising barrister or a justice of the peace aspires to do judicial work with criminals, he might not unreasonably be expected to attend some lectures and to read some books on penology and psychology. Before the war the Tavistock Clinic arranged courses of lectures for magistrates in psychology and its application to problems of delinquency.[1] Similar courses might be arranged in many centres. A list of the more simple books could be given to all those aspiring to the magisterial Bench. A distinction might be made between justice of the peace and court justice (an old title in another connexion) and only those who had made the necessary studies could be made court justices ; the others could witness signatures and do the other useful executive work of a justice. Court justices would be the successors of the Justices of the Quorum of olden days without whom the other justices could not handle the more difficult cases.

It is a comforting fact that a little psychology is not a dangerous thing, provided, of course, that the amateur makes no attempt to make psychological examinations. The essence of what is required is that the magistrate shall understand the need for psychological assistance in certain cases and be able to appreciate such reports or evidence as may be given. Even a slight knowledge of psychological principles might assist a magistrate to prevent his or her unconscious impulses from influencing a sentence ; with elementary training a magistrate would be on guard in regard to this danger. It would, of course, be better if those on the Bench could submit themselves to a prolonged course of psycho-analysis, but this is not likely to be practicable.

If some such reforms were introduced in regard to magistrates, legal and lay, a most useful beginning would

[1] At the course that I attended we were never more than eight in number.

have been made. There would also result great benefit to the community, since magistrates deal with most ' first offenders '. Once this step were taken, those higher up in the judicial hierarchy might be influenced. Thus by stages we should arrive at a trained Bench. Such progress would be preferable to the substitution of some secret treatment board for judicial sentencing, for such a board would have difficulty in securing the confidence of the public. But if there should be in the future no progress towards a trained Bench, then the creation of treatment boards is likely to become a widespread demand.

A treatment board would labour under the disadvantage that it had never seen the delinquent in the background of his offence ; it would know only at second hand and from written documents what the delinquent had done. Such important details as what the delinquent said when first challenged by the police, his demeanour during his trial, whether he gave evidence himself, and so on, would probably not be known by the treatment board. But all such details are of importance and have to be considered in the assessment of the sentence. I see considerable dangers in a system where sentence is passed by a board of experts who only see the delinquent in some place of observation. When delinquents are in custody, it is extremely difficult to estimate their fitness to be at liberty. It is a commonplace of prison life that many men and women behave excellently in prison, but quickly return on account of fresh crimes once they are released. The governor of a large prison once told me of a man whom he had had in his keeping several times ; in the effort to prevent any further crimes, the governor gave particular attention to him ; on the morning of release the governor had a long talk with him, but the talk ended with the pathetic request of the man : ' Will you keep my job open for me ? ' In places of custody most inmates seem deserving of sympathy. I have never been in a prison, Borstal Institution, or even a remand home, without wondering whether it was really necessary for the inmates to be there, but such feelings quickly gave way to a realization that I knew nothing about these people. It may reasonably be doubted whether even highly skilled psychiatrists and social workers, equipped with a paper statement of a prisoner's record, can be in a position to decide whether or not a prisoner can be trusted with his liberty. The desire in most prisoners to regain their liberty is so strong that they would co-operate in any tests that might be applied. The qualities that enable men and women to use their liberty without being a danger to others are subtle and difficult to test; the chances of error are great indeed.

If, as I believe, it would be impracticable to introduce any wholesale system of sentencing by treatment boards, there is one direction in which a valuable experiment could be made. Those who are found guilty of the graver sexual assaults might well be left in the hands of an expert treatment board. There would not be any great opposition, I think, to a bill in Parliament which proposed that in such cases criminal courts should pass only an indeterminate sentence and that it should be left to experts to decide when the offender can with reasonable safety be trusted with his liberty. Under our present methods the public, and especially the children of those who cannot provide constant supervision, are ill protected against men who commit grave sexual assaults. Such assaults sometimes cause devastating results in the lives of the victims, though as was said in an earlier chapter, such results could be minimized if the victims could receive psychological help. There has never been any attempt to think out this difficult problem, so at present our laws dealing with it are grossly inadequate. On 28 March 1933, the then Recorder of London described our present law for dealing with grave sexual assaults as ' anomalous and indefensible '.[1] I remember one case that illustrates this and the consequent dangers to children. In January 1934, I committed a man for trial

[1] The chaos existing in regard to the sexual offender was dealt with by me in a paper before the Medico-Legal Society in July 1934.

at the Central Criminal Court on the following charges :
taking a boy of 6 into a park and keeping him there all
night ; enticing away a boy of 5, keeping him all night,
stripping him and torturing him ; there was a third charge
of a similar nature. This man was sentenced to penal
servitude for five years. Such a sentence is an inadequate
protection to the public, since after less than four years,
with or without psychological treatment, this man would
have been released whatever his self-control. In bad cases
of sexual assault the sentence might well be such that the decision of the actual length of imprisonment will depend upon
examination by psychological experts. In effect this would
create a treatment board for this purpose. With the exception
of this type of offence, it is difficult to see the necessity for
extra-judicial sentences, provided that judicial sentences are
given with knowledge and as the result of training.

A scheme whereby recruits for the criminal Bench received
training in penology would go far to put an end to the bad
record of this country in the sciences relating to the treatment of delinquency. Up to the end of the last century,
it has been stated,[1] ' there was not a single text-book on
English criminal law that dealt either with the problem of
punishment in particular, or with the sciences allied to it
in general '. Even if this statement is an exaggeration,
there is no doubt that English minds have been directed
very little towards these vital problems. When, for instance, from 1909 onwards, the American Institute of
Criminal Law and Criminology began to publish trans-
lations of ' important treatises on criminology in foreign
languages ', there was no lack of material, and the many
volumes of the Modern Criminal Science Series are the
result. Had the editors wished also to publish such treatises
written in the English language, there would have been
a dearth of material. Since then much work has been

[1] *Penal Reform in England*, p. 5. In the narrower field of prison
reform much work of world-wide repute had been done. Such
names as John Howard (died 1790) and Elizabeth Fry (1780-1845)
carried the reputation of this country all over the world.

16

done in the United States, but comparatively little in England. In pre-Nazi Germany and Austria a considerable amount of research work was done, and it is worthy of note that when shortly before the war the London School of Economics and Political Science included penology in its curriculum, it was a refugee from Nazi oppression, Dr. Hermann Mannheim, who gave the lectures. During the war a hopeful movement was set on foot in the University of Cambridge, where the Faculty of Law appointed an expert committee to consider the promotion of research in criminal science. In 1940 the first volume, *Penal Reform in England*, was issued under the auspices of the committee, a beginning to a number of volumes of ' English Studies in Criminal Science '. From such a movement many suggestions for improvements in the working of our penal laws should emanate. The progress made would be greatly accelerated if those who are prominent on the criminal Bench would co-operate in the movement.

Once a substantial and well-supported movement towards the study of penology and criminal psychology takes place, many of the leaks in our present administration of the criminal law would quickly be stopped. For instance, one of the reasons why the criminal Bench in this country has for so long been blind to the very existence of these sciences has been that the Bench is left almost entirely ignorant about the consequences of its decisions about sentence. Except in the case of delinquents on probation (and then only during the actual period of the probation order) the Bench receives no information about the later conduct of those with whom they deal. There is no machinery whereby a judge or magistrate can be informed, for instance, that a week after the expiration of a probation order a delinquent repeated his offence.[1] A judge or magistrate

[1] A youth was once bound over at Kingston Assizes for stealing a motor-car. Within a few days he appeared before me on a similar charge. We had the utmost difficulty in getting into touch with the judge concerned and were then told that the matter must stand over to the next Assizes, three months later.

does not know if a delinquent whom he has sent to prison makes good on his release or not. If the system of judicial sentences is to defend itself against those who would transfer the duty of sentencing to treatment boards, then it seems a matter of great importance that systematic information about the results of sentences should be made available to those who passed the sentences. (Perhaps it is merciful to the Bench that no such information is at present provided.) A magistrate, for instance, could only benefit if he could be informed that, for instance, nine months after he sentenced T. P. to prison for six months, T. P. being hitherto ignorant of prison life, T. P. again committed a similar offence. Such information would encourage the magistrate to keep some records of his cases and to scrutinize the various sentences that he gives. Nothing could be more stimulating to the judicial study of penological science. At present it is difficult for any one on the Bench to follow up any of his cases. I experienced difficulty in obtaining some of the information about my own cases that are included in Chapter 3.

The amount of official information that is published about crime and sentences in general is defective. Even by a study of the annual volumes of official criminal statistics and the annual reports of the Prison Commissioners, valuable as these publications are, no one on the Bench, and no outside student of penology, can obtain much information of the results of this or that penal policy. No information is given concerning the proportion of probation cases that break down soon after their supervision ceases, about the immediate or ultimate effects of prison sentences on the shocking number of young people who are sent to prison, about the numbers in prison of the different religious denominations, and so on indefinitely. Probably the thirst for information of the penological student could never be satisfied ; he would want to know what crimes are more frequent in towns than in the country, and vice versa, at what ages first offenders are most prominent in certain crimes, how many brothers and sisters each delinquent had, how many delinquents came from broken homes, and so on. But even if a student's appetite for information is excessive, there can be little doubt that existing information is too meagre.[1]

Another result of our lack of system is the absence of adequate case papers. During the war a psychiatrist, a refugee from Germany, visited me at the South-Western court for the purpose of continuing his researches into individual delinquent cases, begun in happier days in Germany. He was shocked when I had to inform him that there were many scattered files about each case ; the police had their records, the probation officers theirs, and other reports were at the remand prison. I could only show him a few scrappy notes about the probation cases in which I was particularly interested. My visitor was astonished, but he had not yet much experience of the English method of ' muddling through '.

There are, therefore, many directions in which progress could be made, once a greater interest in penological problems was aroused in the Bench. Without such an increasing interest, the developing sciences concerned with delinquency are likely to result in a demand for taking from the Bench all duties to sentence, save in trivial cases. Such a demand would be regrettable and would be contrary to our national tendencies. But that is no reason why those on the criminal Bench who decide the fate of delinquents should not know the elements of penology and psychology. No reasonable person will demand that our Bench shall be expert in these sciences, but some acquaintance with them is necessary in order that the services of experts shall be utilized and their evidence and reports understood. Our Bench is an amateur Bench after the

[1] In his book *Social Aspects of Crime in England between the Wars*, Dr. Hermann Mannheim devoted many pages to a scientific criticism of the annual official volumes *Criminal Statistics*. On p. 18 he also stated that ' after having worked his way through a few thousand records of probation cases, it became clear to the author that this material was neither uniform nor detailed enough for scientific purposes '.

facts are proved, and an amateur Bench it is likely to remain. But even an amateur golfer takes lessons and does not rely on common sense to teach him to keep his eye on the ball.

APPENDIX

THE difficulties in introducing in the higher courts a general system of remands after verdict, mentioned in Chapter 6, could be surmounted in the following ways. The ideal solution would be the drastic one of amalgamating both urban and rural Quarter Sessions with Assizes,[1] thus creating regional courts. It is difficult to find any reason other than historical development to justify the administration of criminal justice on a three-tier system—magistrates' courts, Quarter Sessions and Assizes. All civil litigation is conducted on a two-tier system—County Court and High Court. Already nothing but the respective dates of Quarter Sessions and Assizes sometimes decides whether magistrates shall commit their cases for trial at Quarter Sessions or Assizes ; one of the results of this is that High Court judges are burdened at Assizes with many cases which Quarter Sessions are competent to try. An amalgamation of all Quarter Sessions and Assizes would result in the existence in all parts of the country of important local courts holding prolonged sittings at regular intervals which would have ample time for full inquiries. High Court judges would then only attend to try such cases, if any, as were of special difficulty. Another benefit would be that the long delays which sometimes even now take place, despite recent legislation, between committal for trial in magistrates' court and trial at Assizes would be abolished.[2]

In some measure Cecil Whiteley suggested this reform in his book *Brief Life*. Those accused persons who cannot be tried in magistrates' courts should, he suggested, ' be committed for trial to the local Quarter Sessions, which should meet monthly '. Then, ' following the practice of the Central Criminal Court, a list of cases should be drawn up which can only be tried by a

[1] When the present building used by the London Quarter Sessions was being planned, Harold Cox, then a member of the London County Council, tried hard to secure the amalgamation of this court with the Central Criminal Court, but legal prejudices and jealousies denied him success.

[2] As to these delays, see, for example, Mr. E. S. Fay's life of Mr. Justice Swift, pp. 75-6.

High Court judge '.[1]   Cecil Whiteley recommended that county boroughs should retain their own Quarter Sessions and that each county should have such a court.   But this recommendation would, so it seems to me, defeat the object in view, since such courts might not have enough work to enable adequate remands to be made.   I would suggest that Recorders, ancient though they be, should cease to do judicial work.   Such towns as wished could still have Recorders, whose duties would be mainly ceremonial, as are to-day the duties of the Recorder of Kingston-on-Thames.   In that town magistrates' courts commit their cases to the county Quarter Sessions.   I realize that this proposal would not be popular with members of the Bar.   To be a Recorder is an honour which barristers prize.   But the system under which Recorders perform judicial work is unsound. Another argument put forward to justify the existence of many Recorders is that some Recorders are later appointed to high judicial office and have obtained valuable judicial experience during their years as Recorder.   This argument seems to me to be contrary to all principles of penology.   The modern idea challenges the whole conception that judges in criminal courts should learn how to deal with delinquents by practising on them. Penology is a science and needs to be studied like other sciences before any attempt is made to practise it.[2]

If Quarter Sessions and Assizes remain separate courts, the question arises how remands for inquiries can be introduced into their working.   The only possible course for Quarter Sessions is to amalgamate town and county Sessions, and in more sparsely populated areas, to amalgamate the town and county Sessions in large areas containing several counties.   Then such a Quarter Sessions would have enough work to make possible the remanding of convicted persons for a week or more.   With a calendar of substantial size, such larger Quarter Sessions could first hold the trials of their criminal cases ; then, while inquiries are being made into those who have been pronounced guilty, the court could dispose of its civil work and its appeals from magistrates'

---

[1] *Brief Life*, pp. 113–14.
[2] One further advantage of abolishing the judicial functions of Recorders is that it would put an end to an undesirable tradition that the local Recorder should be briefed whenever the municipal authority needs to be represented in the higher courts.   Some years before the war of 1939 there arose serious difficulties in Liverpool as the result of this tradition.

courts ; the court would then occupy itself, at least a week after the trials, with the reception of probation officers' and other reports about the guilty, and with this help sentences would be passed.

In order to obtain Assizes in all parts of the country that have sufficient work to demand sittings of more than a week, the only way is to restrict severely the number of Assize towns. The only reasons for Assizes in every county are historical. Because of this undue respect for historical customs, the pre-war system of Assizes resulted in Assizes being held in such places as Hunting-don and Hertford, Ruthin and Mold (the latter towns only ten miles apart), while such towns as Hull and Southampton had no Assizes. There were many protests against the waste of time that such a system involved. Thus Lord Wright, a High Court judge for seven years, advocated the amalgamation of Assizes. He complained that judges had to visit fifty-six towns and that some of these caused ' several days of judicial time ' to be wasted.[1] Lord Justice Mackinnon, a High Court judge for thirteen years, made similar criticisms in his book, *On Circuit, 1924–1937*. It should be explained that in making these protests these much respected judges were thinking mainly of saving judicial time. Perhaps the High Court Bench, and lawyers generally, would accept an amalgamation of Assizes if they realized that this was the only practicable method whereby adequate inquiries could be made. If the plea for the abolition of Assizes at many small towns could be placed on this ground, perhaps the local patriotism of authorities in such towns would give way in the interests of the scientific treatment of delinquency.

[1] *Second Interim Report of the Business of the Courts Committee*, 1933.

INDEX

Abortion, 217
Accused, questioning of, 169
—— statements by, 168–73
Acquittal of guilty, 163–4, 168, 197–200
Acquitted, treatment of, 163–4, 189
Adler, Dr. Alfred, 4, 5, 68, 115, 203
Adolescents, 11, 40
—— evidence by, 191–202
—— trial of, 187–91
Advocacy, 197–9
Aggression, 7, 8, 11, 16–17, 107, 215, 217
Aichhorn, August, 181
Air-raids, 5, 6, 11
Allers, Dr. R., 3
Alverstone, Lord, 207
Ambivalence, 10
American Institute of Criminal Law, 221
American law, 22, 33, 36, 154–6, 213
American Law Institute, 182, 213–14
Anxiety, 7, 74, 81, 96, 120
Approved Schools, 40, 50, 165, 189
Army, 98
Arson, 157
Aschaffenburg, Professor G., 189
Assizes, viii, 144, 150–4, 196–8, 226–8
Atkin Committee, 29–33, 158
Avory, Mr. Justice, 153

Bancroft, G. P., 153
Banister, H., 67
Barnes, Harry Elmer, 112
Barristers, methods of, 197–9

Beccaria, 100
Bed-wetting, 11, 42
Bench, appointment of, 206, 217
—— criticism of, 203–9, 217, 222
—— emotions of, 153, 156, 215–18
—— opinions of, 101, 217
—— position of, 174, 215–6, 222
—— questions by, 169
—— reports to, 154, 177–9
—— supersession of, 32, 165–80, 213–14, 220–4
—— training of, 32, 124, 157, 205–9, 212–25, 227
Bigamy, 217
Birching, 217
Biron, Sir Chartres, 197
Birth-control, 91, 94
'Black Market' cases, 105
Books on psychology, xv, 179
Borstal, 83, 88, 101–2, 117–19, 154, 219
—— Association, 118
Bramwell, Lord, 28
Burlingham, Dorothy, 11
Burt, Dr. Cyril, 147

Cadbury, Mrs. Barrow, 182
Cairns, Huntingdon, 159
Caldecote, Lord, 30
Calvert, E. Roy, 205
Cambridge Faculty of Law, 222
Capital Punishment, 37, 104, 158
Care and Protection Cases, 24, 165–7, 189, 201
Carr-Saunders, A. M., 40
Cautions to accused, 168–70
Central Criminal Court, 44, 152, 187

229

Ceremony in court, 174–6, 190
Chancery judges, 208
' Change of life ', 11
Character, witnesses to, 130
Child guidance clinics, 43, 53, 126, 183–5
Child witnesses, 191–202
Childbirth, 5–7
Childhood, 7–11, 56, 115
Children, trial of, 186–90
Choice of court, 190–1
Christianity, 21, 161
Clarke Hall, Sir W., v, 76
Clinics, weaknesses of, 60
Coddington, Dr. F. J. O., 146
Coitus interruptus, 91, 93
Collective unconscious, 4
Colquhoun, Patrick, vi
Common sense, 208–9, 225
Compulsion neurosis, 76, 115
Conscience, 117
Consent in probation, 49, 110–111, 113
Contradictions in evidence, 170
Controlling disease, 27–34, 158
Conviction, 108, 201
Co-operation of patient, 35, 48–49, 56, 60–1, 86, 90, 129–137, 220
Costs, payment of, 109
Court, Dr. A. C., 61, 64, 91, 94
Court, psycho-therapists at, 61–62, 114
Courts, structure of, 174
Cox, Harold, 226
Crawford, Archibald, 199
Crichton-Miller, Dr. H., 4
Criminal intent, 187–90
Criminal Justice Bill, 20, 48, 111, 149, 154, 217
Criminal Lunatics Act, 29
Criminal Statistics, 152, 223–4
Cross-examination, 167, 171–3, 194, 198
Culpability, 34, 158
Cure, 58–9, 68, 79, 100

Dais, 174, 194
Demeanour of delinquents, 146
Deodands, 22
Determinism, 31–3, 112
Deterrence, 101, 103–7, 208
Diagnosis, 38
Docks, 176
Doctor-patient relationship, 53, 67
Doctors, help of, 49, 52, 59, 141, 157
Dreams, 4, 165
Drunkenness, 127–9

East-Hubert report, 34, 38–48, 67, 131
Education, 7–10, 16, 19, 117, 210, 215
Education authorities, 145, 182, 202
Elkin, Winifred, 148
Ellis, Havelock, 112
Embezzlement, 213
Encephalogram, 36
Environment of delinquents, 58–9, 73, 79, 140–2
Environmentalists, 112, 123–4
Ensor, R. C. K., 207, 213
Erewhon, 32, 99, 104
Evacuation, 5, 11, 182
Evidence, contradictions in, 170, 197–8
—— giving of, 167, 170–6, 187–200
—— of minors, 191–202, 187–200
Exhibitionism, 15–16, 67–80, 90–2, 133, 137, 139, 144

Father, influence of, 126
Fear, 6, 170, 174–6
Ferri, Enrico, 114
Feversham Committee, 52
' First offenders ', 69, 94, 109, 219
Fixation, 16–19, 54
Flogging, 217

Flügel, Professor, 179
Forgetting, 3, 202
Free Association, 62, 165
Freewill, 20–35, 62, 100, 158
Freud, Anna, 11
Freud, Dr. Sigmund, 2, 6, 10, 15, 31, 62, 68, 137, 160
Fry, Margery, 50, 99, 136

Gardiner, Major G., 153
Gillespie, Dr. R. D., 113, 206
Glueck, Professor Sheldon, 124–125, 213
Goring, Dr. Charles, 123–5
Guilt, admission of, 154, 168–9
—— feelings of, 8, 16, 64, 111, 114–18, 211
—— inadequacy of, 161–7
Guilty, acquittal of, 163, 168, 197–200
—— more pleas of, 154, 166, 169
' Guilty but Insane ', 29, 34, 37, 158, 209

Hadfield, Dr. J. A., 15
Hadfield's case, 27
Haldane, Lord, v
Hamblin Smith, Dr. M., 142, 156
Hart, Dr. Heber, 36, 168
Hate, 10
Hatred of criminal, 99
Healy, Dr. W., 63, 99, 118, 126, 205, 213, 215
Heredity, 4, 87, 102, 124–5
Hewart, Lord, 28–30
Hollander, Dr. Bernard, 37
Homicide, juveniles and, 186–90
Homo-sexuality, 17, 64, 72, 75, 79, 127, 131, 157
Hopkins, Dr. Pryns, 217
Hostels, 86, 96
Howe, Dr. Graham, 63, 126
Hubert, Dr. W. H. de B., see East–Hubert Report

Hypnosis, 166
Hysteria, 89

Illegitimacy, 25, 86, 106, 126, 177
Imaginery invalids, 35, 132, 211–12
Imprisonment, 46–7, 58, 94
—— effects of, 46, 50, 219
—— necessity for, 113
—— of youths, 109, 119, 223
—— preliminary steps, 142–52
—— results of, 92, 101, 119–20, 223
and see Prisons, Treatment in
Incapacity for crime, 187–90
Indecent assault, 72, 78, 139, 195
Infanticide, 23–5
Inferiority feeling, 42, 71, 73
Inherited unconscious, 4, 102
Inhibitions, 10, 64, 202
Insanity, 20–37, 131, 158
Instincts, 4, 7, 138, 170
Institute for Scientific Treatment of Delinquency, ix, 53, 58–60, 81, 85, 89, 93, 96, 129, 133
Institutions, 48–50, 117, 121, 137
Investigation of cases, 34, 142–158, 187, 227–8
Irreclaimable criminals, 44–5, 48, 82, 111–14, 124–6, 134–7
Irresistible impulse, 27–35, 158
Ives, George, 38, 114

Jackson, Dr. R. M., 205
Jacobi, Dr. Jolan, 4, 18
Judges, see Bench
—— advice by, 26
—— in juvenile courts, 190, 200
' Judges' Rules ', 168
Jung, Dr. C. G., 4, 15, 32, 102, 170, 216
Jury, xvi, 29, 35, 186–200

Justices, 206, 218, *and see* Bench
— Royal Commission on, 206
Juvenile court panel, 182–3
Juvenile courts, 108, 148–9, 154, 173–7, 181–7, 190, 200, 203
Juvenile crime, 40, 183–4

Klein, Melanie, 10

Langdon-Brown, Sir W., 200
Large families, 125
Law, assumptions of, 158, 160
Lawyers, training of, 154, 200
—— methods of, 171–3, 197–9
Lay magistrates, 56, 149, 183, 206, *and see* Bench
Lay psychologists, 67
Legal aid, 173, 194
—— education, 154, 205–15
Livingstone, Sir Richard, 2, 214
Lombroso, Cesare, 102, 113
London Police Courts, 150, 155
London School of Economics, 222
Love, 10, 15–18, 75–8
Lunacy, 20–37

McCardie, Mr. Justice, v, 29, 142
McDougall, Professor W., 32
McIlroy, Dame L., 5
Mackinnon, Lord Justice, 228
Macmurray, Professor J., 14
McNaghten Rules, xiv, 25–31, 157
Magistrates Association, 24, 206
Magistrates' courts, 24, 36, 65–66, 171, 174–6, 193, 206
Mannheim, Dr. H., 40, 44, 127, 141, 213, 222, 224
Masturbation, 73, 76
Mathew, Theobald, 208
Matrimonial disputes, 12, 18, 64, 90, 125, 141, 195
—— courts, 125, 173, 195, 211

Maule, Mr. Justice, 26
Mead, Frederick, 172
Medicine and Law, 21–3, 31–2
Medico-Legal Review, 143, 188, 207, 220
Memory, 3, 202
Mental defect, 20–37, 158
—— treatment, definition of, 49
Mexican law, 213
Money-Kyrle, Dr. R. E., 8, 179
Morris, Albert, 114, 213
Motives, 14, 16, 22, 66, 70, 76, 114, 161–2, 170, 210
Motoring offences, 106, 162, 171, 199, 212, 217
Munsterberg, Professor, 167
Murderers, 34, 104, 116, 158, 162, 187

National Association of Probation Officers, 11, 149
Neurosis, 13, 54, 76
Nuisance cases, 127–8

Oaths, 175, 195
Obsessional neurotics, 96
Open-counter shops, 184
Oxford's case, 28

Page, Leo, 113, 128, 145, 149
Pailthorpe, Dr. Grace, 47, 107
Paranoiacs, 54
Parents, attitude of, 10, 15–18, 139–40, 201
—— education of, 185
—— quarrels between, 85, 88, 195, 210
Pathological liars, 85
Pearce, Dr. J. D. W., 186
Penology, 154, 209, 222–5, 227
' Peter Pan ' cases, 79
Phillipson, Coleman, 33, 100
Physical effects, 20, 97
—— illness, 57, 70, 81, 83, 95
Planning, v
Plato, 2, 102
Play, 16

Play-therapy, 184
Police, attitude of, 80, 116, 144
—— cautions by, 168–70
—— inquiries by, 143–8
Pre-conscious, 3
Pre-trial inquiries, 143–8, 227–8
Press, xi, 36, 76, 140, 169, 216
Presumption of innocence, 105, 144
—— of responsibility, 22–35, 187
Prison Commission Reports, 50, 119, 223
—— staff in, 119
—— treatment in, 41, 45–7, 137
Probation, and conviction, 108, 201
—— and fines, 109
—— and punishment, 108–10, 137
—— breach of, 47, 53, 84, 87, 121, 128, 133–6, 222–3
—— consent to, 49, 110–11, 113
—— danger of, 107, 121, 128
—— inquiries before, 144–54, 177–9, 228
—— misunderstanding of, 107
—— records of, 222–4
—— scope of, 45
—— terms of, 48–9
—— treatment during, 45–63, 71–98, 121, 158
Projection, 13, 216
Prostitution, 127
Psycho-analysis, 2–3, 6, 40, 62, 114–15, 138, 140, 161–7, 218
Psycho-neurosis, 56
Psychopaths, undiscovered, 42–44
Psychosis, 54
Psycho-therapy, conditions for, 46–7, 126, 129–30, 134–6
—— methods of, vii, 62
—— object of, 4, 19
—— results of, 41, 57–8, 69–98, 121–2

Punishment, 99–122
—— and reformation, 101, 109, 112–13, 117–20
—— as deterrence, 101, 103–7
—— danger of, 55, 114–17, 211, 217
—— demand for, 100, 137–40
—— denial of, 107
—— for life, 113
—— inadequacy of, 116, 163
—— limitations of, 16, 19, 28, 55–6
—— necessity for, 100, 102–7, 112–13, 119
—— Probation and, 108–10, 137
—— psycho-therapists and, 53
—— trials without, 166

Quacks, 68
Quarter Sessions, viii, 144, 150, 196–200, 226–8
—— in London, 44, 150, 152

Rank, Otto, 6
Rapport, 47, 60–1, 74, 82
Reaction character traits, 55–6, 62
Recidivism, 41, 42–4, 55, 80, 113, 124, 136, 142, 221
Recorders, 150, 220, 227
Rees, Dr. J. R., 1, 113, 125
Reik, Theodor, 115, 161, 165
Remands, see Investigation
Reports to courts, 154, 177, 204
—— simplicity in, 178
Repression, 3, 12, 16, 18, 19, 117, 137, 202
Resistance, 40, 55, 61, 76, 130
Results of psycho-therapy, 41, 57–8, 69–98, 121–2
Rhodes, Dr. E. C., 40
—— Henry T. F., 1, 66
Romilly, Sir Samuel, 101
Ruggles-Brise, Sir E., 101

Schools, 8
Security, 7, 11, 13, 75, 126

Self-love, 14, 129
Self-responsibility, 20–35
Sentences, 41, 113, 114, 205–9
—— length of, 127, 133
—— results of, 222–3
Sex, children and, 15–16, 65
—— education in, 16, 72, 141
—— Freud's view, 15
—— ignorance of, 64–5, 85, 92, 141
—— Jung's view, 15
—— restraints on, 106
Sexual intercourse before marriage, 82
—— offences, 65, 92, 131, 157, 191–202, 220
—— —— committee on, 202
Shaw, Bernard, 99, 100, 104
' Shell shock ' cases, vi, 12, 57
Short treatments, 63, 64, 81, 157
Sin, 21
Social Services, 132
—— Committee, 173
Soliciting, 75
Statements by accused, 168–173
Stephen, Sir J. Fitzjames, v, 21, 27, 30, 99, 172
Step-parents, 83, 134, 211
Sublimation, 17
Success, standards of, 58–9, 68
Super-ego, 114, 117, 138
Suttie, Dr. I. D., 15, 110

Taft, Henry W., 167
Tavistock Clinic, ix, 53–9, 63, 70, 72, 75, 218

Text-books, xv, 179, 221
Treatment boards, 213, 219–23
Trial, problems of, 167
Trials, supersession of, 165–180
Truancy, 42
True, Ronald, 29, 37

Ulman, Judge J. N., 213
Unconscious, 3–5, 12, 19–20, 35, 102, 166, 202
Uncontrollable impulse, 27–35, 158
Unemployment, 69–70, 82–3, 134, 140, 144
Unwanted children, 25, 88, 125

Valentine, Professor C. W., 9
Victims in trials, 137–40, 191–203

Walker, Kenneth, 32
War-time crimes, 104
Watson, John A. F., 146, 174
Weaning, 7, 17
Weihofen, Henry, 22, 26, 36
Wexberg, Dr. Erwin, 123
Whiteley, Cecil, 198–200, 226
Witness-box, 176, 193, 196
Witnesses, youthful, 191–202
—— characteristics of, 167, 170–5
Woodworth, Professor R. S., 39
Wright, Lord, 228

Young, Dr. H. T. P., 39, 46

Zillboorg, G., 1, 23, 27